D0760844

America's Airports

Number One:
Centennial of Flight Series
Roger D. Launius, General Editor

America's
Airports

AIRFIELD DEVELOPMENT, 1918–1947

Janet R. Daly Bednarek

Texas A&M University Press

COLLEGE STATION

Library of Congress Cataloging-in-Publication Data

Bednarek, Janet R. Daly (Janet Rose Daly), 1959–
    America's airports : airfield development, 1918–1947 / Janet R. Daly
Bednarek. — 1st ed.
        p. cm.
    Includes bibliographical references and index.
    ISBN 1-58544-130-9
    1. Airports—United States—History—20th century. 2. Airports—United
States—Design and construction—History—20th century. 3. Urban renewal—
United States—History—20th century. I. Title.
    HE9797 .5.U5 B43 2001
    387 .7'36'097309041—dc21
                        2001000831

Contents

Acknowledgments

While this book project began with a question—why municipal airports?—the question began after a conversation with Roger Launius, NASA's chief historian, in the early 1990s. We ran into each other at an American Historical Association conference in Washington, D.C., and began to talk about all the great topics not yet covered in aviation history. One of those topics was airports. Being an urban historian by training and an aviation historian by circumstance, the more I thought about it, the more I saw a way to combine both fields in one project. Then in 1995 Roger was working on a project for Texas A&M University Press on innovation in aerospace history. I asked for a chance to research and write an essay on airports. It seemed I was going to be spending three summers in the Washington area and I wanted to take full advantage of the research opportunities thus offered. Out of that initial essay on airports grew the book on airports.

As I worked on the essay and then the book, a number of people offered important help and support. First, I want to thank staff members of the library and archives at the National Air and Space Museum. Mary Pavlovich and Paul McCutcheon from the library along with Dan Hagedorn, Melissa Keiser, and Brian Nicklas from the archives provided tremendous amounts of valuable and cheerful research support. Of course I would not have had the chance to work as closely with the library and archives staffs had it not been for the aid received from the museum's Aeronautics Department. Tom Crouch, Dom Pisano, and Rick Leyes all supported my gaining official researcher status at the museum. Those fine gentlemen, as well as Peter Jakab, F. Robert van der Linden, and Dorothy Cochrane all expressed interest in the project and continuously assured me that others would also find it of value. I am proud to now consider those people my friends.

While I did a great deal of my research at the National Air and Space Museum, I also spent time working at the National Archives and the Library of Congress. The staffs at both those institutions proved unfailingly helpful and supportive. I especially want to thank the many individuals at the Library of Congress who retrieved volume after volume of bound aviation, city planning, and engineering journals. In Dayton, the interlibrary loan folks at my home institution, the University of Dayton, proved lifesavers on occasions as I sought any number of obscure publications. I must also thank Dawne Dewey and the staff of the archives at the Paul Lawrence Dunbar Library at Wright State University. Wright State has an extensive collection of aviation material, the staff knows it well, and they are very willing and eager to share it with researchers. I would also like to thank the staff of Texas A&M University Press.

My colleagues at the University of Dayton offered support and encouragement over the long process of bringing this project to completion. Both the Society for American City and Regional Planning History and the Cincinnati Seminar on the City gave me the chance to present many of my ideas. I received important feedback in both forums. Most valuable, though, in terms of colleagues and peers were the two anonymous readers of the manuscript. Both challenged me to better focus and organize my ideas. The final manuscript benefited tremendously from their suggestions. Of course for any remaining errors in fact or interpretation, I take full responsibility.

Finally, I must thank my family. In particular, my brother, John R. Daly, gamely acted as my research assistant, along the way learning more about Omaha's airport than he ever wanted to know. And in many ways this project would not have been possible without my husband, Mike. First, it was his Air Force career that provided me the "opportunity" to spend three summers (not to mention every other weekend and school holidays) in Washington. Second, he rescued me from innumerable technological crises caused by my often less than expert use of the personal computer. And last, his good humor acted to pull me through even the most difficult moments. I dedicate this book to him and all the many members of my Daly and Bednarek families.

America's Airports

Introduction

Why municipal airports? This book project began with that seemingly simple question. How and why did airports, in particular the major or primary airports serving urban areas and the nation's major airlines, become a responsibility of local governments, for the most part city governments, in the United States? The existing literature on airports touches on that issue, but usually indirectly. A good deal of the literature focuses instead on primarily either the architecture/engineering of airports, federal aviation policies, or the histories of individual airports or limited groups of airports. Many of these works also focus on the period after 1945, a time by which the idea of local public responsibility for airports had been firmly established. To a great extent these works either take for granted the fact that cities assumed responsibility for airports or simply point to the Air Commerce Act's 1926 prohibition of federal aid to airports.[1] Research into the basic question, however, revealed that the answer was far more involved and complex. It was an answer that evolved over time as the result of the interplay between local actions and federal actions and policies, urban boosterism combined with the aviation enthusiasm of the period before 1945, as well as the economic realities of airport operations. In the end, municipal airports became defined as local, publicly owned facilities, the maintenance, improvement, and operation of which also involved federal funding and regulation.

Similar to the other works on the subject of airports, this will concentrate on the history of the primary airports serving urban areas. Urban areas generally have any number of secondary airports. These facilities are both publicly and privately owned and operated. They principally service general aviation activities such as private flying, aerial photography, flight instruction, aircraft maintenance, police and fire department helicopter operations, and charter companies, among others. And while the stories of these secondary airports are undoubtedly also interesting, the focus in this work will center on cities' major or primary airports—what people generally mean when they mention going to *the* airport.

During the 1990s a number of works appeared focused on the architecture and engineering of airports in the United States and Europe. David Brodherson's 1993 dissertation examined early ideas and designs for the "landside" parts of airports—access roads, terminals, and facilities/devices designed to move passengers from the terminals to the airplanes. He argued that while many design ideas were not fully realized, the 1920s and 1930s represented an important formative period in the history of airport architecture.[2] In 1996 Deborah Douglas produced a dissertation dealing with early airport history (1919–39). Her work focused in part on airports and technology and included an extensive section on the evolution of airports as systems of technologies. She clearly demonstrated the growing complexity of airports, a development that came relatively rapidly between 1919 and 1939. She concluded with an examination of New York's La-Guardia Airport that defined it as the first modern airport.[3] Several books also were published during the 1990s dealing with airport architecture. The first, edited by John Zukowsky, covered airports in the United States, Europe, and Asia. This 1996 work had essays exploring both "landside" and "airside"—runways, taxiways, aprons—architecture and design.[4] The following year Marc Dierikx and Bram Bouwens published a study focused on airports, particularly airport architecture, in Europe. The work was centered on an examination of the history of Schiphol Amsterdam.[5] And in 1999 Marcus Binney produced a work that highlighted the architecture of new airports and terminals planned and/or constructed during the 1990s.[6]

The Brodherson and Douglas dissertations, as well as one by Douglas Karsner (see below), included sections on federal aviation policy before 1945. By far the most in-depth examination of federal aviation policies, though, was Frank Robert van der Linden's dissertation on the role of the Post Office, especially under the leadership of Walter Folger Brown, in the shaping of the airline industry in the United States. Van der Linden's work strongly established that between 1926 and 1934, federal aviation policy reflected the ideals of the Progressive Era as well as the vision of the associative state of Herbert Hoover.[7] Drawing on the work of Ellis Hawley, van der Linden argued that during the Hoover era federal aviation policies sought to establish a business-government relationship based on voluntary cooperation in order to promote efficiency and standardization.

The result of such cooperation would be an aviation sector that would open "new vistas for the business and an expansion of the national economy."[8]

A number of other works presented case studies of individual airports or limited groups of airports. Two of the earliest dated from the 1970s. They were Richard Doherty's history of Chicago-O'Hare International Airport, a facility developed after World War II, and Charles Bonwell's work on St. Louis's Lambert Field and the evolution of its "airside" and "landside" architecture.[9] One of the better published works dealing with individual airports was *A Dream Takes Flight: Hartsfield Atlanta International Airport and Aviation in Atlanta* by Betsy Braden and Paul Hagan. Especially when dealing with the pre–World War II history of the airport, Braden and Hagan connected the story of Atlanta's airport with the development of both the aviation industry and federal aviation policy.[10] Another good work, but one that dealt primarily on the post–World War II era to 1970, was Douglas Karsner's 1993 dissertation. His work, focused as much on aviation in general as on airports in particular, included case studies of airports in Detroit, Tucson, and Tampa. While he concentrated on the period after World War II—as that was when, according to the author, airports really began to have a significant impact on cities—Karsner, similar to Brodherson, identified the period before World War II as being an important formative one.[11] Most works on airports resembled that by Richard Olislager. In 1996 he published a coffee-table book on airports in the American Southwest. In addition to providing an overview of airports in that region—as well as lots of photographs—the book contained short histories of a number of individual airports.[12]

None of these works focused specifically on how and why the airports they studied were essentially local public responsibilities. If they focused on the question at all, as noted, they pointed to the Air Commerce Act of 1926 and its adoption of the "dock concept" as a justification for forbidding federal aid to airports. The concept held that airports were most analogous to docks. While river and harbor improvements had been federal responsibilities, as would the construction and maintenance of the airways, docks had been built, maintained, and improved at the local level.[13] While the passage of the Air Commerce Act and the adoption of the dock concept were important milestones in the history of airports, the full answer as to how and why airports became the responsibility of local governments is far more complex. These works on airports and federal policies, nonetheless, did provide a number of valuable ideas, helpful in understanding the early history of airports. Brodherson and Karsner, especially, contributed the important conclusion that the period before 1945 must be viewed as formative. Important ideas, relationships, and policies were expressed or witnessed initial development before 1945. However, whether talking about architecture or the influence of airports on shaping the modern city, the realization of the hopes, dreams, and expectations of airport enthusiasts was not in any way met until after 1945. It was also during the period before 1945 that the basic relationships between cities, states, the federal government, and airports were worked out. This period, thus, provided the foundation for the postwar development of airports. Douglas showed how airports represented a relatively rapidly developing system of technologies. And as airports became more complex, they also became more expensive. And van der Linden demonstrated the influence of progressive ideas and associationalism on federal aviation policies, particularly between 1926 and 1934.

So, why municipal airports? Local government responsibility for airports was one that evolved over time. Beginning shortly after World War I, local interests—both public and private—began to establish the first primitive landing fields. Those fields represented the origins of the nation's municipal airports. The local interests were responding initially to the needs of the first "customers" for airports—the Post Office and the military.

Between 1919 and 1926 both the Post Office and the military encouraged local interests to build airports. As will be explained in more detail in chapter 1, they did so because, to a great extent, they had no choice as neither had budgets large enough to build the facilities necessary to support either the air mail program or military aviation training. In the absence of federal funds, both turned to those they deemed most likely to agree to help build airports. Emphasizing particularly the idea that airports were going to be essential to any city's ability to continue to grow and to compete with urban rivals, the Post Office and the military lobbied cities hard.

As a result, by the time the Air Commerce Act formally adopted the dock concept as policy in 1926, at least seven years of practice had already established a strong local role in airport construction. In a way, thus, the Air Commerce Act simply formalized in policy the practices already in place. By 1926, practice and policy may have clearly defined airports as a local responsibility, but they had not yet defined airports exclusively as a local *government* responsibility. Through the 1920s, both local private interests and local governments—often, though not always, working together—built the nation's airports. Between 1926 and the late 1930s, a number of factors would come together to create a situation that vastly favored the local, public ownership and operation of the nation's major airports. They included the failure of airports to operate at a profit, the response of states to the aviation enthusiasm of the late 1920s with the passage of airport enabling acts, and New Deal relief policies that eventually mandated public ownership of any airport receiving federal relief funds. The idea that local governments would build, own, and maintain the nation's airports, thus, was one that evolved between 1919 and the late 1930s. Therefore, the definition of "municipal airport" must also be seen as an evolving one.

In addition to addressing early on the needs of the Post Office and the military, cities building airports throughout the 1920s and 1930s were also responding to the new technology of aviation much as they had to other new transportation technologies. For example, while his focus was primarily on city governments and their actions regarding the advent of such technologies as the streetcar and the automobile, Eric H. Monkkonen argued that, in terms of all forms of transportation, "city governments subsidized and in other ways encouraged new technologies."[14] Obviously streetcars and then automobiles had far more extensive influences on the shaping of the modern cities than did airports, especially during the formative period before 1945. Nonetheless, Monkkonen, though briefly, included aviation and airports among the numerous transportation technologies he looked at that had benefited in a somewhat traditional way from city government aid.[15]

In many way cities responded as they did to the emergence of aviation within a traditional urban booster framework. Urban boosterism—the effort to promote the growth and development of one's city, one that often included a sense of competition with rival cities—has been a theme throughout American urban history. During the formative period of airport development, urban booster arguments promoting airport construction abounded in the literature. Airports emerged by the late 1920s as one of *the* facilities a city had to have in order to achieve its "destined" growth and development and to match or, better, overwhelm its urban rivals.

However, in addition to the fact that cities built airports within the context of their general actions toward transportation technologies and traditional urban boosterism, the urban response to aviation also reflected the influence of what Joseph Corn called "the winged gospel." In his landmark work, *The Winged Gospel: America's Romance with Aviation, 1900–1950,* Corn documented the great enthusiasm, bordering on worship, with which Americans greeted the advent of the flying machine. Particularly before World War II, both pilots and planes captured the imagination of Americans and helped inspire great dreams for the future. The winged gospel was the collection of beliefs about the nature and role of aircraft and their pilots, and what the airplane could and would do for individuals and for humankind. Women and African Americans, for example, saw in aviation a new, highly prized field of endeavor not yet clearly dominated by white males in which they could make a mark and, ideally, find a path to greater equality in American society. The gospel included a vision of a peaceful future in which both society and humankind itself had evolved to a higher order. At its extreme was a vision of the far distant future in which a superior race of humans lived their lives in the clouds. For the near future, the gospel predicted a world in which the airplane would become as common a form of personal transportation as the automobile. This vision became one of the strongest and most enduring myths in the history of aviation. In the more mundane present, the gospel and its accompanying "airmindedness" inspired such things as model airplane contests to attract children to the field of aviation and the development of aviation-centered school curricula. The enthusiasm, according to Corn, was widespread in American society and marked it, especially in the 1920s and 1930s, as being particularly "airminded."[16] A close examination of the history of local action on airports, as well as policies dealing with aviation in general and airports in particular, revealed both the influence of the winged gospel and the real limits to its reach.

Cities built airports from 1919 onward in large part because local aviation enthusiasts, particularly those belonging to the business elite, pushed, prodded, and demanded action. While also reflecting more basic urban booster instincts, these local elite evidently bought into the expansive promises of the winged gospel as well. In addition, states acted quickly in the wake of the enthusiasm, bordering on hysteria, following Charles Lindbergh's solo flight across the Atlantic by passing the laws that enabled local governments to own and build airports. And, despite the fact that airports proved far more expensive and far less profitable than promised, cities and aviation boosters continued to seek means to maintain and improve their airports during the 1930s by turning to the federal government for aid.

At the national level, a number of federal aviation programs and policies also clearly demonstrated the influence of the winged gospel. Perhaps the most obvious was Eugene Vidal's efforts while serving as director of the Aeronautics Branch to encourage the design and manufacture of an airplane cheap enough and safe enough to fulfill the dream of "an airplane in every garage."[17] If Vidal's program was designed to provide the planes, then the Civilian Pilot Training Program (1939–46), promoted by the head of the Civil Aeronautics Authority, Robert H. Hinckley, was designed to provide the pilots. Though the program also came to be justified on the theory that the newly trained pilots could rapidly contribute to national defense in case of war, the original idea behind the program was to provide a means to open up the world of aviation to young Americans.[18] When it came to airports, for example, the Federal Airport Act of 1946, as will be shown, also reflected the beliefs of the winged gospel. It emphasized smaller airports—those that could be used by what was sure to be a growing number of general aviation pilots following World War II—over larger airports serving primarily the nation's commercial airlines.

The history of airports, though, also clearly demonstrated the limits to the influence of the winged gospel. The limits became particularly visible during the 1930s, a period that generally saw a diminishment of enthusiasm for airports. Corn's book examined how a number of women and African Americans came to embrace the winged gospel, but it did not determine the degree to which different social and economic classes came to hold to the beliefs of the gospel. As will be shown, studies done of the local politics of airports in Omaha, Nebraska, and Muncie, Indiana, clearly demonstrated that while the middle and upper classes, particularly the elites, in those cities supported airport construction, the support was far less strong among those cities' working and lower classes. This suggests that the winged gospel appealed more to the upper and middle classes, those mostly likely to have the opportunity to participate in aviation, than to the working and lower classes.

Other evidence of the limits to the winged gospel came in the form of legal challenges. The late 1920s and the 1930s witnessed a series of lawsuits dealing with the very legality of publicly owned airports as well as asserting the claim that airports represented a nuisance. While courts generally ruled in favor of airports, the challenges were real and viewed as serious. To some extent, airports played the same role in relation to airplanes as garages, filling stations, and parking lots did to the automobile. Americans clearly embraced the automobile but proved far less enthusiastic about garages, filling stations, and parking lots, especially when such facilities located near their homes. In much the same way a number of Americans may have embraced the airplane, but they were far less enthusiastic about airports, whether located nearby or not.

And while certainly a number of federal officials as well as a number of members of Congress could be counted among the true believers in aviation, the same was not true of federal officials and members of Congress in general. This was particularly apparent when, again, it came to the Federal Airport Act of 1946. The aviation enthusiasts may have written into the act the bias in favor of smaller airports, but they were not successful in convincing Congress to fully fund the program created by the act. Clearly Congress—and the federal government in general—was far more "autominded" than "airminded."

As cities began to construct airports, that activity attracted the attention of members of the emerging profession of city planning. When looking at planners' periodic interest in airports, one can see a number of elements of the general history of airports. First, planners definitely defined airports as being local. However, whereas urban aviation boosters generally focused on the role their airports would play in gaining their city a place in the emerging national system of aerial transportation, city planners, especially in the late 1920s and early 1930s, saw airports as parts of a regional or metropolitan (essentially local) system of transportation. That reflected the fact that in some ways city planners also bought into the winged gospel's promise of a future in which airplanes would serve as forms of personal transportation. While planners were wrong about the future of the personal airplane, during the formative period they developed a number of the very basic ideas dealing with the planning of airports. They also provided cities with a tool that would become important in the postwar period, airport zoning.

Though airports became defined as primarily the responsibility of local governments, throughout the formative period the federal government played an important, growing, and evolving role. As noted, the two most important first "customers" of airports in the United States were the Post Office and the military. Over time, the role of the federal government in the establishment, maintenance, and improvement of airports increased. Between 1926 and 1933, the federal government took the first steps toward developing national-level policies and programs concerning aviation. In 1926 Congress passed the first legislation regulating aviation in the United States and created an aviation bureaucracy within the Department of Commerce. Reflecting the associationalism van der Linden identified as shaping aviation policy during this time period, the Aeronautics Branch proceed to offer limited help to cities interested in building and operating airports.

The first federal financial aid to cities and their airports came with the New Deal through several of its relief agencies, particularly the Civil Works Administration, the Federal Emergency Relief Administration, and the Works Projects Administration. The aid was indirect, though. It paid almost exclusively for labor to work on airport projects, not for needed material or equipment. By the end of the 1930s city leaders were actively lobbying Congress for more and more direct federal airport aid. Congress in essence authorized such aid in 1938 when it called for a national airport plan and a program for civilian airport improvement. Concerns about the growing federal deficit and the gathering war clouds in Europe derailed the effort, however. The first major federal aid for airports came only with the war-preparedness efforts of the early 1940s and with the war itself. Following the precedent set by the wartime aid, Congress established a long-term program for federal aid to the nation's municipal airports in 1946.

With every increase in aid came an increase in the number and kinds of federal rules and regulations cities had to agree to and follow when it came to the airports. Even when basically all the Aeronautics Branch could offer was advice, local regulations dealing with aviation gradually came to conform to those poli-

cies established in or promoted by Washington. For example, local aviation ordinances specifically mentioned the regulations established under the Air Commerce Act. And, reflecting the Progressive Era desire for standardization, the
Aeronautics Branch helped promote and publicize uniform acts dealing with
aviation and airports that cities and states could and did use as models. With the
coming of New Deal moneys, cities found themselves having to deal far more
with federal rules and regulations. The federal aviation bureaucracy in the form
of the Bureau of Air Commerce and then the Civil Aeronautics Authority could
and did force cities to bring their airports into compliance with federal guidelines. The rules and regulations only became more complex as federal aid increased.

In addition to the federal aviation bureaucracy, cities also forged a relationship with another branch of the federal government, the military. Due to this
connection, the history of municipal airports in the United States can be seen in
some ways as a case study in evolving civil-military relations. As noted, between
1919 and 1926 the military, particularly the Army's air arm, aggressively sought local help. To fly and train, the military needed available aviation facilities around
the country. Neither the War Department nor the Department of the Navy had
the budget to build such facilities. Of necessity they turned to the nation's cities.
The Army Air Service in particular established programs aimed at encouraging
local interests to provide airports. The military's role was less visible from the late
1920s through the late 1930s, but it continued to locate units, especially those of
its reserve components, on municipal airports, and representatives of the military
when called upon offered advice to cities. From the late 1930s through the end
of World War II military needs helped justify the first major programs for direct
federal aid to municipal airports. Although both the development of airports in
general and wartime spending on airports in particular had a certain regional fla-
vor, the defense-related aid during the 1940s brought significant improvements
to airports all over the country. And the continued military value of airports provided part of the justification for the postwar airport aid program.

The growing and evolving relationship between cities and the federal government in a variety of areas, including airports, brought a response from the
states. States traditionally had played something of a mediator role between cities
and the federal government. That role had been challenged by the New Deal
and its direct aid to cities.[19] During the debate and negotiations over the terms of
the Federal Airport Act of 1946, states and their congressional allies sought to
shape the legislation so that states played their traditional mediator role in terms
of airport funding.

As city governments took on greater responsibility for airports, eventually coming to own them, the means by which cities would manage their airports also changed and evolved. Initially, airport management was an additional duty taken on by an existing department within city government, frequently a department dealing either with streets or, more controversially, parks. Increasingly, though, cities created separate aviation and/or airport departments or commissions to handle the job.

Finally, just as the relationships between cities, states, the federal government, and airports evolved and grew more complex over time, airports themselves grew more complex, as demonstrated particularly in Douglas's dissertation. In 1919 airports were rather simple affairs, consisting mostly of large, open fields with a minimum amount of not very sophisticated equipment. That changed with the development of airport lighting, radio-navigation equipment, the need for a durable all-weather landing surface, passenger demands for greater comfort, weather reporting equipment, and a host of other aviation advances that came with the 1920s and 1930s. Airports were initially promoted as inexpensive. Within a few short years, however, the costs of building and maintaining a full service, up-to-date airport escalated rapidly. Throughout, cities bore the burden of the ever increasing costs. That fueled the drive for direct federal airport aid in the late 1930s.

This work seeks to provide an overview of the early history of municipal airports within the United States. While it focuses on airports in general, examples were drawn from the experiences of a wide variety of individual municipal airports. They included airports located in some of the nation's largest cities, as well as those near smaller, medium-sized cities. There is no claim that the individual airports included in this study constitute a fully representative cross-section of America's municipal airports. The examples used in the study are, in many ways, those airports that captured the attention of the aviation journals of the day. They also include those few airports that have received the attention of historians and other scholars. An effort was made, though, to include airports from both larger and smaller cities and from each region of the country. The nation's major airports, those in New York, Philadelphia, Washington, D.C., Chicago, Atlanta, Dallas, Denver, and Los Angeles, to name some of the largest, may indeed represent the airports closest to the center of and most vital to the nation's aerial transportation system. Their prominent position, however, makes them somewhat special rather than typical. The examples drawn from the histories of the large number of airports at the nation's smaller, medium-sized cities—Milwaukee, Dayton, Omaha, Tulsa, and Wichita, among others—may in some ways be more typical. And to a certain extent, though one that should not be emphasized too greatly, there was a certain regional variation in the development of municipal airports in the United States. In the end, though, as is often the case, the examples used also represent those cities for which information on the airports was the most readily available to the researcher. However, it should also be kept in mind that, especially during this formative period, it may have been difficult to find any typical airport or set of airports. While developing within a broad framework of federal action and the same general economic conditions, airport developments were largely driven by local politics, conditions, and structures.

Overall, the relationship between cities and airports was one that evolved over time and proved quite complex. This study does not claim to have definitely asked, let alone answered, all the important questions about municipal airports in the United States during the formative period of 1919 through 1947. However, it does attempt to offer some answers and an exploration of the most obvious and important issues. This history of airports in the United States is one that has received little attention. Some work has been done over the last thirty years, and particularly in the last decade, but much remains. The author hopes that this work offers a sense of the possibilities and a starting point for future explorations.

1

Pioneer Efforts

World War I to 1926

When the first cities began to build airports in 1919 they were treading on new ground. Like airplanes, airports were novelties. Cities had few examples, if any, to follow. In many ways, therefore, the earliest municipal airports grew out of very individual experimentation on the part of many cities. Over the first few years of airport development, cities had to devise ways to build and finance airports, sometimes stretching existing municipal powers to their limits. Different cities came up with different answers as to how best to accomplish the job. Although it was generally acknowledged that airports should be built locally, what exactly constituted municipal airports, how they should be built and financed, and what their relationship to their sponsoring cities should be had to be worked out gradually. The idea that "municipal airport" meant only an airport owned and operated by a city did not come about until the 1930s.

Both the Air Service and the Post Office played important roles in prodding local interests to build airports. Each had a deep concern in the development of a nationwide system of air transportation—one in the name of national defense and the other in the name of commerce and communication. Neither, however, had the funds needed to build airports. Of necessity they turned to the nation's cities to help them in fulfilling their goals. Local interests responded to the requests by the Post Office and the Air Service due both to urban boosterism and to the aviation enthusiasm of the age.

The period between 1919 and 1926 witnessed many important firsts in the history of municipal airports. Most obviously, the first municipal airport appeared. In addition, this era also saw the passage of the first federal laws, the first state airport enabling acts, the first municipal ordinances regulating aviation in general and airports in particular, and the first arguments supporting the idea that airports were a local (and ideally a local government) responsibility. While this time period also included some of the earliest calls for federal action on aviation and, to an extent, on airports, by 1926 it had been fairly firmly, but not exclusively, established that local governments (primarily cities, but sometimes counties or city-county combinations), with or without federal aid, would take the lead in building the nation's airports.

A Word About "Municipal Airports"

Outside Dayton, Ohio, on a piece of land now within the confines of Wright-Patterson Air Force Base, is the location of what one author has called the world's first airport, the Huffman Prairie Flying Field.[1] After their triumph on the remote outer banks of North Carolina in December, 1903, Wilbur and Orville Wright sought a location nearer their home to further test and refine their invention. A local landowner, Torrence Huffman, agreed to let the brothers use a pasture he owned outside of town, just off the interurban rail line, as long as they were careful not to let the horses and cows stray. The brothers agreed, and during the next two years the Huffman Prairie Flying Field witnessed the first regular flights of a manned, heavier-than-air flying machine. Before becoming part of Wilbur Wright Field during World War I, the flying field also served as the location of the Wright brothers' flying school and exhibition company.[2]

Calling the Huffman Prairie an airport may, indeed, be a bit of an exaggeration. The location was basically an open, level field, wide enough and long enough to accommodate the takeoff and landing requirements of the early Wright flyers. Over the years the brothers built three hangars on the site (1904, 1905, and 1910). Generally speaking, though, the Huffman Prairie Flying Field probably was quite similar to the other fields being used at that time for land-based aircraft.[3] In the years before World War I, with the exception of a few military training fields and perhaps a few private fields, airfields remained rather simple, informal places. As the Wright and Curtiss exhibition companies toured the country, for example, they frequently operated out of airfields that had only become airfields in anticipation of their arrival. In the early days any flat, open piece of land—including golf courses, racetracks, and fairgrounds—could and did serve as airfields. As long as flying remained exhibition-oriented and experimental in nature, such arrangements worked fairly well. All that changed with the need for military pilots and then, more important, Post Office pilots to fly from one location to another on a fairly regular basis and find upon landing fuel, shelter, repair help, and, in the case of the Post Office, facilities for handling the mail.

In 1919 representatives from three aviation organizations in Atlantic City, New Jersey—the Aero Club of America, the Aerial League of America, and the Atlantic City Aero Club—joined together to establish the nation's first municipal "Air Port." As envisioned by its founders, the Atlantic City Air Port would fulfill more than a dozen purposes, including serving as a "municipal aviation field, an aerial mail station and aerial police station for Atlantic City," and provide an example of a "model air port" for other cities to follow. The founders apparently had dreams of their field being a great port of entry for land aircraft, seagoing aircraft, and dirigibles, public and private. In short, like many who would follow them, the founders of the Atlantic City Air Port believed that in creating that municipal aviation facility they would bring all sorts of profitable aviation activities to their city.[4]

Following the announcement, however, Atlantic City and its Air Port seldom, if ever, appeared again in any of the magazines and journals covering aviation activity in the United States. Atlantic City is still credited with creating the nation's first municipal airport, but most of the dreams of its founders apparently were not fulfilled. Atlantic City appeared neither on Post Office nor Air Service routes in the early 1920s. The condition of the field in 1919 also suggested that the founders' dreams needed much work before they would be fully realized. The same article announcing the creation of the Atlantic City Air Port described it as basically 160 acres of flat, cleared land. While it was said to have an entrance "only 2,000 feet from the Boardwalk," no mention was made of any hangars or any other equipment or facilities on the field. Perhaps, therefore, the greatest legacy of the actions of the people of Atlantic City was in their use of the term "air port."

Air port, airdrome, airfield, landing field, aviation field, and, eventually, airport were all terms used to describe the aviation facilities being built in or near America's cities beginning in 1919 to serve the needs of the Post Office, the military, private fliers, and a very few commercial aviation concerns. Many of the earliest municipal aviation facilities were barely more complex than the Huffman Prairie Flying Field as they consisted mainly of enough land to allow for aircraft arrivals and departures, a hangar, and perhaps some refueling supplies and equipment. Gradually, however, the term *airport* became the one used most frequently in relation to these facilities. No matter how simple they may have been to start with, all those local facilities looked forward to a time when they would serve as "air ports," as places where airplanes, along with mail, cargo, and passengers, could arrive, depart, and be serviced, much in the spirit of the hopes expressed by the founders of Atlantic City's air port. During the early 1920s all the terms listed above were used—largely interchangeably—to describe what were being built, but by the middle of the decade "airport" emerged as the most commonly used word. For example, the Air Service began the decade calling the more developed aviation facilities it wished cities to build *airdromes*. There is no clear indicator in the literature, but it would be a good guess that the Air Service favored that word as a result of its wartime experience in Europe, where it was one of many terms used to describe aviation facilities. Also used was the term *aerodrome*, but Samuel Langley, of the Smithsonian and a pioneer American aviation experimenter, had already misused that word in naming his powered aircraft models, including the one that plunged unceremoniously and very publicly into the Potomac River on December 8, 1903. The Army might have been particularly sensitive about using that term as it funded Langley's efforts. Regardless, by 1923 the Air Service began to use the term *airport*.

Just as all the terms listed above were used in the early 1920s, so the following discussion of airport development in the early 1920s will use those terms. However, by the end of this early period, and especially after 1926, the use of the term *airport* came into general use in the United States and will be used more generally in the discussion. Where distinctions are called for, they will be made. But generally it should be understood that whether called an air port, airport, landing field, airdrome, airfield, flying field, or aviation field, the facilities created in this early period represented the foundations of America's municipal airports.

Finally, most of the pamphlets, articles, brochures, and other literature calling for the construction of municipal airports in the early 1920s spoke of the responsibilities of cities to take action. For the most part, however, while much of the literature spoke to the desirability of having local governments build and own the airports, the reality was somewhat more complex and diverse. Until the late 1920s, which witnessed a wave of state enabling acts appearing on the books, with few exceptions cities did not have the power to construct and operate municipal airports. Therefore, when the Air Service, Post Office, or other individuals or groups called upon cities to create municipal airports, they generally ended up speaking not so much to the local governments as to local civic organizations and/or organizations of aviation enthusiasts within the cities. Many of the earliest airports, and even some created after the passage of a large number of enabling acts in the late 1920s, came about as a result of actions spearheaded in the private sector. And although many of those early airports were in essence private ventures, they were thought of as the municipal airports of their cities, and many, as was generally the original intent, were eventually bought by or donated to the local city governments. As a result, though the text will refer to a city taking action on an airport, through the mid-1930s the term "city" could refer to a local government (municipal or occasionally county) or local civic interests. It should be clear from the context which definition of the term should be kept in mind.

The Air Service and Early Airport Development

The role of the Post Office in establishing the nation's aerial transportation system, including early airports, has been widely discussed and accepted in the literature of aviation history. Less attention has been paid to the role played by the military, particularly the Army Air Service, between 1919 and 1926. A number of the earliest airports came about as a result of requests from the military. The requests largely grew out of the fact that the military did not have a budget large enough to build the necessary facilities. To further the end of prompting local action, the Air Service created programs aimed specifically at encouraging local interests to provide facilities it could use in the training of its pilots. The Air Service also published and distributed some of the earliest "how-to" literature on airport design and construction. While the military often worked in cooperation with the Post Office, its early, separate role in the establishment of airports is important to note.

During World War I the Army needed to train its fliers not just to fly, but to fly over long distances and from one location to another. In part to that end, and in part out of the need to train a large number of pilots rapidly, the War Department built a number of flying field-training bases throughout the country. After the war, the need for continued training led the Air Service to engage in two programs, both of which involved encouraging cities to establish airfields that could be used by military pilots. One program was the Model Airway, and the other, the Air Service Reserve Flying Field Program.

In material dating from the final days of World War I, the Air Service indicated difficulties in providing its pilots with cross-country flight training. The main problem seemed to be a lack of landing sites. Pilots on cross-country training missions often found themselves facing the prospect of having to land their planes on any available piece of vacant ground. To prove the point, in early November, 1918, the Air Service offered the example of a flight by Lieutenant Albert O. Spencer between Payne Field in Mississippi and Birmingham, Alabama. Sixty miles short of his destination, weather and a broken gas line forced Lieutenant Spencer to find somewhere to land his plane. The lieutenant broke out of the clouds over a small town, where he made a forced landing in a vacant lot. Townspeople, hearing the approaching plane, apparently ran out onto the improvised "airfield." To avoid hitting anyone, the lieutenant had to quickly turn his airplane. Unfortunately, that action resulted in a collision with a telegraph pole. A couple of broomsticks proved sufficient to repair the structural damage, and following further repairs to the gas line, Lieutenant Spencer was ready to take off. The "airfield," however, was too short, so he had to guide his aircraft carefully between telegraph poles and onto an adjacent cornfield. The new "airfield" afforded him just enough space to take off while avoiding hitting a nearby warehouse. And that was not the end of the lieutenant's adventure. In attempting to complete the flight to Birmingham, Lieutenant Spencer, again looking for adequate landing facilities as darkness approached, nearly put his plane down into a pond and finally did land his aircraft in a wide, deep ditch next to a road.[5]

At the end of November, 1918, the Air Service announced a program in which its pilots would begin to make "a series of cross-country flights to cities in their sectors to chart air lines, make air maps and gather valuable air statistics." The pilots would also "incidentally . . . locate Sites for landing fields and airdromes." The landing fields would "become a part of a great chain that soon [would] 'air link' every important community in the country from coast to coast." The airdromes would offer "shelter to visiting flyers" and would help "house the equipment the Air Service [would] bring back from overseas."[6]

The Air Service apparently saw a distinction between simple landing fields and what it called airdromes. A landing field was an area designed to, or simply large and flat enough to, allow the arrival and departure of airplanes. An airdrome was a more fully developed facility including hangars and refueling equipment in addition to an adequate landing area. By late December, 1918, the Air Service's *Weekly News Letter* indicated that at least one city, Tucson, Arizona, was willing to cooperate with the Air Service in creating an airdrome that could be used by military fliers.

In December, 1918, Air Service pilots mapping a southern transcontinental air route reported that Tucson had "a perfect landing field." They described it as two hundred acres of leveled land located two and one-half miles from the city. They also indicated that the city was willing to build a hangar.[7] In early 1919 the

Tucson Chamber of Commerce organized an Aviation Committee and the local newspaper began to promote the city as "'an ideal place for aviators.'"[8] In May, 1919, the mayor of Tucson received a letter from the U.S. Air Service formally requesting that the city build "a permanent airfield." A few months later a local councilman, Randolph E. Fishburn, convinced the city council to finance and build one. Apparently, the Chamber of Commerce donated the money to the city to fund the airfield "with the chamber's blessings." The available documents indicate that the new airfield was built not on the original landing field described in December, 1918, but on an eighty-two-acre site four miles south of the city. On November 20, 1919, the municipally owned airfield opened for business, both military and civilian. During its early years the Aviation Committee of the local Chamber of Commerce operated it.[9]

The program begun by the Air Service in 1918 in response to the adventures faced by pilots such as Lieutenant Spencer and that resulted in the construction of a very early municipal airport in Tucson soon grew into an ambitious plan to create a vast network of mapped, marked, and developed airways and airports across the country. To organize the establishment of those airways, and to promote the construction of the municipal airports and other landing fields needed along with them, the Air Service created an Airways Section within its headquarters in late 1920. The Air Service charged this new office with a number of responsibilities. For example, it was to advise on forest patrol and it coordinated "all other civilian activities of the Air Service." Its primary responsibility, though, was to "construct and supervise airways [and] municipal landing fields."[10] The first "Model Airway," constructed in early 1921, stretched from Bolling Field in Washington, D.C., to McCook Field in Dayton, Ohio, and necessitated the creation of a number of different facilities along the route.

The Air Service believed that the creation of a network of airways across the country was vital to both national defense and to the further development of aircraft and aviation in general. As envisioned, the airways would be open to all users—military and civilian, both private and commercial. The creation of the airways included "the location of landing fields and all accessories, including radio direction finding, radio communication, aids to night navigation, housing and maintenance of equipment."[11] While many of the stops along the airways would be military airfields, the Air Service also envisioned the establishment of municipal facilities, which, if possessing "all accessories," could appropriately be called airports.

Material explaining the new model airway program included a list of dozens of cities and towns in Maryland, Ohio, Virginia, and West Virginia in which the Air Service wished to see local authorities take action to aid in the construction of the first airway. Not all cities would be asked to build full airports. Most cities and towns would be asked merely to identify and mark the location of suitable landing areas where, in an emergency, planes could land.[12] And as a later report explained, many of the landing fields created as a result of that program were "merely farm land or unimproved facilities on which landings could be made."[13] For example, Rockville, Maryland, was said to have a "good landing field just west of the town but the stumps should be removed from the center of the field."[14] Other landing fields still needed markers so that they could be identified as landing fields from the air.

Several other towns, such as Hagerstown, Maryland, and Moundsville, West Virginia, however, were encouraged to create more developed facilities. By early 1921 each town had "come forward with available landing fields and preparations [were] now being made for erecting the hangars and gas and oil stations, and marking the fields." So, only a few of the towns along the new airway did or were expected to construct what might be called municipal airports.[15]

Those circumstances reflected a number of factors, including the state of aviation technology in the early 1920s. Given the planes of the day, especially the World War I surplus aircraft flown by the Air Service, any cross-country flying required—for safety, if not for absolute range limitations—providing places for the planes to land every 150 to 200 miles for servicing and refueling. Safety also dictated the presence of a large number of intermediate emergency landing facilities. Airplanes could and did break down frequently in those days. Many a farmer's field of that pioneering time found itself host to an unlucky pilot and aircraft. Therefore, the building the first Model Airway required the construction of intermediate facilities in such places as Cumberland, Maryland, and Columbus, Ohio. As the Air Service attempted to extend the airways nationwide, other cities and towns would be asked to provide either emergency landing fields or airports.

The Air Service's airway program continued until 1926. That year saw the passage of the Air Corps Act and the Air Commerce Act. The first piece of legislation transformed the Air Service into the more independent Air Corps. The second piece of legislation transferred the duty to create a national system of airways from the newly established Air Corps to the newly created Aeronautics Branch within the Department of Commerce.

Once moving beyond the creation of the first Model Airway in 1921, it becomes difficult to separate the influence of the Air Service from that of the Post Office in the promotion of the development of municipal airports. By the early 1920s both were actively engaged in the process of developing air routes across the United States and often coordinated their activities. Both efforts involved visiting cities throughout the country and trying to persuade local leaders to construct the desired facilities. Undoubtedly a number of cities received visits from both Post Office and Air Service officials. There was, however, another program, this one sponsored by the Air Service Reserve, that provided additional examples of early military influence in the creation of municipal airports.

In 1921, when Air Service Reserve officials approached the city, Pittsburgh, Pennsylvania, was ready to listen. The city's responsiveness grew out of the fact that its urban rival, Cleveland, had a place on the Post Office's developing transcontinental airmail route, and Pittsburgh, which did not have a landing field, had been excluded. Critics argued that the city found itself in that predicament because it had not acted quickly enough to meet the needs of the Post Office. However, in late 1921 the city saw an opportunity to make up for its tardiness by participating in the Air Service's Reserve Flying Field program.[16]

The Air Service suggested the creation of a Reserve Flying Field program in a 1920 report to the Secretary of War. During that year, Congress had provided for the training of Air Service Reserve officers (pilots) who could be called to active duty in case of emergency. Since those reserve officers needed to fly in order to train, the Air Service argued that the government needed to establish a number "of small, Federal [sic] owned or supported flying fields in the vicinity of populous centers, where the majority of Reserve officers [resided]."[17] During the following fiscal year (1921–22), a program to create federally supported fields got underway. Under the program the War Department financed the construction of facilities on the field while cities provided the land, which the Air Service leased for one dollar per year.[18] Advised on the existence and terms of the new Air Service Reserve Flying Field program—for instance, that fields could be used by both military and civilian pilots—Pittsburgh's Chamber of Commerce opened talks with the War Department.[19]

The problem was that in 1922, when negotiations began, the city lacked the power to purchase land for an airport. At that point, the Aero Club of Pittsburgh stepped in, leased the land that the city and the War Department had identified as the most suitable for an airport, and, in turn, sub-leased it to the War Department. The new airport, Rogers Field, was named in honor of Calbraith Rogers, a Pittsburgh native and the first person to fly coast-to-coast.[20]

Under the Air Service Reserve Flying Field Program, which faded away as appropriations for military aviation dropped in the early 1920s, a number of cities established facilities. In addition to Pittsburgh, they included Boston, Massachusetts; Kansas City, Missouri; Santa Monica, California; Cincinnati, Ohio; Louisville, Kentucky; Seattle, Washington; and Columbus, Ohio. The Air Service decided which cities would participate in the program on the following criteria: "population, number of Reserve Officers resident in the community, proposed location of Air Service units in the Organized Reserves and National Guard, location in relation to the proposed system of National Airways, and the interest and spirit of cooperation displayed by the community."[21] As indicated by the final criteria, the Air Service may have had some say in the location of the fields, but it was also dependent upon the cooperation of cities—cities wanting to gain a foothold in the evolving world of aviation by establishing an airport.

While neither the Model Airway nor the Reserve Flying Field programs proved great generators of municipal airports in terms of numbers, there was one final, important way in which the Air Service directly promoted the establishment of municipal airports throughout the United States. Before responsibility for creating a national system of airways shifted from the Air Service to the Aeronautics Branch, the Air Service compiled and published more than six hundred airway bulletins. The bulletins contained maps of and information describing major landing fields, including municipal airports, throughout the country. In addition, the Air Service had files on four thousand additional available landing sites in the United States.[22] Most important, in 1923 the Air Service published and widely distributed a basic how-to manual on airport construction for America's cities. Titled "Airways and Landing Fields," the Air Service information circular described the Air Service's Model Airway program, provided a map of all the proposed routes, and suggested to cities "How An Airport Should Be Built."[23]

The "how-to" section of the information circular began by making a quick reference to both "a thoroughly modern air terminal" and "a minor airport." It did not explain the differences between the two but did indicate that any facility calling itself an airport, whether minor or thoroughly modern, needed to meet certain minimum standards. The standards included those for location, size, shape, character of ground, approaches, markings, and accommodations.[24]

An airport, according the Air Service, should be located "within reach of ground transportation facilities, for the aerial transportation of passengers and merchandise [was] closely linked with these conveyers of commerce." The site should also provide for future growth. Initially, it "should allow a clear, unobstructed area of about 2,700 feet along the direction of the prevailing wind, if not in all directions." Pilots could take off from shorter fields, but safety dictated allowing for extra room in the case of the loss of an engine on takeoff. The best shape for a field was square, allowing for roughly equal lengths for landings and takeoffs in any direction. Fields could also be L-shaped, rectangular, or triangular. The circular included a sample diagram of the sizes and shapes of the "Four Types of Ideal Landing Fields."[25]

The ground needed to be "firm under all weather conditions" as well as "level and fairly smooth." Cities should avoid building their airports in locations where obstacles such as tall buildings, trees, or telephone and telegraph poles and wires would interfere with planes either approaching or departing the airport. The field itself should be clearly marked in a number of ways. A large white circle, filled with lime or a similar compound, should be placed at the center of the landing area. Within the circle, long, wide panels should be used to indicate to pilots the directions for takeoffs and landings. All airports should also have some kind of wind indicator on the field. That could be either a wind cone, a wind "T," or a smudge fire. Airports should also have "communication by telephone with nearest city or town, transportation facilities, gasoline, oil, and sundry supplies." Hangars and shops could be added "as the use of the field develops."[26]

As noted, Air Service efforts to establish municipal airports often overlapped with those of the Post Office. They also occasionally overlapped with projects aimed at supporting naval aviation. The Navy did not seem to have any programs equivalent to the Model Airways Program or to the Air Service Reserve Flying Field Program. Its aviators, though, still needed some land-based facilities, especially along the coasts, and the Navy did work to provide such. Seattle's earliest airport came about as a result of efforts by the Navy, the budding Boeing Company, King County (Seattle's home county), the Seattle Chamber of Commerce, and the Air Service Reserve.

Navy officials first traveled to the Seattle area on behalf of naval aviation in 1916. A Naval Commission, charged with locating sites for navy air bases, examined a number of prospective areas. William Boeing, who built and flew his first aircraft that year, aided the commission by providing topographical maps and transportation to each of the sites. After deliberation, the commission decided upon Sand Point, 210 acres of land along Lake Washington. The war apparently delayed the project as no action was taken until 1920. In that year the Board of Commissioners of King County purchased the Sand Point site and offered it to the Navy "on the sole condition that substantial improvements be made on the land." The Navy, however, proved unable to win the necessary funding from Congress. Therefore, the county offered to lease the land to the Navy for one dollar per year "without the original reservation as to the improvements." The county and the Navy finally signed a lease in December, 1922, that stipulated both the Air Service and commercial aviation interests could use the land.[27]

After that point the Sand Point facility became part of the Air Service Reserve Flying Field Program. The Air Service Reserve, with the permission of the Department of the Navy, established a "reserve airdrome" on the 29 acres of the site that had been cleared. The Air Service provided a steel hangar, and King County paid to have it erected on the site. The end result was described as "one flying field, not quite completed, but serviceable at no expense to the Government." And those from the Seattle area who worked so hard to establish that first facility found "the fact that planes [were] actually flying out of Sand Point [was] good reason for rejoicing and self-congratulations."[28]

Throughout the early 1920s the Air Service (and occasionally the Navy) was clearly aiding and encouraging cities across the country to build municipal airports. The Air Service circular in 1923 provided early, important guidelines for cities to follow. While many of the airports cities then built began as "minor airports," a number established in this early period would grow into some of the nation's larger, more important airports. In addition to the Air Service and Navy, another government agency actively promoting the establishment of airports was the Post Office.

The Post Office and Early Airport Development

The Post Office also found itself placed in the position of turning to local interests for the airport facilities it needed due to limited budgets. Similar to the military, the Post Office found some willing partners in cities. In this case the local interests were anxious to become part of the planned airmail system. The promise of airmail, and especially the urban booster arguments tied to that promise, led local interests, including city governments, to act on airport projects.

In the 1917–18 budget, Congress gave the Post Office $100,000 to conduct airmail experiments. Although it would eventually own its own planes and hire its own pilots, in order to get started as soon as possible, the Post Office borrowed both planes and pilots from the U.S. Air Service, which saw flying the mail as a training opportunity. On May 15, 1918, flying from a makeshift field between the Potomac River and the Tidal Basin in Washington, D.C., the first government airmail plane took off for New York. That first airmail plane's pilot set off in the wrong direction and then crash-landed about twenty-five miles away in Waldorf, Maryland. Despite that rather dismal first performance, the airmail service, sought after for years by businessmen, soon established itself as reliable and valuable.[29] But, in order for the service to expand, it needed not only more planes and pilots but also a network of airports to receive and service the planes and handle the airmail bags. To that end, Post Office officials, like Air Service officials, traveled about the country along proposed air routes, attempting to entice cities into building a municipal airport. Sometimes officials from the Post Office and the Air Service crossed paths. Atlanta, Georgia, represented one such case.

In 1921 Air Service officers arrived in Atlanta as part of the ongoing efforts to survey and promote extensions of the military airway system. One route they envisioned stretched from Washington, D.C., to San Diego, California, with important intermediary airports at a number of locations, including Atlanta. While a couple of local groups, including reserve army officers and the Chamber of Commerce, responded favorably, Atlanta's new mayor, William Sims, declared the project too expensive and it quietly died. In 1924, however, the military approached the city once more. It wanted to establish an airfield at the existing arsenal south of the city and to explore again the possibility of the city establishing an airfield. This request might have also involved the Reserve Flying Field program.[30]

The Air Service's proposals failed to overcome local opposition. The possibility of connecting with the emerging airmail network, on the other hand, proved a stronger incentive for action. At the same time Air Service proposals faltered, Atlanta businessmen expressed a strong desire to bring airmail service to the city. A local newspaper pointed out that the Post Office had rejected one proposed route (Atlanta to New York via Washington, D.C.) because Atlanta had no official airport.[31] As far as can be gathered from the literature, an "official" airport was any local airport—publicly or privately owned or leased—with a minimum level of development that a city formally named its official airport.

Mayor Sims remained reluctant to commit the city. He argued that the site proposed initially cost too much, even with the county picking up half the tab. Then in December, 1924, a local aviation pioneer, Asa G. Candler, offered the city a deal on his property, an abandoned racetrack that had been the site of aviation exhibitions. The city could have the land rent-free for two years; all it had to do was pay the taxes. Still the city failed to take action. Local pressure increased, however, and in February, 1925, several local civic groups, backed by the senior U.S. senator from Georgia—who promised that if Atlanta became part of a government airmail route, the government would pay for the airport—mounted a coordinated campaign to gain such a facility for the city. Asa Candler again offered his land, and on April 16, 1925, Mayor Sims, on behalf of the city, signed a lease for the property, which became Atlanta's municipal airport. The city would have to wait another year, however, before the airmail finally arrived.[32]

As the airmail service grew during the early 1920s and the commercial potential of air travel became more easily imagined, several cities, in ways similar to those seen in Atlanta, took action to establish municipal airports. Chicago, an early and important stop on the growing airmail service network, represented an important example of municipal involvement in airport finance and construction tied to the airmail program. In 1916 the Aero Club of Chicago financed and developed an airport at Eighty-third Street and Cicero Avenue, calling it Ashburn Field. When the Post Office announced plans for airmail service to Chicago, the club hoped that the Post Office would use Ashburn Field as its terminal. Considered too remote, it lost out to Grant Park along the Chicago waterfront, which had been used as an aviation exhibition field. In 1919, the club went to the city of Chicago hoping to persuade the city council to invest money in Ashburn Field in order to establish it as Chicago's municipal airport. That plan failed in the wake of a disastrous blimp crash that soured many on the city council to the whole idea of aviation.[33]

During the first eight years of operation, the airmail service in Chicago shifted between three airports—Grant Park, Checkerboard Field, and Maywood Field, the latter two located west of the city limits. Following the establishment of round-the-clock airmail flights in 1924, many civic leaders in Chicago became determined that the city build a municipal airport within the city. Charles Wacker, chairman of the City Plan Commission, went to the city council in July, 1924, asking that it lease some property owned by the Board of Education for use as an airport. The city council initially took little action. But in early 1925, with the passage of the Kelly Act, which transferred responsibility for carrying airmail from the Post Office to private commercial operators, the council moved quickly to sign a lease, and early the following year it approved $25,000 for improvements to the field, which then became Chicago's municipal airport.[34]

Atlanta, Chicago, and a number of cities across the country responded to the Post Office's call for municipal airport facilities, just as other cities built airports to aid the Air Service. The number of cities establishing those very early municipal airports, while not great, was remarkable. In 1919 no cities had the power to establish a municipal airport. Therefore, another important part of the history of this pioneering era is the story, first, of how some cities established airports in the absence of enabling legislation and, second, of early state actions allowing for municipal airports.

Cities, States, and Airports

When the Post Office and the Air Service tried to recruit cities to build airports, few responded. For one thing, simple as they were (still often open fields with perhaps a single hangar—only a few airports, even as of 1926, had lighting) the early airports cost money. And although the Post Office apparently hinted at eventual government reimbursements, no money flowed into municipal coffers to help pay expenses.[35] Second, cities had never built airports before and, as noted in the Pittsburgh example, had no authority to begin to do so. In the United States, cities are creations of the states in which they are located. Even with home rule, the powers of cities are (and were) limited by their charters. Before a city could build an airport, it either had to find a way to stretch its existing powers or it had to be enabled by the state specifically to build an airport.

When Pittsburgh officials ran up against the problem of no municipal authority to build an airport, private interests stepped in initially to keep the airport project on track. The city, however, also took action. In 1923 Pittsburgh's solicitor drafted two bills that were then sent to the state legislature. One enabled counties to purchase land for airports and the other enabled cities of a certain class to do so as well, both within and outside city limits. Why the city sent forth both bills was unclear. Perhaps proponents wanted to double their chances for success, believing that even if the state legislature rejected one bill it might approve the other. Or perhaps, as subsequent actions suggest, the city of Pittsburgh needed some assistance and hoped to persuade the county of Allegheny to help in the airport project by either taking it over entirely or sharing the costs. Either way, both bills passed, and in 1923 the city and county entered into talks that produced a city-county agreement to purchase the Rogers Field site and operate a city-county airport. Despite some local opposition, mostly from the Fox Chapel Country Club and the elite Shadyside Academy located near the site, Rogers Field opened as a city-county airport in June, 1925.[36]

Pennsylvania was not the first state to take action as Indiana passed the first general airport enabling act in 1920.[37] Kansas, Nebraska, and Wisconsin passed the necessary legislation the following year. Pennsylvania then acted in 1923 along with Minnesota (1923), followed by Washington (1925), Kentucky (1926), and Ohio (1926).[38] However, most states took no action before 1927.

The state enabling laws passed up through 1926 generally allowed cities (or cities of a certain size or class) to establish municipal aviation fields or airports.[39] There were variations, though, concerning which local governmental unit could establish the airport (city and/or county) and under what conditions it could be established. The Kansas, Nebraska, Ohio, and Pennsylvania laws specifically allowed cities to establish airports. Laws in Indiana, Washington, and Wisconsin enabled cities or counties to take action, and Pennsylvania also passed a law specifically allowing counties to establish airports.[40] Minnesota, on the other hand, passed a very restrictive law. The Minnesota act applied only to rather large counties—more than 5,000 square miles and with populations exceeding 200,000—with areas experiencing fire dangers. The act specifically noted that the facilities would serve those involved in fire patrol work. Minnesota law did not allow for municipal airports until 1927.[41]

In Kentucky, the state took the lead under the law, but it also allowed for local action. Kentucky's 1926 legislation created a state air board and gave it the responsibility to "provide air ports and air routes together with the necessary equipment, markings, personnel, etc., for the State of Kentucky as best suits the interests and future of aviation, both commercial and military." The board could act alone, but it was also authorized to work with "counties, cities, or incorporated towns, private corporations, voluntary unincorporated associations or individuals" in establishing airports. Further, the act allowed for "the fiscal court of any county and the governing body of any city or incorporated town" acting alone, jointly with each other, or with the state air board to establish airports.[42]

Before 1927, though, in the absence of any enabling legislation in most states, cities had to employ various means to get their airports built. As a consequence, during the early years, the term "municipal airport" came to mean a local airport, but not necessarily a local, publicly owned airport. For example, answering the urgings of a local civic group, the state of Massachusetts passed a very narrow law enabling the state's department of public works "to Construct and Lease to the United States Government an Airplane Landing Field on the Property of the Commonwealth in East Boston."[43] Boston's first "municipal airport" thus began as a project built and owned by the state of Massachusetts for the Air Service Reserve Flying Field program. The city did not take over the airport until 1928.[44]

Omaha's Chamber of Commerce provided that city with its first municipal airport in 1920, a year before the state passed the necessary enabling legislation, by raising money to build a hangar on property it rented from another civic organization, AK-SAR-BEN, which operated a racetrack on the land. That airport, created for the use of the Post Office, helped establish Omaha as an important link on the emerging transcontinental airmail network. The city itself did not build a municipal airport until the late 1920s, after the original AK-SAR-BEN field had been abandoned.[45]

St. Louis civic leaders also took action similar to that of Omaha's. St. Louis's civic leadership exhibited a very early interest in aviation activities. In 1909 and again in 1910 the city hosted major balloon races. In the latter year the city's Chamber of Commerce also arranged for the grading of a field and the erection of a grandstand so that the city could host an exhibition by the Wright Company. In 1918 the Chamber of Commerce, in concert with the Missouri Aeronautical Society and the city of St. Louis, raised $28,000 to grade a landing field and provide a hangar for the Post Office's new airmail service. Those funds provided for the preparation of a 100-acre field in a section of Forest Park and the shipment and reconstruction of an Army hangar on the site. The first airmail plane arrived on August 16, 1920.[46]

Both the airmail and the airfield disappeared within a year. The airmail route was the victim of budget cuts; the Forest Park site judged too small. Even before the Forest Park site opened, however, many of the same people involved in its establishment also developed another, larger airfield eleven miles northwest of the city's downtown area. In June, 1920, several members of the Missouri Aeronautical Society, including Major Albert Bond Lambert, William and Frank Robertson, and Randall Foster, opened an airfield on 160 acres of land Major Lambert leased from its owner. Lambert then paid to have the field cleared and graded, arranged for the improvement of adjacent roads, and erected hangars. He offered the free use of the field, named the St. Louis Flying Field, to any and all aviators. In 1923, the St. Louis Flying Field, expanded through the temporary leasing of 316 additional adjacent acres, played host to the International Air Races. When the original lease expired in 1925, Major Lambert purchased approximately 170 acres of land and continued to offer his now privately owned field free of charge to all aviators.[47]

All along, however, Major Lambert wanted the city of St. Louis to take possession of the field. With the Forest Park site closed, Lambert's field was, essentially, functioning as the city's municipal airport. The Robertson brothers operated their Robertson Aircraft Corporation on the field, offering both passenger and air freight services. When airmail service resumed, the mail landed at the Lambert-St. Louis Flying Field, as it was known after 1925. Several other flight schools and charter companies also located on the field. Major Lambert had to wait until 1928, though, before the voters approved the bond issue and the city purchased his land, along with additional acres, and took control of the airport. Rear Admiral Richard Byrd helped the city christen its aviation field, Lambert-St. Louis Municipal Airport, in 1930.[48]

Therefore, the earliest municipal airports came about by various means, including being built by a city (even in the absence of enabling legislation), by a city-county combination, by the state, or, most commonly, by a local civic group or private individual in the city's name. The general idea was, though, that airports should be built by local interests, preferably with strong ties (formal or informal) to the local government. By the time the Air Commerce Act formally adopted the "dock concept" in 1926, which gave responsibility for the nation's airports to the local level, practice had already firmly established the idea of local airports.

Why Cities and Municipal Airports

If cities lacked the specific power to build and operate airports, why all the early, continued insistence upon municipal airports as the means to building a network of landing fields throughout the country? First, as noted, both the military and the Post Office encouraged cities, or more generally at first civic groups within cities, to build airports. Although the Post Office, in particular, sometimes vaguely promised future federal aid—a promise that cities tried to force the federal government to honor—it, as well as the military, clearly lacked budgets large enough to build the needed facilities. In the absence of federal funds, those organizations turned to the governmental body or to local interests with close ties to local governments they deemed most likely to agree to help build airports. Second, cities acted on airport projects because of urban boosterism. Airports emerged in the early 1920s as the newest important facility a city must have in order to keep up with or even surpass its urban rivals. And, finally, many involved in early airport projects were not only urban boosters but also evidently swept up in the general aviation enthusiasm of the day.

In the early 1920s Post Office officials traveled across the country trying by various means, including broadly hinting at possible federal aid, to entice cities to establish municipal airports. As noted in the Atlanta case, even a U.S. senator suggested that the federal government would reimburse cities for the expense of providing airports.[49] Neither the Post Office nor the Air Service had the funds to spare, however. A number of cities, including two in particular, did try to force the federal government to make good on implied promises of aid. In 1926 representatives from Omaha, Nebraska, went to Congress and testified on behalf of a bill that would have reimbursed the Omaha Chamber of Commerce for the expenses it incurred when, at the behest of the Post Office, it created Omaha's first airport. Representatives of firms from Salt Lake City, Utah, who also sought reimbursement for expenses, joined the Omaha representatives.

In May, 1926, the House of Representatives considered two bills. One bill provided reimbursement to the Omaha Chamber of Commerce; the second bill, for reimbursements to a number of firms in Salt Lake City, Utah. Both cities had built airports at the express request of the Post Office and both had been assured by Post Office representative John A. Jordon—referred to in the hearings as Colonel Jordon—that all expenses would be reimbursed.

John A. Jordon worked for Benjamin Lipsner, the first superintendent of the Air Mail Service. Lipsner was appointed by Otto Praeger, the man contemporaries and historian William Leary have called the "Father of the Air Mail," who served as the second assistant postmaster general of the United States in the early 1920s. As Praeger planned for the expansion of the Post Office's airmail service, Lipsner faced the task of persuading cities to provide adequate facilities. To that end, Lipsner sent Jordon to cities along each planned route extension. Jordon was told to "contact the post master at each city, secure introductions to officers of the Chamber of Commerce and wealthy businessmen, and arrange for newspaper publicity." He was also told to cultivate a relationship with the wealthy women in town. Lipsner believed that they sometimes could be persuaded to take action more quickly than the men.[50] Jordon, though not authorized to do so, also apparently made promises about money.

Testimony at the hearings considering the Omaha and Salt Lake City bills indicated that they were not the only cities seeking reimbursements. Two years before, seventeen cities, most along the Post Office's transcontinental mail route, had pushed Congress to vote funds to pay them back for their expenses. The postmaster general, Paul Henderson, was in favor of the first bill, but Congress failed to pass it. The 1926 hearings did not specify exactly why the first bill failed to pass, but its $277,000 price tag might have had something to do with it. The postmaster general did not favor the 1926 Omaha or Salt Lake City bills, however. While he still felt that the government should reimburse the cities, the increased economy drive within the government would not allow for it. Further, if those two cities should be reimbursed, then the other cities could also come forward and press their claims once again. And, since the Post Office foresaw future expansion of airmail routes, all cities on those new routes would also expect to have their expenses covered by the Post Office or the federal government.[51]

William Leary's history of the Post Office's experience establishing the nation's airmail service made it clear that despite the ballyhoo that often surrounded it, the Post Office's airmail service suffered under tight budgets throughout its existence.[52] It, like the Air Service, depended on cities and the civic groups within them to provide the needed fields. The Post Office did have an advantage, though. It was far easier to convince cities and civic groups of the economic value of airmail to a community than the value of a military airfield. Fortunately for the Post Office, many cities jumped at the chance of securing a place on the airmail route and provided the needed facilities. However, year by year the Post Office struggled to convince a reluctant and tight-fisted Congress to give it the funds necessary to expand and improve its airmail service. The Post Office seldom received all the funds it felt necessary to operate its service on a day-to-day basis and to provide what it considered the most necessary improvements such as beacon lights, two-way radios, and other developing technologies aimed at enhancing safety and reliability. Funds for airports simply were not available.

The Post Office may have wanted to help cities finance airport construction, but the political climate of the early 1920s would not allow for it. The Post Office had to come to rely on cities or groups within cities taking on the financial burdens. The Air Service was not in much better shape when it came to funding. It would also need help from local groups when it came to providing needed facilities. To its advantage, though, it entered the 1920s with a history, albeit a short one, of cities acting eagerly to provide the Air Service with needed facilities, at least in time of war, at little or no cost and with no expectation of reimbursement.

During the war the Air Service needed to build a number of military aviation facilities throughout the country. Congress voted the needed funds, and Brigadier General George O. Squier, aided by Colonel Benjamin Foulois, immediately began to make plans to construct training fields. Foulois soon tapped Lieutenant Colonel Clinton Edgar to handle the task of inspecting and examining proposed flying field sites. Edgar and the site-selection board he formed traveled across the country examining sites and opening negotiations with "local business groups, chambers of commerce, or individuals for leases and options." What the board found was that in most places with potential sites, local interests had formed committees to deal with the Air Service, to handle acquiring options or leases on land, and to gather other information.[53] In a number of cases, the Air Service acquired the land for its new flying fields at very little cost because of the actions of those local committees.

In Dallas, Texas, for example, local civic leaders convinced the Air Service to build a training field near the city by arranging to present the Air Service with six hundred acres of land. Following the donation of land, the Air Service established Love Field.[54] Dayton, Ohio, persuaded the Air Service to establish three facilities in and around that city by means of arranging for inexpensive land upon which to build what became the Fairfield Air Depot, Wilbur Wright Field, and McCook Field.[55]

With the end of the war, the Air Service found itself still in need of facilities. However, its budget was far smaller, and it continued to shrink throughout the early 1920s. If it was to gain and maintain the facilities it required to continue to fly and train, the Air Service needed to encourage cities to extend the help they provided during wartime into the peacetime period. Both the Air Service and the Post Office had to get cities to see the value of building airports.

The letter the Air Service sent to Tucson, Arizona, in 1919 asking the city to establish a landing field was also sent to thirty-one other cities. That letter, dated April 30, clearly indicated that the Air Service and the Post Office expected cities to build "the primary facility for operation of aircraft in their vicinity" that would allow for the development of "aerial intercity transportation, express service, mail service, emergency service and local photographic mapping or aerial protection." The Air Service and the Post Office would cooperate with cities, but that was it. And even their ability to cooperate was somewhat limited, at least at first. The 1919 letter indicated that they would cooperate only with those cities "where the aerial mail service [required] stations or where stations [were] required for cross-country use of the Air Service." That did not mean, however, that other cities were discouraged from also establishing landing fields. Rather, the letter seemed to suggest as many cities as possible should begin constructing fields but that both organizations were limited in the amount of help they could provide and would have to concentrate their efforts on those cities that most closely met the military's and the Post Office's needs.[56]

In July, 1919, the *American City* printed a letter to the editor from Major H. M. Hickam of the Air Service explaining the War Department policy in more detail. That letter listed the thirty-two cities to which the April letter had been sent and, again, encouraged other cities to establish landing fields as well. Major Hickam's letter also included a copy of what appeared to be an early version of the 1923 information circular on airfield construction. Called "Specification for Municipal Landing Fields," the document offered cities advice on where fields should be located, their size and shape, the character of the ground, the approaches, markings, and accommodations. In addition, it included a sample diagram of several different landing fields. Clearly, the most the Air Service had to offer was advice.

With the creation of the Model Airway Program in 1921, the Air Service stated up front that it did not have the funds to build the needed facilities along its proposed airways. Rather, it asserted that the "small expense" that would accompany the creation of the airways "should fall on those who will receive the direct benefits of its existence and operation such as the communities, organization, and individuals along the route." It concluded: "Therefore, Chambers of Commerce, Clubs, Lodges, and all civic or fraternal organizations together with public spirited citizens should take immediate action to install a landing field, by calling on the Army Air Service and by organizing volunteer labor to put the project through."[57] Reflecting another theme that ran throughout the early literature dealing with airport construction—that it would be not only relatively inexpensive but also relatively easy—the Air Service suggested that the Boy Scouts could be very helpful. The long list of tasks the Air Service wished the Boy Scouts volunteers to fulfill—air marking, weather reporting, helping aviators after forced landings and accidents, aiding with night navigation, reports on current conditions at municipal and emergency landing fields, and welcoming pilots at the emergency fields—also suggested just how small a budget the Air Service had for its airways program.[58] Small wonder it came to rely on the kindness of cities and civic groups.

In one of the very first books published on the subject of municipal airports—George Seay Wheat's *Municipal Landing Fields and Air Ports*—the chief of the Army Air Service, Major General Charles T. Menoher, reflected the Air Service's position and argued for municipal airport construction. He appealed to the booster element in cities by noting that any city failing to build an airport would find itself losing out in the coming age of aerial transportation. He further asserted that the nation needed a network of landing fields "established under municipal control by cities and towns" in order to promote commercial aviation and make it safer. Finally, he stated that municipal airports also contributed to national defense.[59] The article seemed to take it for granted that municipally owned airports were the way to go.

Arguments supporting municipal construction of airports appeared as early as 1920. In that year not only was Wheat's book published, but R. Preston Wentworth, an aerial photographic engineer, wrote a short article for *U.S. Air Service* titled "Have You a Little Landing Field in Your Community?" He asserted that cities had to provide an aviation field in order to ensure that they would become a "future air port." He called the construction and dedication of municipal landing fields "a civic duty."[60]

More specific arguments for why cities should shoulder the responsibility for airport construction appeared in two early articles by Archibald Black, a consulting engineer, who apparently ranked as one of the first, if not the first, engineers specifically interested in airport construction. In the first article, "Has Your Town a Landing Field?" written in 1923, Black argued that cities must take action to build airports as "many cities have only one or two really suitable sites for air terminals" and unless the city establishes its ownership over it, the site will undoubtedly come under the control of the first commercial airline to enter the city. That airline would then act to prevent others from entering the city, which Black deemed as "not a very healthy condition for the city."[61]

In a second article, written in 1925, Black appealed to the booster element. He argued that cities needed to act immediately to provide landing fields lest they lose out in the competition with their urban rivals. As in the 1923 article, Black asserted that cities could provide themselves with landing fields at minimal cost. All a city had to do was purchase the land and prepare it for use by aircraft. Hangars and other equipment could wait, but every city that intended to remain a thriving, progressive city needed at minimum to have a municipal landing field on the map.[62]

Black's articles also hinted at why airports should be built by the public sector rather than the private sector. Airports, though supposedly inexpensive to build, were unlikely to make money, at least in the short run. The private sector could not be expected to provide a large number of airports if they were expected to be money losers. As has often been the case, governments, especially local governments, have been expected to step in and provide the kind of services that could not be provided at a profit by the private sector.[63]

Both of Black's main points—that cities needed to build airports in order to remain competitive and that airports should be built by the public sector—were echoed in other literature on airports from the early 1920s. Charles Whitnall, the secretary of the Board of Public Land Commissioners in Milwaukee, Wisconsin, made an argument quite similar to Black's in favor of public (meaning municipal) ownership of airports in a 1926 issue of *National Municipal Review*. Whitnall asserted that commercial airports could put cities at a competitive disadvantage. If a commercial operation was the first to establish an airport, it would place the airport at the prime location and favor its own airplanes. That could then make it difficult for planes not associated with the commercial operator to find adequate landing facilities. Cities would be served best by providing one, central airport, publicly owned, at which the operators of many different airplanes could arrive and depart.[64]

The appeal to the booster element was also quite evident in the literature. Boston's mayor, James M. Curley, made it clear he and many others in Boston believed the city had to build an airport in order for it to maintain its position as a great gateway of transportation. Mayor Curley pointed out to the readers of *Aero Digest* that Boston was, and had long been, "a commercial gateway of the United States." Steamship lines and railroads both reached out from the city, making it "an industrial focal point" and "contributing factor to the prosperity and welfare of the nation." With the rise of aviation, Boston must also become the "logical airport for the northeast." The city, along with all other "forward looking communities throughout the country," must build facilities for this new form of transportation. As the mayor concluded, the leadership of Boston must "leave no stone unturned in making Boston the great aeronautical center of New England."[65]

As Boston saw itself becoming an aeronautical center for New England, Chicago saw itself becoming "The Nation's Airport." In an article describing plans to construct a municipally owned airport on the city's lakefront, Charles S. Rieman of the National Aeronautic Association clearly used booster arguments to justify the project. He argued that just as it had been important in the past for cities to maintain railroad terminals and harbor facilities, in the present (1923) cities must have airports. Cities that failed to build airports would find themselves unable "to take advantage of the economic benefits resulting from the nation-wide use of air navigation in this country which is now being organized and brought into being." Chicago, according to Rieman, "fully intends to secure for herself the emoluments and prestige to be derived by linking up of the cities and towns of this country in a network of air lines."[66]

Yet another city vying to emerge as an aeronautical center was Philadelphia. S. B. Eckert, chairman of the aviation committee of that city's chamber of commerce, predicted that his city, once it had the proper facilities, would emerge as the "leading airport of the East." As he put it, "New York is just a little too far from Washington, while Baltimore is not as convenient to New York as Philadelphia." Obviously, boosterism was pushing Philadelphians to take action. When Eckert wrote his article in 1923, Philadelphia had not yet acted to build a municipal airport. However, a group of "progressive citizens" representing the Aero Club of Pennsylvania and the Chamber of Commerce were working on it. When they succeeded, then Philadelphia could take "her rightful position in the very front of the aeronautical development."[67] Whether speaking of existing facilities or promoting future action, boosterism played a role in encouraging construction of municipal airports.

Hiram Bingham, U.S. Senator from Connecticut, developed yet another argument supporting municipal airport construction. Bingham envisioned a federal (in a literal sense of the word) approach to aviation. He declared that each level of government in the United States, local, state, and national, had specific responsibilities. As he saw it, "towns must build municipal airports, states must provide safe air routes, and the Nation must furnish aids to air navigation and improve navigable airways and air harbors." While it was conceivable that the national government might establish "a few large airports for the great centers of population"—at the time New York City was struggling to find a site for its municipal airport and many hoped the national government would transform nearby Governors Island "into a great federal airport"—by and large Bingham declared it the responsibility of cities and towns to aid the development of aviation in the United States by providing the airports.[68]

The arguments in favor of publicly owned municipal airports versus commercial and/or private airports remained somewhat vague and various during this early period of airport construction. In fact, commercial and/or private airports far outnumbered public airports until the late 1920s. But it was clear that at least two prominent forces behind aviation development in the United States, the military and the Post Office, preferred and promoted the idea of local, publicly owned municipal airports. Boosterism and the desire to attract as much aviation activity to the city as possible by providing public aviation facilities played a role as well. During the next phase of airport construction (1926–33), the arguments favoring local, publicly owned municipal airports would be strengthened and more clearly articulated. Cities, too, became more enthusiastic about the idea.

City and State Regulation of Flying

Once cities began to take on the responsibility of providing aviation facilities, they also saw a responsibility to pass ordinances regulating aviation activity within, and in the skies above, them. A few states also took action to regulate aviation. Although many others argued that any regulation of aviation must come from the national level, cities and states believed that, especially in absence of federal laws before the passage of the Air Commerce Act in 1926, they needed to take action.

From the very early 1920s, many argued that aviation had to come under federal regulation. Airplanes traveled the skies of the United States heedless of municipal or state borders. One of the very earliest texts on aerial laws argued that because air traffic was not only interstate but international in nature, all regulations regarding it should be made by the government in Washington. Any state or municipal laws passed dealing with aviation should coordinate with the federal law.[69] The National Advisory Committee for Aeronautics echoed that view in its 1920 annual report that called for a national aviation policy, including federal regulation of all aspects of aviation.[70] The preference for federal over state or local regulation of aviation remained throughout the period covered by this study. The problem was, however, that until 1926 the federal government failed to pass any legislation. Before the advent of federal action, many cities and states felt compelled to fill the void.

A number of states, including Kansas, Kentucky, Maryland, New York, and Ohio established boards or commissions designed to regulate (or propose regulations for) aviation. Kansas established its state aircraft board in 1921. That board—unlike the Kentucky state air board described earlier that only dealt with airports—had broad powers: "It shall be the duty of the board to supervise, regulate and control aerial navigation, and said board shall have full power to inspect aircraft, to prescribe and determine the qualifications of pilots, to prescribe uniform traffic rules and regulations, and markings for all aviation fields hereinafter authorized to be maintained, and all powers and authority necessary to the performance of the duties imposed herein, and to the carrying out of the provisions of this act."[71]

The 1921 Kansas law also empowered cities to establish airports, forbade "trick flying or aerial acrobatics" over "any city or center of population," and declared that any violation of the act would be punishable as a misdemeanor.[72]

Connecticut, which passed the very first law regulating aviation in 1911, updated its legislation in 1921. The 1921 Connecticut law was quite similar to the Kansas act. It ordered that all aircraft flown in the state be registered by the state, that all pilots operating in Connecticut had to be licensed by the state, limited stunt flying over populated areas, regulated the dropping of objects from airplanes, and established rules governing right-of-way for aircraft and lighter-than-air aircraft.[73]

Maryland established a state aviation commission in 1921. A member of the commission asserted that its greatest task was "the compiling of laws and drafting of local statutes for submission to the next legislature." A great concern, as in Kansas and in Connecticut, was with stunt flying. The Maryland commission, though, disagreed with some actions being taken by other states. Commissioners did think that an aircraft ought to be registered in each state in which it was operated, but pilots need not be licensed by each state. They believed that licenses authorized by the Aero Club of America ought to be valid anywhere in the United States.[74] The same article explaining the activities in Maryland also described actions being taken in New York State. There both the city of New York and the state legislature had before them in 1921 ordinances and bills dealing with the regulation of aviation.[75]

And New York City was not the only city moving to regulate flying activities in the skies within its boundaries. *U.S. Air Service* reported in November, 1920, that Fairbanks, Alaska, had "formulated a set of rules governing the conduct of spectators at airplane landing fields, and also certain rules for the aviator to follow."[76] And at least one city, Omaha, Nebraska, passed a rather extensive municipal ordinance governing flight activity.

The city government in Omaha passed a municipal ordinance in October, 1921, very similar in scope to the state laws passed in Kansas and Connecticut. The title of Ordinance No. 11170 read: "An ordinance regulating the operation of aircraft within or directly above the corporate limits of the city of Omaha, Nebraska, and providing for the formation of a board of control for the operation of aircraft to be hereafter designated the 'Air Board' of the city of Omaha: and providing penalties for the violation of the provisions hereof."[77]

Section 2 of the ordinance set out the rules and regulations. Those included requiring any pilot operating an aircraft in Omaha to hold a license approved by the city's Air Board, limiting stunt flying and outlining rules for the operation of aircraft in the air (for example, what to do when meeting head on or when overtaking another aircraft) and on the ground (for example, while taxiing at the municipal airport). The ordinance also prohibited aircraft from landing on "public highways, parks or public grounds, and in no private estates, unless with the previous consent of the owner of the property." All private flying fields had to be approved, in writing, by the Air Board.[78]

The Air Board had five members: the mayor; the Superintendent of Police, Sanitation, and Public Safety; and three other individuals who were required to be experienced pilots. The city's Air Board had broad powers:

> The Air Board shall have authority to enforce the rules and regulations of this ordinance; to examine pilots as to their qualifications for operating aircraft; to act temporarily on new conditions which should arise, not mentioned herein, until the City Council shall have an opportunity to amend this ordinance; to issue licenses for the operation of aircraft and for the establishing of flying fields and make and enforce special rules for same; to regulate the height of structures or obstructions in the vicinity of flying fields that tend to make the use of the field unsafe and to appoint special representatives to assist in enforcing the terms of this ordinance.[79]

In the absence of state and federal action, Omaha, an early stop on the Post Office's transcontinental airmail route, felt compelled to take some control over the new activity happening in the skies above it.

Conclusion

By the time the federal government enacted the first important pieces of legislation dealing with aviation—the Kelly Act in 1925 and the Air Commerce Act in 1926—much had already been accomplished and many important precedents had been set. According to one count, by 1924 eighty of the nation's larger cities had established airports.[80] Those airports had been built under a variety of different circumstances and involved a variety of different means. Nonetheless, the general idea that local interests, either public or private, should build airports had been firmly established. Federal aid, though promised, failed to arrive. Federal regulation, though called for, failed to materialize. In the absence of both, and with encouragement from the Air Service and the Post Office, cities had embarked on the task of creating the landing facilities needed for the promotion and development of aviation in the United States. While both federal aid and regulation would come later, well into the 1930s, after 1926 cities increasingly shouldered the burden while hoping eventually to reap some benefits.

2

The Era of Airport Enthusiasm, 1926–33

Between 1925 and 1927 three things happened that together contributed to an explosion of municipal airport construction activity. First, in 1925 Congress passed the Air Mail Act (or the Kelly Act). Responding to calls that the time had come to transfer the airmail to the private sector, Congress voted to turn responsibility for carrying the mail to commercial carriers, who would work under contract for the Post Office. The following year Congress passed the Air Commerce Act. That piece of legislation created within the Department of Commerce an Aeronautics Branch (later the Bureau of Air Commerce), and it formally made airports a local responsibility. Those acts by themselves worked to stimulate some cities to begin to look at constructing a municipal airport. However, action remained at a rather low level until the energizing influence of Charles Lindbergh's solo flight across the Atlantic. Lindbergh's feat fanned the flames of aviation enthusiasm all over the United States. In the wake of his flight, and subsequent promotional tour of the country, city after city rushed to jump on the aviation bandwagon.

With the outburst of enthusiasm for airport construction came a number of important developments. First, state after state passed the necessary enabling legislation. The state legislation generally gave local governments—particularly cities, but in some cases counties—a central role in airport development. A few state governments, though, also took direct action to stimulate airport development. Second, the Aeronautics Branch began its work involving the construction of the nation's airways and, in general, promoting aviation activity. In relation to airports, the actions of the Aeronautics Branch reflected the progressive ideals, including standardization and efficiency, and the associationalism current within the Hoover-era federal government. Further, Aeronautics Branch literature favored the local, public ownership of airports. And airport managers held a number of meetings at which they attempted to work out some of the general principles of airport operation.

Despite the attempts to promote standardization, variation remained at the local level. Cities continued to work out for themselves how and by whom their airports would be built. A certain level of regional variation also appeared as western cities, to an extent, seemed to take more aggressive action than cities in other regions. However, the regional variation is most correctly viewed as a tendency rather than a major difference as cities in all regions of the nation became involved in airport projects.[1] There was also a great deal of variation in how cities managed their airports. And there was controversy as a dispute arose between those who felt airports could be managed as parks by park departments and those who defined airports as strictly transportation facilities that must be managed by air transportation experts. Adding heat to the controversy was the objection raised by park proponents to the idea of using park land for airports.

As city governments began to take greater responsibility for airports, arguments in favor of municipal ownership became much stronger and more elaborate. Many of the arguments reflected the spirit of the Air Commerce Act and the dock concept. Most, but not all, accepted the idea that airports ought to be both local and publicly owned. Additional arguments in favor of public ownership included the belief that public airports would treat all users fairly and equally and the notion that only local governments could resist the temptation to sell airport land in the event that it might receive a higher return if used for an alternative purpose. Courts also upheld the legality of public ownership of airports. However, even in the face of all the arguments in favor of local government action, it was clear that local private interests, inspired by urban boosterism and the winged gospel, continued to play a major role.

States, the Federal Government, and Municipal Airports

Before many cities could act to build a municipal airport, state legislatures needed to pass the necessary enabling legislation. Between 1927 and 1929 at least thirty-three states enacted general or specific enabling acts. Some state acts allowed all cities of a certain class to construct and own airports; others enabled a specifically named city within the state to do so.[2] While the acts varied from state to state, all allowed cities and occasionally some other sub-state jurisdictions such as counties to own and operate airports. City ownership of airports, as a result, became familiar. "Municipal airport," however, still remained something of an evolving term. While it seems most cities after 1926 chose to own their airports, some cities continued to lease land or to allow private interests to build and operate airports and call the result "the municipal airport."

Although most state acts basically gave cities the power to acquire and manage airports, some states also took a more direct and active role in airport development. As explained in the previous chapter, Kentucky law created an Air Board that had the power to purchase, lease, or otherwise acquire and manage airports. That board could act alone or in cooperation with "counties, cities, or incorporated towns, private corporations, voluntary unincorporated associations or individuals." In 1927, Michigan also empowered the State Administrative Board "to establish landing fields and airports upon any lands owned by the State of Michigan, suitable therfor [*sic*]."[3]

Several other states took even more aggressive action, seeking to impart some order to the creation of airports within their respective territories. Virginia's 1928 legislation dealing with aviation, for example, required that all airports established in the state receive a permit from the State Corporation Commission. Apparently, Virginia acted in the spirit of recommendations made by a director of the Daniel Guggenheim Fund for the Promotion of Aeronautics. The Guggenheim Fund, established in 1926, provided moneys for a number of projects aimed at promoting aviation and, especially, aviation safety in the United States. Among its many activities, it awarded grants to a number of universities to establish programs in aeronautical engineering, it funded a Model Air Line, and it supported the research in blind flying that led to the world's first instrument-only flight by Jimmy Doolittle in 1929. The fund did not show a great deal of interest in airports, but fund director Harry Guggenheim promoted a plan that called for a nationwide system of landing fields. Under the plan, landing fields would be located every ten miles. That way, in case of an emergency such as an engine failure, airplanes would always be within a short distance of a safe landing site. Such an extensive program had little hope of finding support. It would seem, though, the state of Virginia saw a certain merit in the idea and, at least initially, sought to create not just a large number of airports within the state haphazardly located, but a system of carefully placed airports. The state, therefore, worked closely with its municipalities as they established their airports and even offered aid in the form of equipment and engineering expertise from the state highway department.[4]

Massachusetts also took action in the name of safety. Under Massachusetts law, the state had the power to regulate airports, including the power to "permit, or prohibit, flying from any emergency landing field or airport in the whole Commonwealth." The state decided to exercise that authority in the wake of the airport enthusiasm following Lindbergh's flight and Richard Byrd's flight over the North Pole. As Robert L. O'Brien, the supervisor of aviation for Massachusetts, reported it, in the wake of those aeronautical feats "so-called airports began to spring up all over the State of Massachusetts." Many of those fields were "absolutely untrustworthy for the regular use of airplanes" but were listed as established airports by Department of Commerce bulletins. The state of Massachusetts decided to try and bring some order out of the chaos by establishing a state rating system for airports based on the Department of Commerce's voluntary rating system. The state further determined that while the Department of Commerce's rating system allowed for extremely small fields, Massachusetts would set a minimum size somewhat above that of the Department of Commerce. The state then went out into the field, surveyed the size and condition of the airports, and, if the state's minimum requirements were not met, notified the owner that flying must end unless and until the needed improvements were made.[5]

Federal law and policies worked to encourage, support, and even demand local action in a number of ways. The Kelly Act, for example, stimulated the creation and growth of commercial airlines. These new airlines, like the Post Office before them, needed local airports. Some airlines, such as Pan American, which had the lucrative contract to carry overseas mail, owned and operated their own airports.[6] Most airlines, though, while experiencing growth, depended largely on local action to provide the needed ground facilities. More important, as noted, the Air Commerce Act implicitly, if not explicitly, determined that local interests should bear responsibility for the construction of airports.

While the Air Commerce Act embodied the dock concept implicitly, all it stated explicitly was that the federal government would not build, own, or finance the construction of airports. In the late 1920s, however, the Aeronautics Branch of the Department of Commerce expressed a strong preference for local, public action on airports. It published a series of bulletins which offered cities, specifically city governments, guidance on how to construct and manage an airport. In fact, Aeronautics Bulletin No. 2 *(Construction of Airports)* stated: "The airport should be a municipal enterprise, just as the maintenance of city docks and public highways is generally recognized as being within the province of the municipality." It went on to state that the Air Commerce Act had indeed "suggested" such when it forbade federal ownership or operation of airports and turned over certain airports established by the Post Office to their municipalities.[7] While the debate over municipal ownership of airports was not closed, the federal government, at least as represented by the Aeronautics Branch, had come down clearly on the side advocating municipal ownership.

The federal government's role in developing municipal airports, though, remained one of providing encouragement and advice. This reflected both the progressive ideals and the associationalism held by many in the federal government in the late 1920s and into the early 1930s. Rather than mandating action or establishing strong regulations, the Aeronautics Branch offered cities help on a voluntary basis in the form of information and suggested standards. The above mentioned Air Bulletin No. 2, for example, provided cities with general ideas about how to select an airport site, how to lay out the field, what types of building and equipment were necessary, how to mark the field, how to light the field, and how to provide for seaplane ports and anchorages. It further encouraged all cities, even small cities, to build at least some kind of airport facility. It stated: "Even the minimum of an airport will provide the first requisite — a marked operating area. There should be no insurmountable difficulty in securing control of the maximum available land and the modest preparation of the minimum requirements for immediate needs."[8]

In the late 1920s and early 1930s, the Aeronautics Branch tried to bring some order and uniformity to the process of airport construction. The Air Commerce Act gave the Secretary of Commerce the responsibility to rate airports in the United States. In response, the Aeronautics Branch developed a ratings system. The system first set down some basic requirements for all airports. Under the system all airports should, at a minimum, have a suitable landing area. It defined such an area as "a smooth, well-drained landing area, sufficiently firm to permit the safe operation of aircraft under all weather conditions, approximately level, and free from obstructions or depressions presenting hazards in the taking off or landing of aircraft," accessible by good road to the nearest town or city, with a wind-direction indicator, adequate markings, runways (if the landing area required prepared or hard-surfaced runways to allow for all-weather operations), drainage, and adequate provisions for fuel, communications, transportation to the nearest city or town, and personnel.[9]

The system then provided for the rating of airports in three areas: general equipment and facilities, size of effective landing area, and lighting equipment. In the first area an airport could win a rating of A, B, C, or D, with A representing airports with the best equipment and D representing airports that only met the very basic equipment requirements. In terms of size, an airport could receive a rating of 1, 2, 3, or 4. To receive a 1, for example, an airport had to have an effective landing area of at least 2,500 feet in all directions or longer if the airport was located at high altitude. Or it could have landing strips 2,500 feet long and not less than 500 feet wide that allowed for landing in eight different directions under all conditions. Again, the landing strips had to be longer if the airport was located at a high altitude. To receive a 4, an airport needed only an effective landing area of 1,320 feet in all directions (or longer at higher altitudes). Or it could have two landing strips, aligned to the prevailing winds, at least 1,800 feet long (or longer at higher altitudes) and 500 feet wide. Finally, airports were rated in terms of their lighting equipment. In that area, airports could receive an A, B, C, D, E, or X rating. A airports had extensive lighting systems including beacons, boundary lights, obstruction lights, a landing area flood-light system, and all-night operation of all lighting equipment. X airports had either no night-lighting equipment or did not operate their lighting equipment all night regularly or on request. Airports rated B, C, D, or E had progressively less extensive lighting facilities than A airports, but they all either regularly operated their lighting equipment all night or offered night lighting on request.[10] Under this system the best overall airports would receive an A1A rating.

The rating system was voluntary, however. The Department of Commerce could issue an airport rating only "upon application of the owners of these facilities."[11] That applied equally to municipally and privately owned airports. The department developed the rating system in 1928, began to offer the rating inspections in early 1929, and announced its first airport rating in February, 1930. The municipal airport in Pontiac, Michigan, received an A1A rating. The announcement of Pontiac's good fortune, however, also indicated that several other airports that had initially applied for a rating had asked that their inspections be postponed. Initial talks with the Aeronautics Branch indicated that those cities' airports would not receive the A1A rating. The cities asked for additional time to improve their airports so that they would receive "the desired rating."[12] That was a key. Cities only applied to have their airports rated if they were certain that they would receive a good rating, preferably the highest A1A rating. That was pointed out in a December, 1932, article in *U.S. Air Services*. The effectiveness of the Department of Commerce's airport rating system in improving and standardizing airports would be limited until all airports—at least all municipal and commercial airports—were subject to a mandatory rating system. That same article indicated that less than 5 percent of the municipal and commercial airports in the United States had been rated by the end of 1932.[13]

In addition to the voluntary rating system, in an effort to promote some level of standardization and uniformity when it came to airports, the Aeronautics Branch published a series of bulletins. For example, the branch's information bulletin dealing with airport management, rentals, concessions, and field rules provided examples of what a number of cities were doing in those areas by reprinting copies of municipal ordinances and field rules. More important, it also offered a "Suggested Uniform City Ordinance" covering municipal regulation of aviation activity in the skies over a city and a list of "Suggested Field Rules" cities might adopt.[14]

The Aeronautics Branch took up the subject of standardization and uniformity more fully in a subsequent bulletin entitled "Suggested City or County Aeronautics Ordinance and Uniform Field Rules for Airports" published a little over a year after the above mentioned information bulletin. This second bulletin, published in October, 1929, opened with a discussion of the need for uniformity. It first recounted efforts on the part of the Department of Commerce to encourage states to pass uniform laws regulating aircraft and pilots operating within their boundaries as federal law at that time only covered aircraft and pilots clearly engaged in interstate activities. The idea was to have states help ensure that all aircraft and all pilots operated in accordance with federal standards. To further that effort, the Department of Commerce wanted to encourage cities or counties to pass ordinances and enforce rules that would ensure that all aircraft and pilots operating within the "immediate vicinity of airports" also met federal standards. The department hoped that this effort would bring operations in and around municipal and commercial airports "in conformity with the requirements of the Federal air traffic rules."[15]

The Aeronautic Branch's message did, to a certain extent, reach the intended audience. In 1928 the city of Omaha, which had passed an extensive ordinance establishing municipal rules and regulations for aircraft and flyers, repealed that early ordinance. A first version of the new ordinance appeared in June, 1928. It was soon replaced by a more extensive ordinance, passed in December, 1928, that had a number of provisions somewhat aligning the city's rules and regulations with those passed by the federal government. Section 12, for example, read: "No aircraft shall be navigated within the corporate limits of the city unless such aircraft has been registered under the Air Commerce Act of the United States." The following section read: "No person shall navigate any aircraft so registered without an aircraft certificate issued under the Air Commerce Act of the United States." While the ordinance did not explicitly adopt federal rules, Section 20 required the following: "There shall be displayed in conspicuous places in all airports a copy of the Air Commerce Law of the United States, and the rules and regulations promulgated thereunder by the Department of Commerce, together with a copy of this ordinance and the rules and regulation adopted pursuant thereto." Finally, Section 23 mandated: "No person shall be employed as a mechanic at any airport without a certificate under the Air Commerce Law of the United States."[16]

Still and all, the Aeronautics Branch could at best only encourage cities to take action. To organize its personnel better to exercise their powers of persuasion, in 1929 it created the Airport Section. That office had five employees, including the section chief. Their job was to "assist municipalities and others interested in airport development in the selection of sites, and to offer advice concerning the proper methods of construction." They could do their job only after being invited to do so by a city or local civic group, though. Members of the section traveled about the country speaking to local authorities and others with an eye to creating "a favorable attitude toward airport establishment." They would then often accompany local airport boosters to help them evaluate potential airport sites. Afterwards, they would send a report to the local community. With only five employees, however, the amount of help the section could offer was limited. The section would not, for example, conduct any engineering surveys of potential airport sites. That was left to whomever the local group could find to do the job.[17]

Sharing Ideas: Early Airport Conferences

The Aeronautics Branch was not the only group interested in standardization and uniformity. As early as 1929 airport managers began to hold conventions at which they sought to exchange ideas and discover the best ways to get the job done. Both national and regional conferences were held in the late 1920s and early 1930s where pioneer airport managers tried to work out the details of their new profession.

The first national airport conference convened in Cleveland, Ohio, organized by the Airport Section of the Aeronautical Chamber of Commerce of America. More than two hundred people attended. An article in *Aviation* reporting on the convention suggested that the new airport managers had come to realize that the "airport business [was] not as simple as it [looked]" and that they had few precedents beyond perhaps the railroad industry upon which to draw. Therefore, they needed to start exchanging ideas among themselves. What they found as they began to exchange ideas, generally, was a great deal of variation. Airports faced a number of issues and most local communities had dealt with the issues in their own ways. Airports, clearly, were more complex than many had earlier imagined.[18]

The Aeronautical Chamber of Commerce of America, Inc., sponsored a second national conference in 1930 in Buffalo, New York. This conference began with the naming of ten committees. Each committee tackled one airport issue and then reported its findings to the convention. The committees met on the first day of the conference and reported their findings on the second. They dealt with such issues and subjects as surfacing and drainage problems, standard accounting systems, lighting, hangar construction, concessions, small town airports, air traffic congestion, and sales and advertising of airports and airport services.[19]

One participant at the convention voiced concerns and opinions that many would echo in the near future. C. O. Sherrill, known popularly as Colonel Sherrill, the former city manager of Cincinnati, Ohio, addressed the convention on its third day. He cited the large number of questions and uncertainties facing cities contemplating building airports. They included questions over how best to manage the airport, whether the city itself should build the airport or a local operating company should do the job, whether only federally approved flying schools should be allowed to operate on the field, and what kind of control, if any, the city should exercise over airport and airport-related activities such as the sale of fuel and the operation of restaurants and hotels. Sherrill concluded that the best answers to all those questions lay in the formulation of a "national policy for the guidance of cities interested in airport development." He called for a national study of airports with the objective of finding "the best way to meet all the problems now perplexing the average city port."[20]

Most of those concerned with airports in the late 1920s and early 1930s were not yet interested in going as far as Colonel Sherrill suggested. In 1931, for example, the Chamber of Commerce of the United States, along with the Aeronautical Chamber of Commerce of America, sponsored a number of regional conferences. None of the lists of recommendations coming out of the seven regional meetings included a call for a national airport policy. The recommendations made at the various regional meetings did have in common a call for all airports to adopt the Uniform Field Rules that the Aeronautics Branch had drawn up and published. They also urged that state aviation legislation require that all intrastate aircraft operations conform to federal air traffic rules.[21]

While these various conferences certainly emphasized a need for standardization and uniformity and may have made a certain amount of progress in that direction, they fell short of providing any sort of comprehensive guidelines to direct municipal airport activities. In the absence of either a federal airport policy or a policy developed by any private organization concerned with airport development, variation was the order of the day.

Variation at the Local Level

If variety is the spice of life, then things were really spicy when it came to the circumstances surrounding the establishment of municipal airports in the late 1920s and early 1930s. Aside from the fact that cities themselves were far more involved in the process, taking advantage of the recent passage of enabling legislation, and the fact that Lindbergh's flight was quite influential almost universally, most airports came into being under rather individual circumstances shaped by local factors. Some cities owned, built, and managed their own airports; others relied on civic organizations to provide the needed facilities; still others operated the airport, but on leased land. Some constructed airports from the ground up; others bought existing airports. Some were pushed to action by requests from the military; others, from requests by the airlines. There was also a certain level of variation across regions, with western cities seemingly the most aggressive. The path chosen was usually the result of the particular circumstances at work in that city at that time. A brief survey of the histories of a number of municipal airports—from cities across the country both large and small—can provide a sense of just how varied the landscape was.

Wichita, Kansas, ranked among those cities inspired by the new circumstances of the late 1920s to take aggressive action to build and operate a municipal airport. Aviation enthusiasts in Wichita, in fact, began pushing for an airport as early as 1919. They argued that they needed a place at which to hold aerial demonstrations and to service aircraft. Also, the Post Office made it clear a city had to have an "official" airport before it could become a stop on the new airmail network. To give the city an "official" airport, the local chamber of commerce bought a seventy-five-acre field just outside the city limits. Despite the fact that Wichita had a substantial amount of aviation industry within its boundaries (Swallow, Travel Air, Stearman, and Cessna all operated plants in the city), the small, suburban field remained Wichita's municipal airport until 1929.[22]

In 1929 the Wichita Chamber of Commerce once again took action to provide its city with an airport that would live up to Wichita's claim of being the "air capital." The chamber helped convince the Kansas state legislature to pass a law enabling all cities of the first class (over 65,000 in population) to "acquire within or without the city limits a municipal airport," which would fall under the jurisdiction of the city's board of park commissioners.[23] With the enabling legislation in place, the city of Wichita purchased 640 acres of land just outside the city limits, six and one-half miles from the downtown. The new airport had four intersecting turf landing strips, allowing for all-direction landing; two measured 4,800 feet in length and the other two measured 4,200 feet and 3,600 feet, respectively. Over the next two years the city and park commission installed an airport lighting system, completed a large brick-and-steel hangar, and began construction of a large airport administration building.[24]

San Diego, California, was another city that responded to the enthusiasm created in the wake of the Lindbergh flight. That city's chamber of commerce had created an aviation committee as early as 1922. In that year, the committee urged the city to use its city plan to reserve area for an airport along the waterfront. The city took no action, though, until 1927. Especially inspired by the Lindbergh flight, as Lindbergh's plane, though named the *Spirit of St. Louis*, had been built by a San Diego-based company, the citizens of San Diego approved a $650,000 bond issue to finance the initial work on an airport. The city located its new airport on basically the same site recommended by the chamber of commerce in 1922. Construction involved "dredging in San Diego harbor and dumping this soil on the tideland airport area." The dredging activity reclaimed about 105 acres from San Diego Bay.[25]

Although the Air Commerce Act specifically forbade federal funding for airports, San Diego, nonetheless, received "federal aid" in the construction of its airport. In addition to the 105 acres reclaimed by the city's dredging efforts, the War Department also conducted dredging operations to reclaim 182 acres of land it owned adjacent to the new airport. Some of that land also became part of the new municipal airport. It seems that adjacent to the municipal and War Department land stood a Marine Corps aviation field. In time of war, a combination of the Marine Corps field and the municipal field would allow for a two-and-one-half-mile-long runway. Named in honor of Colonel Lindbergh, San Diego's municipal airport soon became a center of both commercial and military aviation activity.[26] Thus, although the Post Office and then the Department of Commerce received the most attention for promoting aviation, the military still played a role.

Another city that received a boost from the military, albeit a nonfinancial one, in the formation of its municipal airport was Oakland, California. In 1927 the Oakland Chamber of Commerce determined its city should take its place as "the local center for Pacific Coast air commerce." It conducted a survey and concluded that a site six miles from the Oakland Post Office, bounded on the north by San Francisco Bay and the south by San Leandro Bay, was the best location for an airport. The chamber then took its findings to the city's Board of

Port Commissioners. The commissioners concurred and in March, 1927, obtained an option on the site. Shortly thereafter, using proceeds from a 1925 bond issue, the Board of Port Commissioners purchased the site, eventually including 825 acres, for $769,000. The first work on the airport site did not begin, however, until after a visit from representatives of the War Department and the National Aeronautic Association (NAA) in June, 1927. F. Trubee Davison, assistant secretary of war for air; Porter Adams, president of the NAA; and Army lieutenant Lester J. Maitland looked over the airport site and then discussed plans for a Army flight to Hawaii with the Board of Port Commissioners. They told the commissioners that if the city could provide a suitable runway on the site (300 feet wide and a mile long) and if that runway could be finished by June 24, the Army would launch its flight from Oakland.[27]

The city of Oakland jumped at the request, which came only a week or so after Lindbergh's epic flight across the Atlantic. While the flight of the *Bird of Paradise* never achieved the level of intense public interest as the flight of the *Spirit of St. Louis*, the Army's Hawaii flight nonetheless focused a great deal of attention on Oakland and its new airport. The city completed the needed runway in twenty-three days, and on June 28, 1927, Lieutenants Maitland and Albert F. Hegenberger took off from Oakland and landed successfully at Wheeler Field, Honolulu, Hawaii, twenty-five hours and fifty minutes later. Several weeks later pilot Ernest Smith and his navigator, Emery Bronte, became the first civilians to fly nonstop from the mainland to Hawaii. And then in the fall of 1927, the participants in the ill-fated Dole flight to Hawaii also began their journeys in Oakland.[28] Sponsored by James D. Dole of Hawaii, the contest, which attracted adventurous but largely ill-prepared pilots, offered a $35,000 prize; two of the four aircraft attempting to win the prize disappeared over the Pacific.

The city began work on developing the site into a functioning municipal airport in September, 1927. Once again, the military aided as the city received advice on the airport plan from Assistant Secretary of War for Air Davison, Lieutenant Maitland, and Major Delos C. Emmons, the commanding officer of the nearby Crissy Army Air Field. The city also turned to the Department of Commerce for advice on how to organize and manage the airport. And the city worked with the Daniel Guggenheim Fund for the Promotion of Aeronautics. The Oakland municipal airport had one of the earliest weather reporting stations in the nation, funded by the Guggenheim Fund and operated by United States Weather Bureau personnel. By 1928 the airport also boasted of four all-steel hangars, a complete airport lighting system, and an Administration Building with a coffee shop, dining room, and banquet room.[29]

That points to another feature of the variation in local airports. To a certain extent, western cities seemed to embrace the idea of airports more completely than cities in other regions of the country. As several historians have argued, Westerners eagerly embraced aviation, both commercial and military. The enthusiasm with which western civic leaders greeted the airplane was based on a number of factors. Westerners had long exhibited a faith in science and technology. Railroads, the telegraph, irrigation works, and other advances had helped bridge the great distances between settlements in the West and had provided the means by which humans could gain some measure of control over the often harsh environment of the region. Transportation technologies in particular had helped draw the region together and afford it closer connections with the rest of the nation and the rest of the world. Aviation was viewed as a way to build upon those earlier transportation links. Also, westerners felt a need to diversify and develop the region's economy. Aviation offered an opportunity for economic diversification through both commercial airline operations and aircraft manufacture. And westerners had a long tradition of seeking federal aid and participating in federal programs that promised material benefits.[30]

Other examples of western cities that embraced the new air age were Tulsa, Oklahoma, and Denver, Colorado. With visions of becoming "one of the principal air centers of the Southwest" a group of Tulsa businessmen began planning the construction of a municipal airport. The committee included C. C. Herndon, the vice-president of Skelly Oil Company. He went so far as to travel to Europe to inspect airports there. Shortly after his return, other leading businessmen in Tulsa formed the Tulsa Airport Corporation. Their goal was to create "for the city an air terminal second to none in the United States." To achieve that end, they held a design competition and awarded the contract for the design of the airport to the B. Russell Shaw Company of St. Louis, described as "among the largest . . . designers of airports in the United States." The Tulsa Airport Corporation would initially finance the airport and then "present" it to the city, which would then purchase it from the corporation.[31]

The plans for the Tulsa airport were indeed grand. Most of the facilities were described as "second to none," "the last word," and "the most forward." They included an all-steel hangar (100 feet by 120 feet), a large gasoline and oil servicing station—as befitting Tulsa's position as a center of the oil industry in the United States—and an extensive airport lighting system. Central to the plan was the design and construction of an elaborate terminal building. The men building the airport in Tulsa reasoned that since travel by air was "acknowledged as the last word in high speed travel," passengers using air transportation "should be accorded equal or better accommodations both at the air terminal and in the air as [were] afforded by other means of transportation." Tulsa's terminal building was designed, therefore, with a main floor offering "a large waiting room with ticket office, baggage rooms, soda fountain and magazine stand as well as telephone booths." On the second floor, the building provided office space for the field manager and for representatives of the Department of Commerce and of airlines servicing the field. The third floor boasted of "a spacious and up-to-date dining room opening on the field side onto a roof garden 60 feet wide and 120 feet long." The fourth floor included space for the dispatcher, the weather bureau, and a radio room. The very top of the building held the 24-inch revolving beacon. The Tulsa Airport Corporation obviously saw their airport as attracting not only national air traffic but a great deal of local traffic as well. The field included parking for 10,000 automobiles.[32] The city of Tulsa purchased the privately financed airport from the Tulsa Airport Corporation in 1931 for $650,000. According to a 1940 article, the Tulsa Airport apparently lived up to the ambitions of its founders as it ranked as one of the few municipal airports in the country to operate at a profit during the 1930s.[33]

Denver's civic leaders acted to create a municipal airport as part of their own ongoing efforts to secure and maintain that city's regional prominence. Transportation had always been an important and sometimes vexing issue in Denver's history. In the nineteenth century, the problem was the railroad. When construction began on the nation's first transcontinental railroad, the route bypassed the city of Denver. The Rocky Mountains looming west of the city were simply too rugged for the rail line to cross. Instead, the route traveled north of the city to Cheyenne, Wyoming. Denver's business community reacted immediately and built a spur line north from their city to connect to the new line. In subsequent years they also helped finance spur lines east and south of the city to connect with other major lines. In the twentieth century, the issue became the air lines. The nation's first transcontinental air route also by-passed the city, again going through Cheyenne. Like the early railroads, the early airplanes found the Rockies west of Denver a daunting obstacle. Once again Denver's business community responded. Anthony J. Joseph founded Colorado Airways and that company won a bid to carry the mail on the Cheyenne-Denver-Pueblo airmail route, linking the city with the transcontinental airway.[34]

Even as the city secured a connection to the transcontinental airway, other civic leaders planned to construct a modern municipal airport. Apparently, Benjamin F. Stapleton, the city's mayor, began considering the idea of a municipal airport as early as 1923. The city's commissioner of parks and improvements, Charles D. Vail, also supported the idea. They believed that the city needed a single, large, municipally owned and operated airport that would act as a "focal point" for the city's aviation activity. Vail toured the country, visiting airports and talking with representatives of the emerging airlines and of the Department of Commerce. Stapleton and Vail eventually came to believe that a site seven miles from downtown Denver, known locally as Sand Creek, represented the best possible airport location. It was removed from the developed area of the city, and land prices were reasonable.[35]

In 1927 Stapleton approached the city council, which was studying the idea of building an airport, and began to push strongly the idea and the Sand Creek site. Neither the site nor the idea of a municipal airport were without local opposition. Some pointed out that a friend of the mayor stood to profit from the purchase of the Sand Creek property. Others wanted the city to build its airport nearer the downtown. And one city councilman opposed both the site and the very idea of building an airport. Despite the opposition, on March 19, 1928, the Denver City Council voted to purchase the Sand Creek property. It did not, however, immediately appropriate the needed funds. Opponents once again attempted to stop the venture, but on March 28, 1928, the council, at the urging of Mayor Stapleton, voted the moneys.[36]

With nearly $200,000 appropriated for construction in its 1929 budget, Mayor Stapleton pushed the city to build the most modern facility it could afford. He wanted it to receive the highest rating from the Department of Commerce. Therefore, the Denver airport opened with two major runways, each well longer than the 3,300 feet suggested by the Department of Commerce for a high altitude airport. The airport also had an elaborate lighting system, including a high intensity beacon atop the administration building that became known as the "Eye of Denver." The administration building was a three-story brick and steel structure. The airport opened with a 121-by-122-foot hangar, painted bright orange for visibility. By the time it was ready to open, the airport had cost the city a total of $430,000. Boosters believed it would secure Denver's regional importance.[37]

The regional variation that did exist, though, should be seen as a general tendency, rather than a sharp difference between the West and other regions. Indeed, cities outside the West could also act aggressively when necessary. The city of Columbus, Ohio, for example, quickly responded when offered the chance to play a role in what it saw as an exciting aviation innovation. In 1928 C. M. Keys, president of the Curtiss Aeroplane and Motor Company, announced the formation of Transcontinental Air Transport, Inc. (TAT). The new airline proposed to use a combination of air and rail to transport passengers from New York to Los Angeles in approximately two days. At the time, the fastest coast-to-coast travel by rail alone took four days. With Charles Lindbergh on board as the technical advisor, TAT promised a revolution in travel.[38]

TAT worked in concert with the Pennsylvania and the Santa Fe Railroads. As night flying was still considered too risky, passengers would board a train in New York in the evening. They would then travel overnight by rail to Columbus, Ohio, where they would board a plane that flew them to Waynoka, Oklahoma, by evening, after a lunch stop in St. Louis and several other intermediate stops. Passengers would then travel by train overnight to Clovis, New Mexico, where once again they would take to the air, arriving in Los Angeles late on the second day.[39] One key to the scheme was the construction of an airport with railroad connections about an overnight train trip's worth of distance from New York. Columbus fit the bill in terms of distance and soon acted to provide the needed facilities.

The new Port Columbus Municipal Airport was built on 320 acres of land, located about eight miles from downtown Columbus, bordered on one side by the tracks of the Pennsylvania Railroad. The city spent $850,000 to develop the airport. Because of soil conditions that would not allow for heavy air traffic under all weather conditions, the airport had paved runways from the very beginning. It also opened with an extensive lighting system. The city built an administration building on the site. It was a 34-by-106-foot, two-story concrete and brick building. One end housed the control tower, which extended yet another story above the main building. The airport plan called for seven hangars on the field, all a standard 167 feet 3 inches wide and 206 feet long. At the time the airport opened, only one hangar was complete, but work had started on the others. The hangars were built on lots that the city leased to interested parties and at the time of the airport's opening, six of the hangar sites had been leased. A municipal hangar would occupy the seventh site. Airport employees included "a manager, an assistant field manager in charge of maintenance and operations, a chief clerk, a hangar clerk, several electricians, a ground crew of six and the caretaker for the administration building."[40] In addition to the facilities provided by the city, the Pennsylvania Railroad constructed "Air Depot Stations" on either side of its tracks. A 150-foot-long covered walkway connected the stations with the airport administration building.[41] The air-rail route across the country operated for only a short time, though, made obsolete by improved, longer-range aircraft and technical improvements that made night flying safer.

Not every city had to start from scratch in order to acquire a municipally owned airport. Some cities simply bought an existing airport. Atlanta, as noted earlier, created its first "official" airport when it leased land south of the city. In 1929, following the passage of a law specifically enabling Atlanta to "purchase, own and operate municipal land fields . . . located within or without the limits of the city," the city bought Candler Field, later renamed Atlanta Municipal Airport.[42]

Even with enabling laws in place, some cities continued either to have local private/commercial interests provide them with their municipal airports or to lease, rather than buy, airport property. Two such examples are Dayton, Ohio, and Los Angeles, California. Following the passage of the Air Mail Act in 1925, several private airports offered to be named Dayton's municipal airport. The city accepted a bid from the Moraine Flying Field, located south of the city, and it, while remaining in private hands, served as Dayton's "official municipal airport" for two years. Following Lindbergh's flight, the city explored the possibility of either building its own airport south of the city or taking over the soon-to-be-abandoned McCook Field site, which was being leased by the Air Corps, across from the downtown. Nothing came immediately of either initiative, and in 1928 the city signed an agreement with the Air Corps for the temporary use of another local army air field. Airmail planes destined for Dayton could land at Wright Field, located east of the city, until the city built its own airport in late 1930 or 1931.[43]

Dayton's business leaders wanted a municipal airport much faster than the city apparently was willing to provide one. Therefore, they took matters into their own hands, incorporating the Dayton Municipal Airport Company in March, 1928. They then sold shares, raising $300,000, and used the money to buy property near Vandalia, Ohio, a small town about twelve miles north of downtown Dayton. In early 1929 the city arranged for the airmail service to transfer from Wright Field to the Vandalia airport. And in the summer of 1929 the city and the Dayton Municipal Airport Company held a dedication ceremony for the new Dayton Airport.[44]

During the 1920s the Los Angeles area witnessed the creation of a number of private and commercial airports. They included the Venice Airport, the Chaplin Airport, and the Los Angeles Metropolitan Airport. After passage of the Air Commerce Act, however, many civic leaders decided that the city needed a publicly owned airport, and in 1927 the California legislature passed the needed enabling legislation. Inspired by Lindbergh's flight, the city council resolved to take action and began to take bids from property owners of potential airport sites. The city looked at twenty-seven different properties before narrowing the competition down to three. However, the council could not come to an agreement over which site to purchase. With the idea that it might purchase up to three separate as yet unspecified airport sites, each serving a different part of the Los Angeles area, the city council put a $6 million bond issue on the ballot in May, 1928. The vague wording of the bond issue, however, contributed to its defeat.[45]

Following the bond issue defeat, the Los Angeles City Council finally settled on a site in Inglewood, recently selected as the location for the upcoming

National Air Races. Once the air races were over, Los Angeles took control of what became known as Mines Field (named after William W. Mines, the real estate agent who handled the property transaction). However, the city chose to lease rather than purchase the land. The recent defeat of the airport bond issue suggested a general lack of support for a city-owned airport. Further, many still objected to the Mines Field site. By leasing, the city could "experiment with municipal airport operations and decide whether or not the Mines site was suitable." The city council approved the lease idea on September 26, 1928, the day after it created the Los Angeles Department of Airports to administer the new municipal airport.[46]

How to Administer the Local Airport

Just as there was a great deal of variation as to how airports were established at the local level, so there was a great deal of variation in how cities chose to manage their new airports. In the late 1920s, early 1930s, the main question seemed to be whether the new airport, be it owned or leased by the city or operated by private interests in the name of the city, should be administered by an existing city department or whether a new aviation department should be created. Other alternatives were also proposed.

One survey done in the late 1920s indicated that most municipal airports were administered by an existing department of city government. A department of public works oversaw airport operations in Albany; Chicago; Detroit; Indianapolis; Kansas City, Missouri; Philadelphia; Richmond; Rochester; Tampa; and Utica, New York. Park departments were in charge in Atlantic City; Boston; Buffalo; Cleveland; Des Moines; Minneapolis; St. Louis; Spartanburg, South Carolina; Syracuse; and Wichita, Kansas. And a department of public service controlled airports in Akron, Cincinnati, Columbus, and Toledo. Other departments charged with airport administration included the Department of Radio Station and Highway (Jacksonville, Florida), Harbor Board (Milwaukee), Board of Port Commissioners (Oakland), and Department of Public Utilities (St. Paul).[47] A Department of Commerce survey in 1928 uncovered a number of other alternative forms of airport management. City-appointed citizen boards or committees managed airports in Hartford, Connecticut; Louisville, Kentucky; Fort Wayne, Indiana; Centralia, Washington; and Lansing, Michigan. The city manager in Stockton, California, directed that city's airport.[48]

Aviation advocates in Philadelphia proposed combining the administration and operation of rail, water, and air terminals under a quasi-public corporation. The plan, put forth in 1929 in "A Plan for the Development of the Philadelphia

Terminal Air-Marine-Rail," called for the creation of a corporation known as "The Philadelphia Terminal." The corporation would be owned by the city of Philadelphia and be governed by a board of directors. The members of the board of directors would be individuals holding elective or other responsible positions within the city. Suggested members of the board included the mayor, the president of the City Council, the presidents of the Chamber of Commerce, the Board of Trade, the Maritime Exchange and the Engineers Club, the director of wharves, docks, and ferries, the chairman of the State Aeronautics Commission, and the "manager or representative of the lessee of the airport." The airport would then be "leased by the city to this corporation at a rental which would be 100% of the net income."[49]

A Harvard study of airports concluded: "A uniform type of airport administration can hardly be expected, nor would it be altogether wise." However, cities interested in establishing airports should look to the examples of other cities as to how best to administer them. As a consequence, the study concluded that the number of different types of airport administration would eventually diminish, as the best forms of administration became evident and widely imitated. The study also concluded, though, that the number of cities creating separate departments of aeronautics would likely increase. At the time of the study, fifteen cities, including Dallas, Los Angeles, Miami, and Memphis, had airports administered by separate departments of aeronautics.[50]

Of all the various forms of airport management and administration, one came under intense fire, at least by city planners. In 1930 at the Municipal Airport Conference sponsored by the American Road Builders Association, U.S. Grant III, director of Public Buildings and Public Parks of the National Capital, presented a paper in which he concluded that municipal park departments were the "best equipped" to purchase, develop, and manage airports. He supported his conclusion with a number of arguments. First, he stated that cities should avoid creating new departments to govern airports when an existing department could do the job. Further, he asserted that most of the tasks associated with acquiring and developing an airport were already being done, and efficiently, by park departments. Such tasks included purchasing land, maintaining large, open grassy spaces, "the construction and maintenance of runways which [were] so nearly like park roads," operating lighting systems, and controlling crowds. And he stressed that airports, like parks, had a recreational value and that cities could "be sure of gaining the greatest return from this use of [its airport] by fitting it into the plan of park development and making it accessible as part of the general park system."[51]

The planning journal *City Planning* reprinted Grant's address in its January,

1930, issue and over the following months a number of individuals contributed short statements either supporting or, more commonly, refuting his arguments. L. H. Weir of the Playground and Recreation Association of America dismissed the idea that the functions of an airport fell within the existing functions of a park department. He began by looking at how parks responded to other forms of transportation, especially the automobile. When the automobile first appeared, it was used primarily for recreation. Park authorities responded by transforming "their carriage driveway systems into more or less extensive automobile pleasure driveways." However, once automobiles became far more common and were driven at far higher speeds, park authorities moved "to preserve their properties from too much intrusion of the automobile so that these properties may the better perform their primary functions as centers for beauty, rest, or activities for the people." No one would argue, Weir asserted, that parks now had the responsibility for building and maintaining highways and other road systems for the use of the automobile. At most, they should be responsible for a limited number of scenic roadways within parks. Airplanes, in a development similar to that of automobiles, were likely to become parts "of comprehensive and complex systems of passenger and freight-carrying air lines with great terminal landing fields equipped with an unbelievable array of facilities and convenience." At most, parks could provide potential landing fields at certain of its facilities, but park departments should not be responsible for "the administration of terminal facilities for air lines."[52]

Gilmore D. Clarke, a landscape architect, saw airports as being primarily transportation rather than recreational facilities. While airports did have a certain recreational function, Clarke concluded that the "recreational value of the airport [was] secondary to it commercial value." Airports, he argued, must be operated at a profit. Parks, on the other hand, were not "business enterprises." Therefore, it would be best to operate the two separately. Further, he rejected the idea of using parks as emergency landing areas. He believed that if parks "were to become emergency landing fields then they would no longer serve as parks, for they would be unsafe places for recreation." Parks and airports should be as separate as possible. The only exception he accepted was the idea that parks might surround airports in order "to insure a border of unencumbered open space."[53]

Leading city planner John Nolen also rejected the idea that airports should be managed by park departments. He offered no definite ideas on how airports should be managed, but he did conclude that "the natural, efficient administration of municipal aviation systems would be from the point of view and for the normal requirements of *transportation* rather than recreation." [Emphasis in original.] Whatever form the management of airports took—public administration, private franchise, or other—airports needed to be administrated as parts of a transportation system.[54]

While the journal *City Planning* did present arguments on both sides of the debate as to whether or not park departments should manage airports, it also asserted that its editorial board rejected Grant's arguments. It presented five points in opposition. First, the editorial board concluded that aviation represented a transportation function, not a recreation function. Second, the management of airports should be in the hands of airport experts, rather than in the hands of someone whose expertise may have some relation to the issues concerning airports, but which was not focused on airports. For example, they argued that park commissioners should not be expected to manage highways simply "because many highways have grass strips on them planted with trees." Third, the editors pointed out that in the past it had also been suggested that other facilities, such as armories or fairgrounds, incompatible with parks be placed within them. They implied that airports, like armories, did not belong in parks. Fourth, if airports were located near parks, there was no reason why park departments could not help airport managers with such tasks as the maintenance of grass, trees, and roadways. Park departments did not need to manage the airports in order to provide those services. Fifth, while some park superintendents may indeed have the executive ability to run an airport, cities would more likely find suitable candidates for the job if they looked beyond park experts. And sixth, the editors believed that it was time for aviation "to stand on its own feet," implying that airport proponents should not try to use parks and park funds to gain their ends.[55]

Other evidence of some conflict between parks and airports came from New Jersey. In 1929 the New Jersey State Legislature supported a bill allowing "the leasing of municipal park lands for airport purposes." The governor, Harry A. Moore, vetoed the bill. He rejected the use of park land for airports for a number of reasons. First, he held that the state had too few parks, especially in its urban areas and it could not afford to lose those parks to alternate uses. Further, parks were a public trust. The governor also stated that the bill opened the way for fraud in allowing valuable park land to be leased for what the bill called "reasonable consideration." And the bill did not restrict the length of the lease. Under the bill, the state could lose the use of the park lands to airport use "forever."[56]

The period between 1926 and 1933, therefore, represented one in which cities began to work out their relationship with their local "municipal" airport. The trend was toward city ownership and management of the airport, but that was not as yet fully established. Arguments in favor of public ownership, however, became stronger and more common.

The Arguments for Municipal (Public) Airports

Even more clearly than during the pioneering period, and despite the still considerable amount of variation in practices, between 1926 and 1933, airports came to be defined as not just local but as locally (or municipally) owned and operated. Nearly all arguments supporting municipally owned airports began by comparing airports to other transportation terminals such as railroad stations and, following the lead of the Air Commerce Act, docks and harbor facilities. This was necessary as the railroad example did not support municipal ownership. Railroad terminals, even the large union stations, were privately owned and operated by the railroad companies which, like the airline companies, were privately owned and operated. Proponents of municipal ownership, therefore, moved on to the example of docks and harbor facilities. As noted, in the case of water transportation, historically harbor facilities, in particular docks, had been both privately and publicly owned and under both forms of ownership were viewed as a local responsibility. As a result, many proponents of municipal ownership of airports began to refer to airports as harbors of the air.[57] (The assumption is that harbors of the air sounded better than docks of the air.) Not all those dealing with the issue of airport ownership agreed with the idea of public ownership, however. In Harvard University's study of airports conducted by city planners Henry V. Hubbard, Miller McClintock, and Frank B. Williams, for example, the authors concluded that while municipal ownership appeared to be the best means of building a network of airports at the present (1930), in the future airports might just as well be provided by private, commercial interests.[58] As will be seen, though, public ownership of municipal airports became far more common than private ownership by the mid-1930s.

Proponents of municipal airports moved on from the transportation terminal example to provide other arguments in favor of municipal ownership. Austin MacDonald provided one of the more concise discussions of an additional point long brought up by a number of different people in favor of municipal ownership. He asserted that municipally owned airports were most likely to treat all aviators, private and commercial, fairly and equally. At privately owned airports, on the other hand, the commercial operators owning the airport or the largest lessor of airport property were likely to be treated best. Other lessors/users were likely to find themselves at a disadvantage.[59]

Further, MacDonald declared that the strongest argument in favor of municipal ownership "[was] that the airport land must be kept in public hands in order to prevent its diversion to other uses." Municipal land values changed over time. The owners of a privately owned airport situated at a prime location might find that within a few years their property would yield a greater return if used for other purposes. The owners, in that case, would be likely to sell. Only a public body could afford to withstand such a temptation.[60]

The definition of a municipal airport as both local and publicly owned thus received further support between 1926 and 1933.[61] In addition to the theoretical arguments in favor of public ownership, courts began to uphold the actual practice of public ownership of local airports and defined airports as a "public purpose."

Municipal Airports and the Courts

Not surprisingly as city after city took action to purchase and operate an airport, some people objected and challenged the actions in court. One of the earliest cases involved the city of Cleveland, Ohio. When the city proposed issuing bonds in order to finance the construction of its municipal airport, the action was challenged on the grounds "that [it] was in violation of the state constitution in that it constituted a raising of money or loaning of credit to or in the aid of a corporation or company." The court ruled in Cleveland's favor. The decision asserted that even if airports were not specifically mentioned in the part of the state constitution allowing cities to build, own, and operate public utilities, the enabling act passed by the state in 1926 did confer upon cities the power to build, own, and operate airports. The court found that the enabling act violated no parts of the state constitution. In several other cases also challenging municipal authority to construct and own airports, the courts found in favor of the cities.[62]

While the cases such as the one in Cleveland dealt primarily with a city's power to build and own an airport, another set of cases touched directed upon the issue of whether or not an airport represented a public purpose. An especially important case dealing with that issue was *Dysert v. City of St. Louis*, decided in late 1928. In the *Dysert* case the plaintiffs first argued that, at best, airports served the needs of a few, wealthy, reckless individuals engaged in private flying activities. Perhaps a few tourists and other travelers might arrive in the city by way of the airport, but airline transportation remained so expensive as to be available only to a tiny minority. The court rejected that argument, asserting instead that in the near future airline travel had the potential to be as common as travel by railroad or motor car.[63]

The plaintiffs also argued that airports could be "better provided through private initiative and private capital." The court rejected that as well, declaring that airports were "a necessary instrumentality in a new method or system of transportation which [required] public aid for its development and final establishment."

The court compared airport construction to aid offered the railroads in the nineteenth century and concluded that, like the railroads, "the increased prosperity of a community which might be expected to result from the new means of travel and transport made the purpose a public one."[64]

Other court cases echoed the opinions expressed in the *Dysert* case. The Supreme Court of Oregon, for example, provided an extensive defense of the idea of airports as a public purpose. In the case of *McClintock v. City of Rosenburg*, the court maintained that the definition of public purpose had and would continue to change over time given "the changing conditions of society, new appliances in the sciences and other changes brought about by increased population and modes of transportation and communication." Commercial air travel had witnessed substantial growth in the late 1920s, and the court expressed the belief that the growth was likely to continue well into the future. It then asserted that: "An airport owned by the city open to the use of all aeroplanes is for the benefit of the city as a community, and not of any particular individuals therein. It is therefore a public enterprise." Public ownership of airports, further, would assure that no commercial airline could monopolize the air travel into and from any city.[65]

The Role of Civic Organizations

Still, despite the calls for action on the part of city governments to establish airports, local civic organizations continued to play important roles in the building of municipal airports. So, while the arguments for municipal construction and ownership of airports strengthened, airports established by local civic groups in the name of the city—and then often turned over to the city—continued to be part of the picture. The actions of these local civic organizations clearly demonstrated the continued influence of urban boosterism and the winged gospel.

The Chamber of Commerce, both at the national level and at the local level, emerged as an important proponent of airport construction, as well as a booster of aviation in general. The Chamber of Commerce's own Bureau of Aeronautics study in 1927 indicated that "activities looking to the establishment of airports, the development of air traffic and transport facilities, the encouragement of aircraft industries and the stimulation of the public use of air transport [were] being carried on in 134 cities through chambers of commerce and commercial organizations." The national chamber even issued a bulletin "which [summarized] the activities now carried on in various communities throughout the country" and offered suggestions to local chambers on how best to locate airports and protect them through the use of zoning.[66]

Two years later, *Aero Digest* published an article outlining the important contributions of local civic organizations to the development of local airports. W. Gordon Kuster, executive secretary of the Birmingham Chamber of Commerce, wrote that the rapid progress in airport construction witnessed in the late 1920s was owing in large part to the work of such local civic organizations as the United States Junior Chamber of Commerce, the National Exchange Clubs, the Elks, and the American Legion. He argued that the most important contribution those and other local groups made to the cause of airport development was what he called "Educational Exertion." Kuster asserted that local groups played an important role in educating "the public to the safety, to the time saving speed, to the convenience and to the manifold utility of air travel." He credited such an educational campaign for the success of airport drives in Columbus, Ohio, and Brownsville, Texas. In Columbus, for example, the educational campaign by local boosters helped guarantee the success of an $850,000 bond issue.[67]

Kuster then went on to describe what had happened in his home, Birmingham, Alabama. He told how the Birmingham Chamber of Commerce drummed up support for an airport project by first targeting one member of the local newspaper staff and then "[pumping] him full of air and aviation, at every opportunity." Once convincing him of the value of bringing aviation to Birmingham, the newspaper staffer was then charged with convincing others on the staff to get on board. In addition, the chamber paid repeated visits to the paper, especially its editorial staff, and held "sincere discussions" on the importance of aviation. Kuster asserted that once the local newspaper was convinced of the importance of an airport project it "often [became] the most valuable aid in achieving success."[68]

Kuster concluded his article by reiterating that educational programs were the most important function carried out by local civic groups in support of airport programs. Those programs were carried out "through the newspaper, by means of luncheon clubs, by actual demonstrations of the commercial possibilities of planes, by cooperation with operating companies, and by the dissemination of an abundance of aeronautical information."[69]

Archibald Black, one of the most active airport engineers and boosters of the late 1920s and early 1930s, saw an even more direct role for civic organizations in the development of local airports. In his book, *Civic Airways and Airports*, published in 1929, he saw civic organizations as playing far more than just a booster-educational role. In those cases where the local government could not, or would not, provide for a local airport, Black proposed that a local "public spirited group of men" control the municipal airport and "make it open to all on fair terms." Further, whether or not the airport ultimately ended up being owned or controlled by the local government, Black believed that any local airport project should begin with the appointment of "an Airport Committee formed of public-spirited men."[70]

Black's suggestions, in essence, reflected the practices of the times. As demonstrated earlier in the chapter, even though states had for the most part passed the necessary enabling legislation, many cities continued to hold off from plunging into full ownership of their airports. Cities such as Los Angeles chose to lease the property upon which it constructed its municipal airport, whereas Dayton civic leaders—Black's group of publicly minded men—owned and controlled that city's municipal airport. While local groups, which had played a pivotal role in the establishment of the earliest municipal airports in the United States, continued to play important roles, the trend was toward municipal ownership or control of airports. Enough variation existed, however, to continue to make "municipal airport" an evolving term.

Conclusion

The arguments in favor of municipal ownership and control of airports coincided with the explosion of municipal action in the late 1920s. They came at a time when municipally owned airports began to match the number of private/commercial airports in the United States. Also a number of court cases from the era bolstered the arguments in favor of municipal ownership of airports by declaring the establishment of a municipal airport as a public purpose.

Theory, practice, and the law all came together in favor of municipally owned airports by the late 1920s. But just as cities gained such strong support for building the airports they dreamed would afford them an important place on the emerging air transportation network, several other factors came together to dampen the enthusiasm and bring the whole enterprise down to earth. First, of course, in late 1929 the country began to experience what would become the longest and most severe economic downturn in its history. Second, cities found themselves involved in several cases that signaled the fact that owning and operating an airport was not quite as simple as some cities had hoped it would be. The late 1920s and early 1930s saw several court cases dealing with issues of liability and of whether or not an airport constituted a nuisance. The early depression years, however, also saw continued experimentation and innovation on the part of cities.

3

Depression and Reality
The Fading Enthusiasm

*I*t was all supposed to have been so simple. Archibald Black had said so in
his pioneering articles in 1923 and 1925. In 1923 the Air Service published a
how-to pamphlet on airport construction that seemed to lay things out
clearly.[1] By the late 1920s cities could also take advantage of a series of
brochures published by the Aeronautics Branch of the Department of Commerce. Buy a property, provide for grading and drainage, build a hangar, and,
basically, a city had an airport. Cities all over the country jumped at the opportunity after 1927, but by the end of the decade found that their simple enterprise
was not so simple after all. Almost immediately the Post Office and the commercial airline companies began to push for a series of costly improvements including lighting, all-weather landing surfaces, two-way radio communications,
among others. Coinciding with the onset of the depression, cities found themselves in the position of facing growing aviation demands and shrinking municipal revenues.

While cities were being asked to spend more and more on their development, airports failed to generate the profits that would have helped to pay for the

improvements. Cities tried a number of ways to increase revenues at airports including leasing land, renting hangars, and providing maintenance. Many even attempted to redefine airports as not simply transportation centers but social and popular recreational centers, in the hopes that such a change would turn the financial situation around. Despite best efforts, though, few succeeded in making a profit.

Additionally contributing to the deterioration of the situation, cities found themselves in court defending themselves in liability and nuisance suits. Courts mostly ruled in favor of airports, but the suits were significant and challenging. The legal and financial situation contributed to a general diminishment in the enthusiasm for airports. Careful studies of local airport projects, further, indicated there were also limits to the winged gospel's ability to inspire support for airport projects.

The Growing Demands for Better, More Complex Airports

The first decade or so of municipal airport construction, 1918 through the early 1930s, witnessed the rapid development of aviation technology. Not only did the planes themselves become larger and faster, but the push to turn aviation into a viable commercial activity necessitated the development and adoption of a number of other technologies. These included radio communication and navigation equipment, lighting systems, and methods of runway surfacing to allow for safe all-weather, day-and-night operations. Just as cities began to build airports in earnest, they were faced with conflicting messages. On the one hand, they were told to get on with the business of establishing airports. As has been shown, many cities responded to that call. On the other hand, their efforts came under criticism for failing to provide the most modern facilities. What was adequate in the mid-1920s was no longer adequate by 1930.

During the 1920s both government agencies and private interests worked to develop the technologies necessary for all-weather, day-and-night flying. Until the late 1920s, pilots flew their aircraft basically under what is now called visual flight rules. Also called "contact flying," pilots retained visual contact with the ground at all times and navigated by picking out and following known roads, railroads, and other landmarks. Some pilots did navigate over unfamiliar territory and in poor visibility, using a compass to keep to their course—a process known as dead reckoning—but they still needed to maintain visual contact with the ground in order to find their final destination and landing area. As aviation historian Richard Hallion pointed out, the ability to engage in blind or fog flying— taking off, navigating, and landing with reference only to instruments in the cockpit—required the development of several new and reliable instruments and other equipment. First, pilots needed a means to navigate from point to point without reference to ground-based landmarks that was more accurate than the use of the basic compass. Second, pilots needed instruments that would allow them to maintain their aircraft in a safe straight and level flight attitude. And third, pilots needed ground-based facilities that would allow them to take off or land under conditions of poor visibility. During the 1920s a number of agencies and organizations worked to provide the needed instruments and equipment.[2]

In 1920 the Department of Commerce's Bureau of Standards, at the request of the War Department, began work on developing an airborne direction finder based on a concept patented by German inventors in 1907. Sometimes called the A/N system, it provided a pilot with aural clues as to position. The system involved using a two-loop antennae that crossed at a ninety-degree angle. One antennae sent out the Morse code signal for the letter A (dot-dash) while the other sent out the signal for the letter N (dash-dot). This produced a four-course radio range. Imagine the airspace surrounding the antennae as being divided into four quadrants. As one moved around the antennae through the four quadrants, one would hear alternately dot-dash, followed by dash-dot, then dot-dash, and finally dash-dot. However, in the area where the signals overlapped, along the lines separating each of the four quadrants, one heard a solid signal where dot-dash merged with dash-dot. If an airport had one of these radio ranges, pilots could fly their aircraft to that airport by following a line of flight in the direction of the airport through which their radio broadcast the solid signal. Pilots hearing either a dot-dash or dash-dot would know to adjust their course left or right until they once again heard the solid tone and were, thus, flying "on the beam." They knew they had arrived at the location of the beacon when, because it did not transmit its signal directly upwards, the pilot entered a "cone of silence." The system had a number of limitations, though, including the problem of static, which might make it difficult for a pilot to determine whether the radio was broadcasting a solid signal or not. In 1926 the Bureau of Standards began work on a system that would, instead, give pilots visual clues as to their course of flight.[3]

Bureau personnel developed an instrument that "consisted of a radio receiver connected to two vibrating white reeds placed parallel to one another." If a pilot was on course, both reeds appeared to be the same length. If a pilot was off course, one of the reeds would appear longer than the other. If left of course the left reed would appear longer, and if right of course the right reed would appear longer. In 1927 the Bureau of Standards began operational trials of the new radio range system of navigation. National Air Transport's scheduled flight between New York and Cleveland began using the new system for navigation. By early 1928, Bureau pilots "were routinely flying 130-mile flights from and to the research station at College Park field, using experimental models of the visual reed indicator to guide their aircraft." These new flight aids—both aural and visual—represented important advances in radio communications and navigation.[4]

Pilots now could fly from one place to another by means of radio navigation. Also, they could listen to their radios for weather reports, thus allowing them to fly around or otherwise avoid bad weather conditions along their flight path. They still needed a means to fly the aircraft and land it safely without the use of visual cues, though. The Daniel Guggenheim Fund for the Promotion of Aeronautics tackled the remaining obstacles to blind flying. Between 1926 and 1929 the fund sponsored research that resulted in the production of the last elements needed for a blind flying system. It set up a "Full Flight Laboratory" at Mitchel Field in New York and borrowed the services of military test pilot James "Jimmy" Doolittle.[5]

Doolittle used a Consolidated NY-2, a two-seat biplane, as his test aircraft. Gradually, the NY-2 received installation of and allowed for the testing of all the remaining equipment and instruments needed for successful blind flying. These included a second visual indicator for the landing area marker beacon, a precision barometric altimeter, and the Sperry artificial horizon and directional gyro. On September 24, 1929, Doolittle conducted the first completely blind flight in history as he took off, circled Mitchel Field, and landed his aircraft while seated in its rear cockpit enveloped by a canvas hood.[6] While it would be several years before all the new equipment and instruments would become in any way standard, the advent of blind flying offered commercial aviation a certain freedom from delays caused by weather and poor visibility. But many of the instruments in the plane depended on ground-based facilities. While the Department of Commerce could provide much of the equipment, municipal airports would soon be asked to help provide those facilities.

Until the complete development and adoption of the technology necessary for full blind flying came about, beacon lights and other lighting equipment provided the means by which airplanes could navigate at night. By the early 1920s both the Army and the Post Office began to experiment with ways of providing a lighted path through the night sky for aviators. In 1921 the Post Office attempted a daring day-and-night dash across the country, carrying the mail between New York and San Francisco. The pilots used only their primitive on-board instruments, dead reckoning, and the "lighted airway" consisted of "bonfires lit along the route by accommodating citizens." It was a night of adventure during which pilot James H. "Jack" Knight emerged as a hero. He flew three segments of the west-to-east route, pushing onward through a blinding snowstorm and fog to cover the distance between North Platte, Nebraska, and Chicago, Illinois. The Post Office's airmail pilots on the west-to-east route had flown the mail cross-country in thirty-three hours and twenty minutes at a time when even the fastest trains took three days to cover the same distance. (The storm prevented the pilots on the east-to-west route from completing their flights.) The success, though limited, of that experiment inspired the Post Office to try and move from "bonfires to beacons," but a cost-conscious Congress was not yet ready to provide the needed funds.[7] Regardless, both the Post Office and the Army, which also conducted experiments with night flying in 1921, continued to press on.

In 1923, the new second assistant postmaster general, Paul Henderson, found money in the budget to revive the idea of night flying and a lighted airway. While many doubted such a technological feat as a lighted airway could be accomplished, Henderson found support for his ideas in the Army. In 1923 two Army lieutenants, Donald L. Bruner and Harold R. Harris, using "rotating light beacons, field floodlights, and flashing markers that enabled pilots to fly from one beacon to another," built a seventy-two-mile experimental lighted airway between Dayton and Columbus, Ohio. In July and August of that year, they attempted twenty-nine scheduled flights and completed twenty-five. With a successful example to draw upon, Henderson began planning for the construction of a lighted airway between Cheyenne, Wyoming, and Chicago. Planes flying from San Francisco could make it as far east as Cheyenne in a day's flight, and planes flying from New York could make it as far as Chicago. It was the route between Cheyenne and Chicago, therefore, that would most likely have to be flown at night.[8]

The nation's first lighted airway took four months to complete. It included a series of different lights providing different information to pilots along the course. First were the giant rotating beacons that marked the landing sites at Chicago, Iowa City, Omaha, North Platte, and Cheyenne.[9] Each beacon stood atop a thirty-five-foot tower and projected a beam of light equivalent to 450,000,000-candlepower at an angle of 2 degrees above the horizon. The beacons were "visible from over 100 miles under ideal conditions." The landing fields also had equally powerful searchlights for the landing areas and floodlights that illuminated the hangars and other buildings. Red lights marked obstructions along the path of flight. The Post Office also constructed thirty-four emergency landing fields along the course, each marked by 5,000,000-candlepower flashing lights atop fifty-foot towers. The intermediate fields also included boundary lights, approach lights (green), and obstruction lights (red). The course itself was marked originally by beacons placed every three miles. With improved equipment, eventually the beacons were located up to fifteen miles apart. When the Post Office tested its new airway system in August, 1923, flights both eastbound and westbound were completed in less than thirty hours. Once regular service began, westbound trips took a little more than thirty-four hours on average, while wind-assisted east-bound trips averaged just over twenty-nine hours.[10]

With the passage of the Air Commerce Act of 1926, responsibility for building a lighted airways system moved from the Post Office to the Department of Commerce. By 1933 its Airways Division oversaw a rapid expansion of the airways system in the United States. By that year the system included "18,000 miles of lighted airways on which were installed 1,550 rotating light beacons and 263 intermediate landing fields."[11] However, the Department of Commerce's responsibility for the airways ended at the airport boundary. The department provided the airport beacon light, but the municipal airport was responsible for providing other night lighting equipment (floodlights, boundary lights, and so on) and the electricity to power the lights. Harvard's airport study of 1930 indicated that on average airports spent $16,935.58 on lighting.[12] That was quite an expense to municipal airports still struggling to break even.

While the Department of Commerce helped provide equipment needed for blind flying and to connect airports to the lighted airways, one type of early improvement's costs fell squarely on the shoulders of municipal airports. As commercial aviation moved toward more all-weather operations and as the airplanes used became heavier and with faster landing speeds, the days of turf landing areas, particularly at any municipal airport hoping for a high volume of commercial traffic, were numbered. Turf landing strips were fine for even the largest planes operating in the late 1920s and early 1930s as long as the weather was dry (no rain or snow) and the volume of traffic was low. However, a turf landing strip could soon become a rutted mess if used too soon after a rain and was very difficult to clear after snow. Also, heavy use could cause stress and damage to even the best maintained turf surface. A more durable and more easily maintained surface was needed.

Airports experimented with a variety of runway surfacing materials in the late 1920s and early 1930s, including cinders, gravel, and asphalt. The most publicized example of providing a prepared runway instead of a turf-covered landing area or landing strip came from Henry Ford's airport near Detroit. In 1929, Ford installed a 75-foot-wide, 2,500-foot-long concrete runway at the airport he built near his factory. Soon other airports, both municipal and commercial, followed Ford's example.[13] Given the demands of scheduled commercial airline companies, which were accompanied by a strong push from the concrete industry, a big booster of paved runways in the 1930s, cities were being asked to do more than seed and mow the landing areas at their airports.

Therefore, though cities may have heard the message that airports were relatively simple enterprises during the early 1920s, by the time cities were ready to take action in the late 1920s, the situation was far different. Airports, at least the ideal types that many would wish to see, had become complex. When cities failed to meet the new, higher expectations, they found themselves coming under criticism.

As early as 1928 advocates of bigger and better airports began to chide cities for providing inadequate facilities. In an article entitled "What Is an Airport?" civil engineer B. Russell Shaw concluded that many of the new municipal facilities were airports in name only. To make his point, he drew distinctions between what he called landing fields, airports, and air terminals. A landing field was "a tract of land comprising less than 100 acres, level but without accommodations except small hangars and gasoline servicing facilities." An airport was a larger field "equipped with hangars, gasoline servicing facilities, telephones, pilots' quarters, rest rooms and a passenger station." According to Shaw, an airport also provided "night lighting, first aid, maintenance equipment, fire fighting apparatus" and other equipment. An air terminal was a facility that had the highest quality airport equipment and was "serving as a terminal on established airlines." It would match in quality and comfort the best railroad terminal facilities in the nation's largest cities.[14]

Shaw concluded that in 1928 the nation had no air terminals and very few airports. The vast majority of the new municipal aviation facilities ranked only as landing fields. He pointed to several features that these municipal fields lacked. First, they lacked adequate landing strips or runways. Shaw stated that, while the entire landing area should remain usable, to accommodate regular use of the landing area, especially by larger planes, and to help control air traffic flow, it would be best to designate either landing strips or runways on the field. The difference between a landing strip and a runway was in width and surfacing. Landing strips were wider — up to 500 feet — while runways tended to be narrower, as narrow as 50 feet. Also, landing strips had grass or turf surfaces, while runways had a prepared surface of some kind — cinder, gravel, oil, asphalt, or concrete.[15] Both landing strips and runways set off certain parts of the landing area for preferred use, although in the late 1920s and early 1930s most airports still allowed for all-way landing. (Once paved runways became the norm, they became the only places in the landing area for planes to use for takeoff and landing.) Shaw found that a number of accidents had been caused "by the promiscuous use of 'all-way' landing fields." Defined landing strips or runways along with definite air traffic rules were needed.[16]

Second, municipal facilities for the most part lacked adequate passenger accommodations. Shaw reminded readers that air travelers were generally prosperous individuals capable of paying premium prices. Too often, he said, these passengers found themselves boarding "a $50,000 airplane by walking through slush or rain and finally getting on board with their clothing wet and in a disagreeable state for the trip." Such conditions, according to Shaw, harkened back to "the old stage coach days." While conceding that some smaller airports might continue to be able to provide only minimum passenger facilities, he declared that all major airports and any air terminal had to do better. They had to build passenger stations that would allow planes to be "loaded and unloaded under cover," so that passengers could board and leave the aircraft in comfort regardless of the weather. He pointed to the terminal building at Tulsa, Oklahoma, as a good example for airports and air terminals to follow.[17]

Shaw concluded by stating that the best strategy was not to "discourage cities, by telling them that their landing fields [were] not airports, but rather to encourage them to make airports out of landing fields that would be capable of handling the largest airliners."[18] He did not, however, suggest how cities would either pay for the needed improvements or finance the construction of more elaborate facilities in the first place.

Shaw was not the only critic of conditions at the new municipal airfields. Also in 1928, Major Hugh J. Knerr, commander of the 2d Bombardment Group, U.S. Air Corps, wrote a critical editorial for *U.S. Air Services.* He stated that on a recent Air Corps exercise in which nine airplanes from the 2d Bombardment group traveled from the East Coast to Los Angeles for the National Air Races, the group spent almost as much time on the ground as in the air. The problem was not with the planes but with the lack of adequate refueling facilities. While that certainly made problems for his men on their trip, he also pointed out that the lack of adequate refueling services would hamper commercial air transportation. Problems with refueling would cause additional problems of congestion on the ground at the airport and difficulty in maintaining schedules. He warned that cities and municipal airports that failed to address that issue might find themselves bypassed by airlines.[19]

His editorial criticized municipal airports on another front as well. He found that most municipal airports were located "at great distances from the business sections of their cities." Therefore, when he and his men landed, they had to spend a great deal of time traveling into the cities to find something to eat. Flying, he said, "[seemed] to create a demand for food that cannot be denied, and yet on the entire route from the Atlantic to the Pacific we did not find so much as a hot dog stand at an airport." He suggested that if cities provided for even a small restaurant at their airports "a paying business will be established and, in addition, a desire to stop at that airport will be created in the minds of pilots who know that it is available." He concluded by encouraging cities to provide "facilities for the comfort and convenience of pilots and passengers" in order to take full advantage of "the fast awakening air-mindedness of the American people."[20]

The complaints continued. A 1930 *Aero Digest* article strongly encouraged cities to upgrade their airport facilities. The author, Wyatt Brummitt, began by comparing air travel to train travel. He stated that railroads had learned how to cater to affluent travelers by providing "club cars, observation cars, compartment Pullmans, extra-fare trains and de luxe [*sic*] terminal facilities." The aviation industry now needed to learn the same lesson. It could no longer assume that time-saving would be enough to draw passengers to airlines. Business travelers might agree that "time was money," but, contrary to initial theory, they were not willing to "overlook the sketchiness of the airports, the general catch-as-catch-can atmosphere of the business and the actual discomforts of starting and finishing his flight." True, more than three million people made commercial flights of some sort in 1929, but the author asserted most of them (97.5 percent according to the author) "were merely joy-hoppers, sightseers or stunt relishers." If commercial aviation was to move beyond serving those seeking short thrills to serving the serious business traveler, it needed to pay more attention to passenger comfort.[21]

The author complained that most airports resembled "a fairly disheartening looking thing." They seemed not to have advanced much since World War I "when any shed large enough to take a Jenny was a hangar and when discomfort itself [had] a sort of prestige." He further lamented that passengers had nowhere to wait for their flights except "a draughty shed," and had to walk to their planes "through mud, dust, or cinders, dodging propellers and wondering whether or not, after all, this flying stuff was worth the candle." In contrast to Major Knerr, he did give airports credit for at least providing a hot dog stand as a "gesture toward animal comfort."[22]

Brummitt further acknowledged that some improvements were being made. A few municipal airports, such as those at Buffalo, Cleveland, and Chicago, were providing at least small, though adequate, airport terminal buildings. And Kansas City's new Fairfax Airport, a commercial facility, had "an impressive structure" costing sixty thousand dollars. He credited some of those improvements with the fact that air travel increased during the first six months of 1930. If air traffic was to continue to increase, more improvements were necessary. He concluded by arguing: "It [better service] quiets the fears which still persist in the minds of many in regard to flying. And it justifies the hopes of those who, though convinced of the practicability of aerial transport, looked forward to a time when flying would cast off its vacant-lot spirit and become an honest, self-respecting business."[23]

Complaints were not limited to lamenting the lack of terminal buildings, restaurants, and fueling stations. Others emphasized the need for meeting much higher standards, even higher than those set by the Department of Commerce, and for adoption of all the latest aviation equipment. Writing in the *Annals of the American Society of Political and Social Sciences*, Austin F. MacDonald admitted that once cities decided to construct an airport, they immediately faced a number of problems and questions. Those included how the airport would be financed and managed, could the airport ever support itself, the number and size of hangars to be constructed, the type of fire-fighting equipment to provide, what system of night lighting would be required, and what kind of repair facilities to provide. He summed up by stating: "The list [of problems and questions] might be extended almost indefinitely."[24] He went on to insist, though, that cities needed to do a better job responding to the challenges facing them.

Austin's rather lengthy treatment of "The Airport Problems of American Cities" included a section in which he outlined the Department of Commerce's airport rating system. He then went on to use the criteria set down in the rating system as a basis for evaluating conditions at American airports in 1930, especially noting how the airports generally failed to measure up to the standards for the highest A1A rating. He gathered information on 181 airports at cities with populations exceeding 50,000 according to 1927 census estimates. He further divided the cities into Group I (populations over 500,000), Group II (300,000–500,000), Group III (100,000–300,000) and Group IV (50,000–100,000).[25] Using that information, he did not paint a very rosy picture of conditions at the nation's major municipal airports.

First, the airports were too small. The Department of Commerce set the minimum area for an airport at 150 acres. MacDonald pointed out, however, that while 150 acres did provide for an adequate area for landing, it allowed no room "for hangars, repair shops, administration buildings, and other necessary structures." He concluded, therefore, that the minimum acreage for an airport should be 250 acres and that 500 or 1,000 acres "would give much more satisfactory results." His study indicated, though, that only half of the airports at the largest cities had areas of 250 acres or more. He found a similar situation with Group II cities. In Group III cities he found that most airports covered only 50 to 150 acres. He further pointed out the significance of that finding by emphasizing that even Group III cities were "among the one hundred largest cities in the United

States." And Group IV cities' airports ranged in size from 50 to 90 acres and "two thirds of them [were] so small they could not possibly meet the size requirement set up by the Department of Commerce for the highest rating."[26]

He then criticized the conditions of the landing surfaces and drainage systems at the airports. Only half of the airports studied had prepared runways, most still relied on grass surfaces. He further concluded that "many fields which [were] classified as grass covered [were] in reality covered only with patches of grass and weeds." The drainage systems were equally inadequate. Most airports had no special system to provide drainage, relying "entirely on such drainage as may be provided by nature." Even when controlling for the size of the city involved, only in Group I cities were a majority of the airports provided with systems for other than natural drainage. What that meant was "that most airports never have satisfactory surface conditions, save for very limited periods." Otherwise they suffered from either clouds of dust or found themselves mired in "veritable seas of mud." MacDonald admitted that providing adequate drainage would be expensive, but he encouraged cities to spend the money rather than simply going with whatever provided the cheapest solution.[27]

He further urged cities to provide prepared runways. He stated that both heavy traffic and heavier planes made hard-surfaced runways a necessity. His study found that hard-surfaced runways were found primarily at airports in Group I cities. Only a few Group II cities' airports had prepared runways. He did note, though, that the smaller the city the less the need for runways as "in the absence of heavy traffic, a well-drained turf field [was] capable of giving excellent results." However, he found generally that whether a city relied on landing strips or runways few airports at any city, large or small, could meet the Department of Commerce's requirements for an A1A airport in terms of landing area. Generally landing strips were "too short, too narrow, and too few," even at major metropolitan airports. And, when they had runways, most airports had too few.[28]

The verdict was the same when it came to airport lighting. Only a few airports by 1930 had met the Department of Commerce's standard for night lighting. While most cities provided an adequate beacon light, they fell short when it came to boundary lights and field floodlights. And, as he had done when considering the size of airports, MacDonald declared that many of the airport lighting requirements set by the Department of Commerce were inadequate. So even if a city met the minimum federal guidelines, MacDonald would argue that they needed to do more.[29]

MacDonald also took airports to task over their buildings. He complained that most airports "[were] still trying to get along with structures which, though far from adequate at the time they were built, [were] even less suited to present needs." And remember, MacDonald was writing in 1930. Most of the airports he studied had only been built in the last few years and already any buildings they had were being judged as inadequate. He found that, generally, hangars were too small. The only good news was that airports were replacing older wooden hangars with sturdier structures. Cities were also beginning to provide suitable administration buildings, but much still needed to be done. And he found that most airports did not provide good repair facilities.[30]

Finally, MacDonald concluded that most airports also fell short in providing many other types of equipment and services. Gasoline and oil services were improving, but most airports still lagged when it came to fire-fighting equipment. Even most of the largest airports still relied on handheld fire extinguishers. He also found radio receiving sets as rare. He did believe, though, that they would become more common in the near future. He suggested that airports could and should equip themselves with "the new radio devise" that made blind landing possible once it moved beyond the experimental stage. Weather equipment was available at most airports, but MacDonald found most of it inadequate. Only at the forty or so of the largest airports could United States Weather Bureau personnel and government-supplied equipment be found. And he concluded that airports needed to develop better systems for controlling traffic on and in the immediate vicinity of the airport.[31]

Given the criticism of municipal efforts and the strong push to provide more, better, and more expensive facilities and services, it was not surprising that the burst of enthusiasm that propelled cities into the airport business after 1927 quickly faded. An article by the assistant editor of *Aviation*, Charles Gale, provided evidence of the bursting of the airport bubble. He looked at a number of figures, all of which suggested that many cities failed to follow through on airport plans. First, although the total number of airports did increase in the late 1920s, nearly half of the cities reporting plans to build airports to the Department of Commerce failed to report completing those airports. Specifically, between July 1, 1927, and July 1, 1929, the Department of Commerce received reports on 1,632 airport projects. As of July 1, 1930, only 678 projects were reported as completed. The author assumed that all the other projects "had fallen by the wayside," thus indicating a failure rate of 45 percent.[32]

The author also compiled some numbers of his own. He took a list of 147 cities proposing to build airports from a July, 1927, issue of *Domestic Air News*. He found that as of the time of his article (December, 1930), forty-six cities had built municipal airports. Another forty cities had new commercial airports. However, sixty-one cities still had no recognized airports. He also followed up on a shorter list from November, 1927. Of the ten communities included on that list, five still had no airports. And yet another list of nineteen cities yielded only ten completed projects.[33]

Growing Costs and the Problems of Revenue

By the late 1920s and early 1930s, alongside articles continuing to boost munici-pal airport construction, a number of aviation journals also began printing ar-ticles dealing with the money problems of the nation's airports.[34] The problems were many and ranged from organizing successful bond drives to finance airport construction to somehow making the airports pay for themselves—or at least break even—once in operation. While a few writers insisted that airports were still reasonable investments for cities, most acknowledged that airports were and were likely to remain expensive propositions.

As late as November, 1929, J. E. Bullard of *Airports* could publish an article on airport financing that still had an optimistic booster tone. In fact, he insisted that cities could acquire airports with what he called "painless financing." He argued that wherever airports were built, the value of the adjacent land rose. He said that some "far sighted men" had even bought as much as a thousand acres and then sold to the city only the amount of land needed for the airport. They then profited from the increased value of the remaining land once the city con-structed the airport. Bullard asserted that cities should follow the example of those men and buy as much land as possible for their airports, up to one thou-sand or fifteen hundred acres. The cost of the land purchase could then be cov-ered either by profits from the airport or profits derived from the rising value of the additional land. As he put it: "As the revenue-producing agencies will grow more rapidly in the vicinity of an airport than at other spots near a city, it is ob-vious that the revenue from the land purchased around the airport site will grow at a more rapid rate than did that from land used by the natural growth of the city."[35]

Bullard did acknowledge that while the bonds for land purchases could be painlessly financed, that was not necessarily the case with bonds issued to fi-nance the actual construction of the airport facilities. Those bonds might have to be paid out of general tax revenues. He did suggest several ways cities could address that situation. First, they could issue long-term bonds. Those bonds could eventually be paid off with revenues from the airport and from revenue re-maining from the surrounding lands once the land purchase bonds had been retired. Another alternative was to build a smaller airport. As long as the city controlled the surrounding land, and could keep the approaches clear of obstructions, a smaller landing area could be used, at least in the beginning.[36]

Bullard concluded by emphasizing "the many advantages a city [derived] from having an airport located near it." He judged the cost of building an airport as "small," especially compared to the annual street-widening projects undertaken by cities. And he insisted that if the site were purchased under "favorable conditions" it "need not cost the city anything" as "the land [would] not only pay the interest on the bonds but also for the land itself." Therefore, there was "no good reason" why cities should not go out and buy as much land as possible for an airport site or sites. If allowed to issue long-term bonds, there would be "no risk to the buyers of the bonds" for even "if the land [failed] to produce the desired amount it [was] a simple matter to sell what land [was] necessary to make up the deficit." Cities could, therefore, come into possession of all the land needed for an airport "without in any way affecting the tax rate or increasing the debt of the city itself."[37]

Such optimistic booster statements became increasingly rare. The same month Bullard published his boosterish article in *Airports*, he and Avery E. Lord published a less optimistic article in *Aviation* outlining the revenue problems faced by a number of existing airports. They began by emphasizing the fact that the nation needed "larger, better and more airports" and that those airports should most likely be provided by the public sector, namely cities. In arguing that last point, they compared airport construction to the provision of highways for automobiles. Just as the automobile industry needed good roads in order to grow, the aviation industry needed airport facilities in order to expand.[38] They failed to deal with the fact that highways were financed largely by states and the federal government, however, not cities.

Having established that the public sector must act to provide airports, the authors then acknowledged that selling that idea to all cities could be difficult. Only a very small percentage of the American population actually used airports and, thus, benefited directly from them. The authors pointed out, for example, that there was only one plane for every thirty thousand people in the United States. Therefore, even though airports also provided indirect benefits, it would be hard to convince taxpayers to "burden themselves with the bigger and bigger bond issues that will be needed unless these ports can show a substantial financial return." Airports needed to become both self-supporting and capable of providing enough revenue to retire the bonds. Some cities, though, had spent so much on their airports—driving up their debts—that other cities had begun to hesitate to build their own airports. It was also clear that costs were rising.[39]

The article briefly repeated Bullard's argument about cities buying large tracts of land with long-term bonds. But the *Aviation* article also acknowledged that, in buying a larger tract of land, cities needed to have a larger bond issue and that "unless a direct revenue [could] be secured from the very start it [might] not be possible to obtain as large a bond issue as [was] required." One answer the authors proposed was that cities buy the land but then lease it to private interests to develop into an airport. They declared that once the city tried to develop the airport, it was engaging in a business activity and the experiences with other municipal business enterprises such as municipal electric light and gas plants suggested that cities "rarely proved successful" in such endeavors. It was best that private capital be used to build the needed facilities on the airport site.[40] Obviously "municipal airport" was still a flexible and evolving term.

The article then examined the revenue situation at a number of airports. The authors first pointed out that "it [was] probable that no public airport [was] as yet actually meeting expenses, to say nothing of showing a net profit." However, some airports, through various means, showed signs of being able to make a profit—or at least stop losing money—in the near future. Newark, New Jersey, for example, leased land at its airport and also charged a variety of fees. Among them, it charged sightseeing companies operating out of the airport a fee amounting to 10 percent of their revenues; it collected two cents on every gallon of gasoline sold; airmail, express, and freight companies paid a penny per pound of cargo hauled; and airline transport companies paid a fixed fee per passenger. While there were complaints about the fees, air traffic at Newark, at the time the official airmail airport in the New York region, continued to grow. The airport was still not making money, but its deficit was low and, if growth continued, it was predicted to earn a net profit soon.

Cleveland's municipal airport, another busy, growing facility, also showed signs of soon turning a profit. That airport charged one thousand dollars per year per "unit of space for the erection of a hangar" and charged also for the use of the municipal hangars and for the use of the night-lighting system. In addition, the Cleveland airport imposed a small landing fee. The Buffalo, New York, airport planned to put itself "on a paying basis" by collecting revenue from "the sale of gasoline, oil and supplies, the rental of buildings and the service of mechanics." The city also planned to lease land at the airport for "building purposes." The city would then provide "taxi ways, sewer, water and light facilities and those who [held] the leases [would] be taxed on a foot-frontage basis to maintain these utilities." In Montgomery, Alabama, the city purchased 1,526 acres of land. Only 925 acres were used for the airport. The city planned to develop the other 600 acres, surrounding the airport on three sides, as a public golf course. The golf course was not expected to create revenue. However, so many people would use the golf course—as opposed to how few would actually use the airport—that it was hoped it would "tend to make the taxpayers willing to stand the cost of the development of the site as a whole."[41]

The Cleveland, Buffalo, and Montgomery airports were municipally owned and operated. The article also included an example of revenue-generating activities from a "municipal airport" owned by a local group of investors and leased to a commercial operator. That example was the Dayton, Ohio, airport. As pointed out in chapter 2, Dayton's "official municipal airport" for airmail purposes had been provided by a group of local businessmen who bought property north of the city, near Vandalia, Ohio, developed an airport, and then leased it to a private operator, the E. A. Johnson Flying Service. The Dayton Airport drew revenue from a number of sources including hangar charges, a five-cent per gallon fee on gasoline as well as a fee on oil purchases, and charges for repair and maintenance activities. The airport also derived revenue from concessions operating on the airport.[42] However, though the article neglected to mention this fact, Dayton's airport still failed to make money for its operator or investors. (See chapter 4.)

In fact, a number of suggestions as to how municipal airports might generate revenue came from actions taken by commercial airports. Two commercial airports presented as examples of how airports in general could earn money were the Fairfax Airport in Kansas City, Kansas, and the Grand Central Airport in Glendale, California, near Los Angeles.

Fairfax Airport was a commercial field owned by the Woods Brothers Corporation, an engineering firm known for its river control work, and operated by Fairfax Airports, Inc., in which the Woods Brothers Corporation owned a major share. In June, 1930, the Fairfax Airport could brag of twenty consecutive months of profit as well as major improvements made to the field. Although the article describing operations at Fairfax concentrated primarily on more or less standard ways for the airport to earn revenue, including hangar rentals, sales of fuel and oil, and leasing portions of the field for use by flying schools and aircraft manufacturers, the author admitted up front that the airport had a unique advantage. Natural gas deposits had been found on the airport property. Fourteen wells produced enough natural gas, sold at the retail rate of 34 cents per 1,000 cubic feet, to heat the airport buildings and fuel the manufacturing plants on the airport and in the adjacent Fairfax industrial district. Surplus gas was sold to The Cities Service Gas Company at the wholesale rate of 18 cents per 1,000 cubic feet.[43]

The author insisted, however, that he mentioned the natural gas on the field only as a way of showing how an airport management might fully utilize any by-products of the airport. As noted, the bulk of the article pointed out how the Fairfax Airport earned revenue from more conventional sources. The Fairfax operators, though, did have a couple of other tricks up their sleeves. For example, the Woods Brothers owned a number of other, smaller auxiliary airfields in the area. They planned to have a flying school open on one of those fields near Weston, Missouri. In the meantime, much of the field was used for growing tobacco. Plans allowed for prospective student pilots to work part-time in the tobacco field, their earnings offsetting some of the costs of their flight training. Once the flight school became fully operational, the Woods Brothers planned to continue to use the land in between the runways to grow tobacco. The author did admit that the idea sounded "weird," but knowing the management style of the Woods Brothers, it was neither "impossible nor improbable." And another unique revenue-generating scheme used by the Woods Brothers was the placement of pay toilets in the new administration building. The author stated that the management estimated that the pay toilets could bring in as much as $2,400 annually. As the author concluded at one point, the "officials of Fairfax Airports, Inc., have adopted or plan to adopt almost every known means for increasing the income of the aviation field."[44]

Grand Central Airport, a commercial airport near Los Angeles, also found itself presented as an example of how an airport might earn money. Showmanship was the key in that case. An article on the airport described its manager, Major C. C. Mosely, as having "a rare type of business mind and a peculiar ability for devising effective showmanship angles." He also had a staff of "idea" or "gag" men to aid him. Grand Central Airport profited from operating a "joy-hop" service that averaged more than five thousand passengers a month. Three Ford Tri-Motors took passengers on six-minute flights for which the passengers were charged according to their weight, a penny per pound. The airport further attracted people to the field for these short rides by "rebroadcasting on the loudspeaker system the position reports broadcast over the radio telephone by pilots coming in on transcontinental flights." Sometimes the pilots would also have passengers get on the radio "and tell of the beautiful landscape or region over which the plane [was] passing." The author argued that any airport could use this, especially to attract greater "Sunday crowds" to the airport.[45]

To further cater to the "Sunday crowds," Grand Central Airport had a special Sunday program from 12:20 P.M. until 7:45 P.M. "with music, news broadcasts, flying model demonstrations, crop-dusting demonstrations, parachute jumps and demonstrations of airport lights." For five dollars, people could ride along in the plane carrying the parachuter and watch him jump. Grand Central Airport, through such actions, catered especially to the local news media. Their Sunday shows offered sources for feature articles. Press often received complimentary flights. The author concluded that those examples of "aeronautical showman-ship" brought "results in good circulation-building stunts for the newspapers, as well as profit to the port."[46]

The managers attending the second national airport conference in 1930 sounded a more cautionary note about the use of concessions and other non-airport activities as revenue-generating sources. While calling concessions "one of the promising sources of airport income," a special committee on concessions at the conference presented rather guarded opinions about their use. First, the committee stated "that municipal airports need to be careful about maintaining a dignified basis of operation, as far as concession were concerned, furnishing mainly transportation, terminal and aeronautical facilities." The committee fur-ther opined that "amusement concessions in any case should be separated from flying activities." It also saw a danger in "concessions running wild under out-side operators at some point adjoining the airport." Under those conditions, the committee believed it would be best for cities to maintain control over con-cessions. When it came to restaurant concessions, it held that they were best handled by "[securing] a guaranteed monthly minimum with a percentage basis beyond that."[47]

As for gasoline and oil concessions, the committee's report of its opinions probably did not gladden the hearts of many struggling airport managers. The committee held that hangar lessees should be able to own and operate their own gasoline and oil equipment, rather than purchasing such from the airport. It did, however, say that the lessees could be barred from selling to transients (meaning planes and pilots landing at the airport on their way to or from some-where else).[48]

Regardless of any innovative thinking on how to raise revenues at an airport, the number of airports, both municipal and commercial, that made steady prof-its was small. Probably typical of many was the story of the struggles of Love Field in Dallas, Texas, to move out of "the beggar class." As told by the city's director of municipal airports, Preston Sneed, despite the fact that by mid-1931 Love Field could challenge Chicago's municipal airport for the title of second busiest air-port in the country, the airport had failed to make money.[49]

As Sneed saw it, the problem of insufficient revenue stemmed mainly from the fact that the city owned only the ground upon which the airport sat. It did not operate any fuel or oil concessions as each company operating on the field sup-plied their own fuel and oil. Further, it owned only two World War I-era hangars, which it leased out. Therefore, the city could not collect any fees for the daily or overnight storage of aircraft on the field. As a result, the airport cost the taxpayers of Dallas $25,000 during the fiscal year ending in July, 1931. Further, the county invested $18,000 building a taxiway. In contrast, the airport earned only $6,700 during the same fiscal year. In the coming fiscal year, the city planned to impose a number of new fees in the hopes that they would help bring Love Field out of the red and into the black.[50]

First, the city found a way to get around the fact that the companies operating on the field supplied their own oil and gas and, thus, did not pay the city gasoline tax. The Dallas city government passed an ordinance "exacting a fee from any concern which used Love Field as a base for its operations, but which handled its own gasoline." That would bring the city $2,500 annually. The city also enacted a fee for the use of the field by flying schools that it hoped would net about $2,000. Further, the city required any pilot wanting to hire out their own plane to take passengers on sightseeing tours to purchase a $50-per-year permit. The expected annual revenue was $700. The city also leased its two hangars for $2,750 each. Sneed further recommended that other transport lines operating through Love Field, but not based on the field and buying little gasoline there, be charged a fee for the use of the airport. That could result in $3,000 in additional revenue.[51]

Sneed argued that the city was able to levy these additional fees without facing strong opposition from the companies using the airport. In fact, he asserted that two of the largest companies, American Airways and National Air Transport, volunteered to start paying some of the fees even before the city government had taken action. As Sneed put it: "Those who pay the tax feel better for it." Apparently, the companies using Dallas were willing to pay something to help the city maintain the airport.[52] After some struggle, Love Field may well have been on its way out of the red. However, it was a major airport not only in the South but in the nation. Whether other municipal airports could adopt similar fees and continue to keep business was unknown.

The Social Role of Airports

Faced with economic pressures, cities tried many ways to convince people that airports were more than municipal money losers or, as contemporary law suits asserted, liabilities or nuisances (see below). In additional efforts to make airports pay their own way and despite the doubts of many airport managers, cities began to emphasize the social aspects of airports. Airports had always attracted crowds of people. Airplanes remained enough of a novelty that people still came out to the airports, especially on weekends, to view those modern marvels.[53]

Aviation enthusiasts concerned with airport finance began to make suggestions as to how airports might provide social and recreational facilities as a means to raise revenues. An article in the *American City* in 1930 suggested that airports take advantage of the crowds they attracted by establishing concessions. The article then listed a number of possibilities including refreshments, a hotel, a swimming pool, "toilets with nickel slot machines" (the assumption is that this was some kind of pay toilet), a merry-go-round, and a barber shop. The success of those concessions depended on the size of the crowds the airport could attract on the weekend. However, if the airport provided such concessions, it might increase the number of people interested in spending part of their weekend at the airport. The article concluded: "There is no reason why airports should not have many of the features of an amusement park, as the visitors to a flying field are there principally for amusement."[54]

The idea of providing social and recreational facilities at airports as a way to make money continued well into the 1930s. In 1935, Grand Central Airport near Los Angeles once again offered examples of actions that might be taken. It used radio advertisements to try to convince people that the airport was a recreation center. The managers of the airport asked: "And why shouldn't an airport profit by satisfying the same needs that have been filled by motion picture theaters, restaurants, bazaars and the higher type of cocktail dispensaries?"[55] Grand Central advertised that it offered a bar, a sidewalk cafe, and a first-class restaurant. In addition, the Los Angeles airport had an advantage all its own that might also help attract crowds. The airport's radio announcements included a list of the Hollywood stars expected at the airport and their times of arrival or departure. Los Angelenos could go to one of their local airports to gaze not only at the airplanes but also at the stars.[56] As late as 1940 *Aviation* published an article that encouraged the construction of airport country clubs that would offer pleasant facilities for private pilots on cross-country jaunts and for other visitors to the airport.[57]

The fact of the matter was that airports had become expensive and complex facilities. Faced with the rapid advance of aviation technology that demanded frequent updates of airport equipment and landing areas, the rising costs of airport operations and the financial pressures exacerbated by the deepening economic depression, by the early 1930s cities could no longer build and maintain airports on their own. The situation made it clear that cities needed help to build, maintain, and equip their airports. And at the same time, legal challenges further complicated the job of operating an airport.

Airports and the Courts

The law states that cities cannot be held liable "for alleged injuries to the persons or property of individuals when it is engaged in the performance of public or governmental functions."[58] Several states passed laws that either declared municipal airports a governmental function or otherwise exempted municipalities from liability.[59] Most states, and most courts, however, viewed municipal airports as a proprietary function of cities. In other words, much as when cities operated electric, gas and water systems, when cities owned and operated airports they "[were] engaged in a private enterprise and not a governmental function and for that reason [were] liable for any injuries sustained by a third party as a result of the municipality's fault, just as any other private airport proprietor would have to be."[60]

In examining the issue of liability, in 1932 the *National Municipal Review* opined that while cities should be held liable for injuries sustained at municipally owned airports, nonetheless such a situation increased the cost of maintenance at most municipal airports. That increased cost constituted a "discouraging element," which, along with the depression, served to put a "decided check" on municipal subsidies to aviation "in the form of the establishment of municipally owned airports."[61]

In addition to being held liable for injuries, cities also found themselves in court defending their airports against the charge that they constituted a nuisance. Many of the earliest cases dealing with that issue involved private or commercial airports. Two important cases, arising in 1932 and 1934, involved municipal airports. The first dealt with the airport leased by the city of Santa Monica and the second dealt with Atlanta's municipally owned airport. In the Santa Monica case the court ruled "that the ordinary use of an airport need not necessarily result in a nuisance." Therefore, airports per se were not nuisances. However, the case did not resolve whether or not certain airport operations might constitute a nuisance. Cities, therefore, might still find themselves faced with injunctions against their airports because certain operations might produce, among other things, dust, noise, danger, and crowds.[62]

A 1934 case in Georgia seemed to lessen the possibility of airport operations being halted by injunctions aimed at preventing nuisances. Atlanta's airport, in place since 1925, had grown during the late 1920s and early 1930s once Atlanta became a stop on the airmail network. In 1934 an adjacent property owner, a Mr. Thrasher, complained that the dust stirred up by the airport made his wife ill, that planes flying low (under five hundred feet) over his property constituted a danger, and that both he and his wife suffered from the noise produced by airport operations. Thrasher wanted the airport declared a common nuisance and put out of business.[63]

The court decision was mixed, but generally supported the airport. The court ruled that the airport did have to do something about the dust and "that Mrs. Thrasher could recover for her illness caused by such dust." On the other hand, as to the issues of noise, and particularly that of over flight, the court ruled in the city's and the airport's favor. On the latter issue, the court declared "that there was no proof sufficient to show that flying at less than 500 ft. was a trespass or a nuisance, and therefore refused to grant an injunction."[64] Cities, however, remained subject to charges that their airports constituted nuisances.

The anti-airport sentiment behind many of the lawsuits indicated that not everyone viewed aviation and airports in a favorable light. The failure of airports to earn a profit or at least break even, especially in light of the general economic depression, further diminished their value in the public eye. Careful study of local airport politics in two midwestern cities further indicates that although the winged gospel continued to influence many, there were limits to how greatly it could encourage favorable action on behalf of individual airport projects.

Airports and Winged Gospel

While some could still be inspired to great flights of imagination when it came to aviation and airport terminal design, particularly once the depression fully gripped the nation, airports themselves proved far less inspirational than the pilots and the planes flying around and to them. In addition, certain case studies suggest that upper-income Americans were, perhaps, more enthusiastic about aviation than were lower-income Americans. Analyses of the controversies surrounding the development of municipal airports in both Omaha, Nebraska, and Muncie, Indiana, suggest that while the cities' elite supported the airports, support was less forthcoming from the working-class citizens of those cities or at least those who claimed to speak for them.

As noted earlier, the concrete industry became a major booster of runway construction in the late 1920s and early 1930s. After all, concrete runways represented yet another market for its product. It was not totally surprising, therefore, that the Lehigh Portland Cement Company sponsored an airport design contest in late 1928. According to the introduction written by Clarence M. Young, assistant secretary of commerce for aeronautics, airports were needed "to link the airways together and thereby make the system complete and effective." However, it seemed to the sponsors of the contest that "the creation of adequate ground facilities was neglected." They hoped the contest would provide cities with "designs of practical as well as inspirational value to guide the development of airports, present and future."[65]

When the Lehigh Portland Cement Company published the winning entries in 1930, they were presented as inspired concepts for airport design. Given the fading enthusiasm and the financial condition of American cities by the early 1930s, however, the designs were probably not very practical. Most all of the designs included elaborate, multistoried terminal buildings, and many also included buildings for hotels and restaurants, amusement concessions, and swimming pools, and called for elaborate landscaping. Virtually all included plans for multiple paved (cement) runways. And one of the plans was truly visionary, if also completely impractical. H. Atwater of New York submitted a design proposal for a circular airport built high above the city streets. His plan looked something like a wagon wheel. The spokes of the wheel were runways built atop a group of skyscrapers.[66] The architects participating in the Lehigh design contest obviously could still be moved to flights of fancy when it came to airports. In many American cities, voters seemed far less enthusiastic.

Studies have been done on airport bond elections in Omaha, Nebraska, and Muncie, Indiana. In both cases, it was clear that a group of local elites provided the primary backing behind the construction of an airport. In Omaha, bond election results demonstrated a sustained opposition to airport development on the part of the city's working class. In Muncie, local officials, backed by petitions and claiming to speak for the majority of the people, failed to authorize municipal funding for an airport.

Omaha was part of the airmail service almost from the beginning. Once the Post Office began building its transcontinental airmail line, Omaha, already a center for mail carried by rail, became a stop. As noted, the city's initial airmail field was provided by the Chamber of Commerce, which established a landing field and built a hangar on land owned by another civic group, AK-SAR-BEN. The small airport remained the city's airmail field until 1924. In that year the Post Office declared it too small for its new night flying operations and announced plans to move the airmail operations to an Army field south of the city at Fort Crook near Bellevue, Nebraska, as of July 1. A little over a week before the scheduled move, a tornado tore through the AK-SAR-BEN airport, destroying the hangar and seven airplanes. For the next six years the Chamber of Commerce would struggle to build a new municipal airport and to bring the airmail service back to the city proper. The difficulties faced by the Chamber of Commerce demonstrated the lack of support for airport development on the part of the city's working-class neighborhoods.[67]

As soon as airmail operations moved to Fort Crook, the Chamber of Commerce's Aerial Transportation Committee began to work to establish a new municipal airport. They immediately identified a potential site—north of the downtown area, along the Missouri River near Carter Lake. The city had the authority to issue bonds to purchase the land as an airport. However, the chamber representatives convinced the city not to do that. Instead, they urged the city to pass an ordinance purchasing the property as park land. Chamber representatives feared the voters were not airminded and would not approve an airport bond issue. Once the city purchased the land, the Aerial Transportation Committee then began to try and transform it into an airport.[68] The committee, however, had no support and no funding from the city until 1926, when the city council turned responsibility for airport development over to Commissioner of Street Cleaning and Maintenance Dean Noyes. The airport remained without specific funding and without any significant development until 1928 when the city voted to transfer the land, originally purchased as park land, to the Department of Street Cleaning and Maintenance. Noyes, an airport booster, used whatever extra money he could find in his budget to make improvements such as grading and drainage to the field. In the meantime, the Aerial Transportation Committee sought private funding for the construction of a hangar. In 1927 it sponsored a subscription drive to raise thirty thousand dollars, and, thanks to a timely visit to the city by Charles Lindbergh and Clarence Chamberlin, the drive succeeded by September, 1927. The hangar was completed in the spring of 1928. The slow rate of progress finally prompted the Aerial Transportation Committee to consider going to the voters for support, something the committee had avoided, fearing defeat at the polls.[69]

The razor-thin margin of victory in the 1928 bond election proved the fears of the chamber group well founded. Despite a massive publicity campaign in the week before the vote was taken, initial returns showed the bond issue defeated by 212 votes. Only absentee votes, which favored the measure by 875 to 508, assured passage of the bond issue by 155 votes. Analysis of the voting demonstrated that Omahans were largely divided by income levels when it came to support for airport development. The working-class wards of the city voted 57 percent to 43 percent against the measure. Wards in the downtown business area and the more affluent western sections of the city approved the bonds by a 60 percent to 40 percent margin. Working-class opposition to bonds for airport development continued in subsequent elections held in 1930, and the margin of victory, especially in the November, 1930, election authorizing an additional $100,000 for airport development, remained small.[70] Omaha's new airport finally opened in 1930, and airmail operations moved to it from Fort Crook at the same time. It was clear, however, that there was a definite and sustained difference of opinion among Omaha voters as to the urgency or even necessity of airport development.

In Muncie, Indiana, local politicians claiming to speak for the majority of that city's citizens thwarted efforts by the business elite to gain municipal funding for an airport. In 1929, Muncie's Chamber of Commerce began a campaign to get the city to develop a municipal airport to replace the small private field that had served the city since 1925. The city council in 1929 voted to establish a municipal department of aviation. Abbott L. Johnson II, local business leader, pilot, and head of the new department of aviation, purchased 160 acres of land north of the city and donated it on the condition that the city develop it into an airport. The city council voted $27,000 to begin the project. In January, 1930, however, a new mayor and council took office.[71]

The new mayor was George Reynolds Duke, a Democrat and the editor-publisher of the local newspaper. He had gained considerable fame in the 1920s for campaigning against the Ku Klux Klan in the city. He had also been critical of the city's largely Republican business leadership. When Johnson submitted a request to the heavily Democratic city council for $125,000 for airport development in 1930, the council voted to approve an ordinance authorizing a bond issue. The council approved the ordinance by a vote of ten to three despite the fact that a local attorney presented a petition with what he claimed were three thousand signatures opposing the bond issue because of the depressed state of the local economy. Mayor Duke vetoed the ordinance, stating that the city could not afford the burden at a time when it had so many other pressing needs. The city council failed to override the mayor's veto. Crucial to that defeat was the loss of support from two Democratic councilmen, both representing the working-class section of the city. Both claimed that they had changed their votes after great pressure from their constituents.[72]

Abbott Johnson II resigned from the city's aviation department in 1931. The following year, he filed suit to regain title to the 160 acres he had donated to the city. His suit was successful, and he and two members of the Ball family, owners of one of the largest industrial concerns in the city, formed a private corporation to develop the airport. Muncie's new "municipal" airport, owned and developed by private funds, opened in September, 1932.[73]

Conclusion

The course of events in Omaha and Muncie not only suggested some limitations to the reach and depth of the winged gospel but also mirrored events on the national level. Generally, municipal support for airport development declined with the onset of the Great Depression, although a few cities pursued extensive airport projects despite the economic conditions. Airport boosters had predicted great benefits for cities. In practice, cities were finding that airports were far more expensive and far less profitable than enthusiasts had imaged. And although courts generally acted in a way favorable to airports, the legal challenges were significant and costly. By the early 1930s it was clear that further airport construction and improvement would have to await either a dramatic upturn in the economy, something that proved elusive throughout the 1930s, or a new source of funding. With the coming of President Franklin Roosevelt's "New Deal," those still interested in airport development turned to the federal government for help.

Figs. 1 and 2. Chicago's 640-acre Municipal Airport (above) and Dallas's 478-acre Love Field (below) show the disadvantages of building an airport in town. Both cities expanded and surrounded their airports by World War II, making any substantial postwar expansion difficult, if not impossible. Courtesy Air Force History and Museum Program

Fig. 3. Wichita, Kansas, dreamed big when it came to aviation. Its municipal airport during World War II covered 1,855 acres. Courtesy Air Force History and Museum Program

Fig. 4. Cleveland was one of the last major cities to build runways on its airport. According to John Woods, *Airport Design,* Cleveland Municipal Airport (1,280 acres) was an all-direction landing field as late as 1940. Courtesy Air Force History and Museum Program

Fig. 5. Tucson Airport, 1939. Tucson forged an early and close relationship with the military, and the city's 1930s-era municipal airport became what is now Davis-Monthan Air Force Base. Courtesy Air Force History and Museum Program

Fig. 6. Brodhead Intermediate Field, Wisconsin (80 acres), was an example of the fields that aviation safety advocates in the 1920s and 1930s wanted located every ten miles along the nation's airways. Ink marks outline the corners of the field in this photograph. Courtesy Air Force History and Museum Program

Fig. 7. Although Randolph Field, Texas, was a military base, its unique layout led city planner George B. Ford to tout it as an example of the importance of aesthetics in airport design. Courtesy Air Force History and Museum Program

4

We Have to Have a Plan
(and Money to Pay for It)
Cities, the Federal Government, and
Airports, 1933–40

Many asserted in the late 1920s and early 1930s that a national system of airways was nearly worthless without airports to act as terminal points. Airways had to go somewhere. However, just as the Department of Commerce worked to complete the airways system, rising costs and falling enthusiasm stunted airport construction, either municipal or commercial. In fact, commercial investment in new airports virtually halted with the onset of the depression, and economic conditions made future private investment in airports highly unlikely. Something had to be done in order to stimulate cities to build, maintain, and continually upgrade airports to serve the nation's airways. First and foremost, cities needed help shouldering the burden of cost. With that came further steps toward the final definition of municipal airports—locally and publicly owned, but also involving federal funding and regulation.

Help first came in the form of federal work relief programs.[1] When Franklin D. Roosevelt became president in March, 1933, millions of Americans were unemployed. Providing immediate relief to the out-of-work ranked high on the list of priorities for his new administration. To that end Congress passed the Federal Emergency Relief Act (FERA), and Roosevelt created the Civil Works Administration (CWA). Those two agencies provided cities with the means to hire labor to work on many needed projects, including airports. While both programs were temporary in nature, the FERA and the CWA began to establish the patterns for federal aid to municipal airports. First, both the FERA and the CWA would give money for airport projects only if the city owned or leased the airport. Thus, the advent of federal aid resulted in a narrowing of the definition of the term *municipal airport*. Second, during the 1930s federal aid to airports came primarily in the form of work relief dollars. While the Public Works Administration (PWA), which created jobs indirectly by funding public works projects, also engaged in airport improvement projects, its participation was relatively small in comparison to the involvement of the FERA, the CWA and, after 1935, the Work Projects Administration (WPA), which were direct federal works programs. Federal aid thus provided airports with manpower but little in the way of materials or the latest equipment. Critics charged that mandating a link between airport aid and work relief limited the value of the program.

The 1930s also saw the introduction of an important new airplane and a change in the rules of the airmail game. In 1933 the Douglas Aircraft Company developed the DC-1 as competition for the newly introduced Boeing 247. Both airplanes employed some of the most advanced aviation equipment available and were built using advanced construction methods. The DC-1, however, had several advantages over its rival, including the fact that it was bigger and had design features that made it more comfortable for passenger use. The prototype DC-1 led to the production DC-2. It quickly demonstrated its value in terms of speed and comfort. American Airlines then turned to the Douglas company and asked it to develop a larger version of the DC-2 that would allow the airline to offer coast-to-coast sleeper service. The result was the Douglas Sleeper Transport, or DST. The "daytime" version of that plane, with capacity for twenty-one passengers, was the DC-3. The DC-3 proved immediately popular, and by the end of the decade nearly 80 percent of all American airlines, plus more than two dozen foreign airlines, operated the plane. The DC-3 made it possible for airlines to make money from passengers only, thus making the airmail subsidy less important.[2]

While the introduction of the DC-3 made the airmail subsidy less important, the passage of the Civil Aeronautics Act in 1938 changed the rules governing the

nation's airmail system. Congress passed the Civil Aeronautics Act in order to reform the way the federal government regulated aviation. Two sections of the act
directly dealt with airports. First, the act removed the ban on federal aid to airports and mandated the drafting of a national airport plan. Second, the act removed responsibility for the nation's airways and airmail system from the Post Office, the Interstate Commerce Commission, and the Bureau of Air Commerce and
vested it in a newly created Civil Aeronautics Authority (CAA). (After a 1940 reorganization, the Civil Aeronautics Authority became the Civil Aeronautics Administration.) The act further ended the old contract airmail system and replaced it with a system of negotiated, noncompetitive certificates. Any airline
holding a certificate could carry both passengers and airmail. That was important for a number of municipal airports, especially those in larger metropolitan
areas with more than one airport (the New York area and the Philadelphia area,
for example), in that it gave the CAA and the airlines more flexibility in determining at which airport operations would be based. Under the old system, the
needs of the Post Office came first. With the new system, the needs and prefer-
ences of the airlines and their passengers could be taken into consideration.[3]

The advent of federal aid for the construction of airports also reflected a new
city-federal relationship developed during the 1930s. As Mark Gelfand argued in
his work, *A Nation of Cities,* the depression helped establish a new relationship
between cities and the federal government. Before 1933 the relationship had
been largely indirect. Most communication between the federal government
and local governments went through the states. With the onset of the depression,
however, a number of organizations representing the nation's cities began to
forge direct ties to the federal government. According to Gelfand, cities desired
direct federal aid in the areas of unemployment relief, public works, and housing.[4] Airports represented another area in which cities wished to establish a direct relationship with the federal government in the form of airport funding.[5]

The more direct relationship, however, also meant the development of
greater federal regulation of airports. With federal regulation came a further evolution in the definition of municipal airport. Early New Deal relief programs
mandated that airports receiving aid be either owned or leased by local governments before funds could be awarded. The WPA took it even further. It required
that airports be owned by local governments in order to receive aid. Therefore,
in the end, as a result of the New Deal, municipal airports came to mean local,
publicly owned airports.

While great changes came along with the federal dollars in the 1930s, some
things stayed the same. Boosterism and the beliefs of the winged gospel still
played a large role in airport development. Although the early 1930s had

witnessed some of the limits to both, especially the winged gospel, those factors still combined to continue to inspire many. New York and Newark, for example, battled throughout the 1930s over which city would be the site of the eastern terminus of the transcontinental airmail route, thus guaranteeing a share of any benefits brought by aviation. Newark, with help from the WPA, poured millions into its airport. Between 1929 and 1939, New York built not one but two new, state-of-the-art airports in hopes of capturing the airmail prize. Many cities justified raising the local contribution necessary for receiving WPA funding on the premise that up-to-date cities needed up-to-date airports. Up-to-date airports, though, were complex and expensive.

The 1930s also saw the construction of the most unusual "municipal" airport in the country. It was unusual in how it was built and how it was managed. Congress and President Roosevelt oversaw the construction of an airport serving Washington, D.C.—Washington's National Airport. It was touted as a "model airport." It did boast of some of the latest technology, but otherwise Washington National was far different from any other municipal airport in the country. The circumstances surrounding the construction of an airport in the U.S. capital city, particularly the prominent role played by government at the national level, most closely resembled the circumstances surrounding the construction of airports in several of Europe's capital cities. Although many European cities, similar to U.S. cities, took responsibility for building and operating airports, the national governments in England, France, and Germany played key roles in building airports for their capital cities of London, Paris, and Berlin.[6] In addition, like the New York and Newark examples, the Washington airport further demonstrated how expensive it was to build a fully modern airport.

By the end of the decade, cities began to lobby the federal government for changes in the structure of federal aid. Proponents argued that "the pick and shovel work [was] largely done." In other words, the manpower funded by the CWA, the FERA, and the WPA could only do so much. The federal government had to realize that airports also needed help to acquire the latest equipment and facilities.[7] New Deal policies had essentially mandated local, public ownership of the nation's municipal airports. Cities had eagerly grasped at the aid that came with the federal relief policies. In the late 1930s they sought to gain more permanent, direct federal aid for their airports.

Airports, the CWA, and the FERA

Hoping to speed relief to the American people, President Franklin Roosevelt created the Civil Works Administration in late 1933. Funding for the temporary program came from the PWA and the FERA. The CWA, like the more permanent WPA that followed, hired people eligible for relief and put them to work on a variety of projects. Among the projects eligible for CWA funding was a landing field improvement program developed by the Department of Commerce. In late 1933, Eugene L. Vidal, the new director of aeronautics within the Department of Commerce, announced a $10 million program aimed at creating or improving landing fields in up to two thousand cities and towns across the country "which have either no facilities or inadequate facilities for aircraft operation." The program only provided labor and materials for the improvement of landing fields. It did not provide for any other kind of airport improvement. Cities wishing to participate in the program had either to provide the land for the new landing field or to own or lease the land containing the landing field to be improved.[8]

Vidal emphasized that it was a work relief program. Of the $10 million allocated to the program, $8 million was for wages, and only $2 million for materials. The CWA envisioned the landing field improvement program providing work for up to fifty thousand people eligible for relief. Cities and states were asked to loan the "road-building machinery necessary for the grading and leveling." And each individual project was fairly modest in scope. Each project was estimated to cost on average $5,000. Of that, most of the money went to provide labor with only $630 spent on average on materials. The landing fields created or improved under the program were to consist of "two landing strips up to 3,000 feet long and 300 feet wide, except in locations where terrain or other conditions [limited] the area to one strip." Each state was "entitled to have a certain number of landing fields established, the number depending on the size and population of the state, and it [was] expected that these landing fields [would] be distributed in such a manner that they [would] be of the utmost service to air men and their aircraft."[9]

As noted in the introduction, Eugene Vidal was a believer in the winged gospel. Along with the airport improvement program, Vidal sponsored the aircraft design competition aimed at creating a safe, inexpensive aircraft. Thus it was much in the spirit of the winged gospel and its belief in the future of personal air travel that the CWA and the FERA placed great emphasis on improving airports and landing fields at the nation's smallest cities. The organizations also emphasized small airports over larger airports. By late 1934, CWA funding and, following the end of the CWA in the spring of 1934, FERA funding for the landing field and airport improvement program had been expanded, and work was under way at 808 landing fields and airports around the country. In addition, more than 1,400 projects had received approval. Among those additional projects were improvements to landing fields at "662 airport sites which [were] either leased or owned by cities and which [were] especially desirable for aeronautics in general as units in a nation-wide network of airports." Of the 662 airport sites with approved projects, 461 were in cities with populations under 5,000.[10]

Especially under the expanded program, cities struggling to finance improvements to their airports could now receive federal aid. There was something of a string attached to the aid, however, and one which served to begin to narrow the definition of "municipal airport." As noted, some cities, such as Dayton, had designated private, commercial airports as their official "municipal" airport. In order to receive aid, Dayton had to agree to lease the Dayton Airport from its private owners. The city signed a lease in 1934 and received $45,000 from the FERA.[11] Thus, in terms of federal aid, a municipal airport now meant only an airport owned or leased by a city.

Airports and the WPA

The patterns established by the FERA and the CWA remained in place under the more permanent work relief program established in 1935, the WPA. The WPA continued many of the projects begun under the earlier programs and initiated a new, expanded airport and airways improvement program.[12] The WPA also further refined federal policy toward airport aid and, in many ways, gave cities their first taste of what it would be like to run a municipal airport under federal regulation.

The definition of a municipal airport further narrowed under the WPA. The FERA and CWA had allowed aid to flow to cities as long as they leased their airports. The WPA declared that under its program "no airports may be constructed or improved unless the land on which they are built is owned by a public agency."[13] Chicago could continue to lease its airport because the Board of Education, a public agency, owned the land. Many other cities, however, had to scramble to purchase their airports in order to receive federal aid.

Los Angeles, under pressure from the airlines that served Mines Field, initiated a program of airport improvement in 1935. It applied for both FERA and WPA funds. The FERA approved the application; the WPA did not because Los Angeles leased the land from private owners. In 1937 the city finally concluded it had to buy the airport, and the city council took the necessary action in September.[14]

City leaders in Dayton also realized that its airport had to become municipally owned in order to receive additional federal aid. The Dayton Airport was in poor financial shape. The Johnson Flying Service, which had run the airport from 1929 to 1933, lost money. Frank Hill Smith, one of the original participants in the formation of the Dayton Municipal Airport Company, took control of the airport in 1932. The company owed him $45,000 and also owed money to a local bank. Between 1932 and 1936 Hill repeatedly petitioned the city government for aid.[15]

The city could do little. It leased the airport for a nominal sum in 1934 in order to be eligible for FERA moneys, but it apparently could not afford to buy the airport in order to receive WPA funding. Dayton's business leaders decided that they would have to take action. Led by James Cox, editor of the local newspaper, a number of Dayton's most prominent businessmen, including several who had been involved in the original Dayton Municipal Airport venture, along with businessmen from throughout the Miami Valley, raised the money necessary to purchase the airport from Hill. The businessmen then presented the airport to the city as a gift in April, 1936. WPA funding soon followed.[16]

Although airport projects originated at the local level, in order to receive funding all projects had to receive the blessings of both the WPA and the Bureau of Air Commerce (or after 1938, the Civil Aeronautics Authority). The Bureau of Air Commerce's predecessor organization, the Aeronautics Branch, had attempted to set standards for airports beginning in the late 1920s. The rating system it established, however, was purely voluntary. In order to receive a rating an airport had to apply to be rated. Generally, only airports assured of receiving the highest rating applied.[17] The Bureau of Air Commerce also published a series of pamphlets with recommendations on such topics as airport management and construction. With the advent of federal aid, however, the Bureau of Air Commerce, the WPA, and, later, the Civil Aeronautics Authority could begin to require that cities take certain actions in order to receive aid. Thus, they moved away from the associationalism of the late 1920s and early 1930s toward greater federal regulation.

Tampa, Florida, one of many cities in that state receiving WPA funding, found its project suddenly canceled. The city of Tampa had signed a lease for the airport with Pan American Airways, Incorporated. Civic leaders defended the action on the grounds that the lease was the only way to get Pan American to return to Tampa. What good was an improved airport, they argued, unless it had air traffic. The exclusive lease with the airline, however, violated WPA policy. If the airport was used exclusively by Pan American, a private corporation, then the money spent on airport improvement in Tampa would be for the benefit of a private corporation, not the general public. The city, at first, refused to cancel the contract. However, it had no money to complete the improvements, and within a week of the WPA action, Pan American and the city canceled the lease.[18] In the resolution announcing the cancellation, the city pledged that before finalizing any future arrangement "for the general management or operation of [Peter O. Knight Airport] by other than a governmental agency" the city would submit the terms to "the bureau of aeronautics of the United States department of commerce, or other like body at that time having jurisdiction of such matters, for its study, criticism, suggestions, and recommendations."[19] Cities still owned their airports, but now city policies had to reflect federal policies if they wanted to receive federal funds.

With the passage of the Civil Aeronautics Act of 1938 authority over the nation's airports shifted from the Bureau of Air Commerce to a successor organization, the Civil Aeronautics Authority. Just as the WPA and the Bureau of Air Commerce could force cities to bring their airport projects in line with federal demands, so too did the WPA and the new CAA. Philadelphia was one city that found out just how powerful and influential the WPA and the CAA could be. While the dispute over the Tampa airport was solved within days, the dispute over the Philadelphia airport took months to resolve and demonstrated just how complicated airport politics had become with the addition of federal moneys and greater federal regulation.

As early as 1929 a civic group in Philadelphia, the Philadelphia Business Progress Association, had called for the construction of an air-marine-rail terminal at Hog Island in southwest Philadelphia. With the help of the WPA, the city began construction of what became the S. Davis Wilson Airport on that site in late 1937. In December, 1938, however, the WPA, acting at the recommendation of the CAA, withdrew funding for the project. The problem was the Navy's ammunition depot at nearby Fort Mifflin. The number one runway at the new airport, equipped so as to allow for blind landings, was directly in line with the ammunition depot. The CAA feared that planes attempting a blind landing at the field on the number one runway might overshoot and crash into the ammunition depot. The Navy also voiced objections to having planes bound to and from the Philadelphia airport flying low over the ammunition depot. The CAA proposed shifting the runway's orientation by 10 degrees.[20]

The mayor, S. Davis Wilson, responded by asserting that the city would complete the work on the airport without federal aid. As the WPA workers left the field, the mayor ordered two hundred city workers to the site to finish the final paving of the runways. The CAA then announced that if the mayor did manage to finish the airport, including the disputed runway number one, it would simply "bar all civilian aircraft from using the runway." The CAA, the Navy, and the WPA all blamed the controversy on the mayor. They argued that he had been told long before of objections to the orientation of the number one runway. The mayor and the city's congressional delegation countered by demanding that the ammunition depot be moved. The ensuing controversy over whether to move the runway or move the ammunition depot, and who would pay for either operation, consumed nearly all of 1939.[21]

During January and February, 1939, the city, the Navy, the WPA, and the CAA worked on developing a solution to the problem. Suggestions ranged from reinforcing the buildings holding the munitions on Fort Mifflin to realigning the runway, to shifting the explosives to another location on Fort Mifflin, to the complete removal of all explosives from the depot. The parties seemingly reached an agreement in March. Under that proposal the Navy would move the explosives to a location off the line of the runway. The Navy insisted, however, that Department of the Navy funds not be used for the necessary new construction. The city apparently agreed to provide the "non-labor cost of building the new magazines," while the WPA would fund the rest of the project. That agreement fell apart in early April when the city refused to pay its share. The mayor argued that the city could not spend funds legally for a project located outside the city and on federal property. He suggested that the WPA fund the project out of "'surpluses in the airport project.'" The WPA rejected that idea, and the city's Works Progress Administrator, F. C. Harrington, called the airport project "'dead.'" Further, CAA officials announced they would most likely never lift the ban on the use of runway number one as long as the ammunition depot remained in place.[22]

Local editorial opinion was strongly critical of the mayor, and negotiations on the issue began again in May, 1939. Late that month a local newspaper reported that the city had agreed to absorb some of the federal costs on certain projects within the city. In return, the WPA would fund the entire cost of relocating the depot. Apparently, however, working out the details of the agreement proved difficult. In July a local newspaper reported that negotiations were still ongoing. Another local newspaper suggested that the city might have been reluctant to come to an agreement because city officials preferred spending city money on the airport. Using WPA money, they felt, would help the Democratic cause. In the meantime, city workers continued to work on the airport site, and in early August the chief of the city's Bureau of Engineering and Surveys announced that the airport would be complete by the end of the year. The CAA finally removed its objections to the project in late August when the city and the WPA came to terms on the compromise solution first worked out in May. The final agreement meant the creation of WPA jobs both at the Navy depot and at the airport. It was estimated that the airport would finally be ready for commercial use in early 1940. The commercial airlines serving the city had already agreed to use the new airport.[23]

The WPA and the Bureau of Air Commerce, followed by the CAA, all desired to achieve some level of uniformity, or at the least a situation in which most public airports met certain minimum standards. Federal regulation of airports remained somewhat limited, but by wielding the power of approval, for example, the two agencies could strongly persuade cities to make certain kinds of improvements. Another obvious "stick" the CAA could employ was to refuse to certify an airport for passenger traffic unless certain measures were taken. The WPA's division of airways and airports drew up a plan that outlined the basic airport needs of the nation. The hope was that the plan would offer guidance to local officials and inspire projects that would bring more of the nation's airports up to what the WPA, the Bureau of Air Commerce, and, later, the CAA considered adequate standards. But officials in the WPA had to admit that the airport program was a relief program and that creating work opportunities, rather than raising standards at U.S. airports, remained the primary focus.[24]

The Airmail Airport War: New York versus Newark

Despite all the changes that came with the 1930s, many things stayed the same. Many civil leaders continued to view airports as absolutely necessary. And they not only had to have an airport, they had to have a modern, up-to-date airport. Only a modern airport would have any chance of bringing to the city such potential economic benefits as the airmail and the airlines. One of the fiercest urban rivalries concerning airports involved New York City and Newark, New Jersey.

The struggle between New York City and Newark over which city's airport would be the eastern terminus of the transcontinental airmail route started in 1927. The Department of Commerce, under Herbert Hoover, expressed concern that the nation's largest city had no municipal airport. While the New York metropolitan area could boast of a number of private and military airfields, none of those were developed enough or close enough to the city to serve as a municipal airport. Secretary Hoover appointed a commission to study the issue in 1927, and the commission submitted its report late that same year. In its report, the commission recommended sites for both primary (six) and secondary (four) airports in the New York metropolitan region, which included parts of New Jersey. One of the sites recommended for a primary airport was in Newark, New Jersey. In 1928 the city of Newark began construction on an airport, which opened in October, 1928.[25]

Prompted by the actions of the city of Newark, together with the enthusiasm generated by Lindbergh's flight, New York City officials decided to begin con-

struction of a municipal airport at another site identified by Hoover's commission, Barren Island, located in Brooklyn at the end of Flatbush Avenue on Jamaica Bay. New York City officials chose the Barren Island site for a number of
reasons. First, the city had planned for a number of years to turn Jamaica Bay into
a major shipping harbor and the city, the state, and the federal governments had
already spent in excess of $100 million on the project. Sand extracted from the
dredging of Jamaica Bay could be used "to raise the level of [Barren Island] to a
height suitable for the airport." This would also place the airport near a major
commercial and industrial development. Second, the city's aviation advisor,
Clarence D. Chamberlin, who flew the Atlantic shortly after Lindbergh, preferred the site. Most important, though, the city chose the Barren Island site because it already owned it. Most of the other alternative sites would have to have
been purchased. Finally, the few other alternative sites already owned by the city
were estimated to have much higher development costs.[26]

New York's new municipal airport, named for aviation hero Floyd Bennett,
opened in 1931. However, the Newark airport, opened in 1928 and only a forty-
five-minute drive from Times Square, had already grabbed the airmail prize. By
1930, it also housed a number of commercial aviation enterprises including, according to contemporary sources, the Eastern Aeronautical Corporation, the
Newark Air Service, Colonial Air Transport, United States Airlines, and Baltimore Airways, Incorporated. It had a U.S. Weather Bureau station and was
equipped with obstruction and beacon lights. And in that same year it emerged
as the busiest airport in the country. Still, New York City was confident that once
its new airport—built to the highest standards—opened, the airmail service, as
well as other commercial aviation activities, would quickly transfer from the
Newark airport to Floyd Bennett Field. That proved not to be the case.[27]

When Newark built its airport in 1928, officials from the city worked closely
with the Post Office to ensure that the new airport would meet all Post Office Department requirements. The Newark airport, thus, was by far the best airport in
the New York metropolitan region when it opened. The airport also had easy access by road to Manhattan. It would be expensive to relocate the airmail operations from the Newark airport to the new Floyd Bennett Field. New York City officials, who had just assumed that the airport's location in New York City was
enough to convince the Post Office to make the move, found themselves having
to convince the Post Office Department that their new, almost $4 million airport
offered facilities superior to those in Newark. Without the airmail, it was highly
unlikely that any commercial airlines would shift their operations to Floyd Bennett Field.[28]

Fiorello H. LaGuardia, elected mayor of New York City in 1933, took up the task of persuading the Post Office to move airmail operations from the Newark airport to Floyd Bennett Field. LaGuardia, who served as a pilot during World War I, was a great aviation enthusiast. He began his fight even before taking the oath of office as mayor in January, 1934. Shortly after the election in November, 1933, LaGuardia and his wife traveled to Florida for a brief vacation. On the return flight, the LaGuardias' plane landed, as scheduled, at the Newark airport. LaGuardia refused to leave the plane. He declared that his ticket said that his final destination was New York City. He would not get off his flight until his plane landed in New York City. Airline officials eventually agreed to fly the plane from Newark to Floyd Bennett Field, where LaGuardia disembarked, garnering publicity for himself and the New York airport. Still, airmail operations continued at Newark.[29]

In 1934 and 1935, LaGuardia led a sustained battle to convince Post Office officials to transfer airmail operations. Both civic pride and money drove the struggle. New York City officials wanted the eastern terminus of the airmail service to be in their city, not in New Jersey. And if Floyd Bennett Field was ever going to make a profit, it needed to attract the services of the major airlines, who would only move to the field if the airmail service moved there. LaGuardia tried arguing that the Newark airport's facilities were inferior to those at Floyd Bennett Field. In 1935 he finally convinced the Post Office to study the situation. The final report concluded that the Newark airport had far better access to New York City, especially the Central Post Office on Manhattan Island, than did Floyd Bennett Field. In fact, almost buried at the end of one of the articles describing Floyd Bennett Field upon its opening in 1931 was the statement that it was "a little over an hour by subway and surface transportation" from Manhattan and the Post Office. Even before further improvements to the road system, the Newark airport was only forty-five minutes from Manhattan and the Post Office. LaGuardia tried to counter the Post Office's findings by conducting his own experiment. He ordered the police department to time the journeys from Pennsylvania Station (across the street from the Central Post Office) to both the Newark airport and Floyd Bennett Field. Unfortunately for the mayor, the police trials indicated that, by several minutes travel time, the Newark airport was "closer" to the Post Office than the New York City airport.[30]

LaGuardia then tried to convince the Post Office to declare Floyd Bennett Field an alternate airmail terminal, to be used when the Newark airport was closed because of weather conditions. When that failed, LaGuardia pushed the Post Office to hold a public hearing on the matter. New York representatives at the hearing, held on December 12, 1935, presented basically two arguments. First, because New York City was the nation's largest and most important city, it had an "inalienable right . . . to a place on the air map of the United States." Second, the city had an airport available to serve as the airmail terminus. In March, 1936, Postmaster General James Farley announced his decision. Airmail operations, because of easier access to Manhattan and because of the costs involved in the transfer, which would not result in improved or less expensive service, would remain at Newark.[31]

Farley's decision spelled the eventual end of Floyd Bennett Field as a municipal airport. It did not mean the end of New York's fight to gain airmail operations. If Floyd Bennett Field was not acceptable, then the city would just have to build another airport that would be acceptable. And that's exactly what LaGuardia and the city of New York proceeded to do. In the meantime, Newark city officials were not sitting idly by. As New York launched its campaign to capture the airmail service, Newark also launched a campaign to keep it.

Just as New York's mayor pulled out all the stops to bring the airmail terminus to his city, Newark's mayor, Meyer Ellenstein, fought hard to keep it in his. In 1935 the city prepared a booklet, printed and distributed by the Fidelity Union Trust Company, outlining why the Post Office should keep its airmail operations in Newark. According to the booklet, there were four reasons: accessibility, facilities, safety, and economy. The booklet emphasized the fact that the Newark airport had far better transportation connections to Manhattan and the Central Post Office than did Floyd Bennett Field. Not only was the New York City field isolated, but its location also introduced hazards to flying. Many of the approaches to the field were over water, making a safe emergency landing by a land-based plane impossible. Further, the tall buildings of lower Manhattan and Brooklyn also posed a hazard. The booklet argued that removal of the airmail operations to the less accessible Floyd Bennett Field would "impair service to 8,000,000 people." In addition, the Newark airport was better served by railroads, an advantage during those circumstances, such as heavy fog, when the mail had to be rerouted to land-based carriers.[32]

The mayor's booklet pointed out all the modern facilities available at Newark. Those included, according to the mayor, "every facility known to the science of aeronautics and the enterprise of air transportation for the safety, convenience and dispatch of field operations." The airport also had a modern terminal building. Moving the airmail operations to Floyd Bennett Field would mean having to duplicate "all ground equipment such as the radio range and radio broadcasting station, the landing beam and the teletype system, and the relocation of all course equipment."[33]

The Newark airport was also pictured as being safer than Floyd Bennett Field. While Floyd Bennett Field had hazardous approaches, Newark's approaches afforded many opportunities for a plane in trouble to make an emergency landing. The Newark airport was equipped "with the most modern safety devices" including "every modern and effective device that inventive genius has contrived for the direction, by radio, of aircraft pilots to their landing fields and in the mechanics of operation in directing their landing and taking off." The booklet also argued that the Newark airport enjoyed better weather conditions, generally, than did Floyd Bennett Field. It asserted that weather records that seemed to give the advantage to Floyd Bennett Field were "grossly in error" as record keeping at that field was not under federal supervision. Instead, the booklet suggested that Floyd Bennett Field experienced "44% more fog hours" than did the Newark airport.[34]

Finally, the booklet argued that the Newark airport was the more economical choice and that it was, in fact, "generally regarded by aeronautical experts as a model of enterprise in commercial aviation." Moving operations to Floyd Bennett Field would only increase costs for the airmail carriers an estimated $200,000 or more. It would also increase costs to the Post Office by $45,000. In terms of local costs, the booklet pointed out that the city of Newark had, often at the urging of the federal government, invested more that $5.5 million in the airport. Revenues at the airport only met operating costs, they did not "meet maintenance charges nor have they produced any return on capital investment." Newark, thus, viewed its airport as its "contribution to the nation in the cause of commercial aviation."[35]

Newark held off the initial challenge from New York City and Floyd Bennett Field, but the fight was far from over. With the WPA money that came available in 1935, Newark continued to improve its airport while New York City continued to invest in Floyd Bennett Field and prepared to build yet another municipal airport. Up until 1935, the goal had been to capture the job of serving as the Post Office's airmail terminal. By the time New York City's new airport opened in 1939 two things had happened that altered the situation somewhat. First, in 1936 the DC-3 came into service. It was the first airplane capable of carrying enough passengers and of operating efficiently enough to allow the airlines to make money by simply carrying passengers. Its introduction made the airmail subsidy less important to the airlines and added to the push to reform the way the federal government regulated aviation. Congress enacted many of the desired reforms when it passed the Civil Aeronautics Act of 1938. That act created the Civil Aeronautics Authority, and, like the DC-3, it also changed the situation faced by the New York metropolitan area airports. In August, 1938, the CAA took over responsibility for the airways and the airmail from the Post Office, the Interstate Commerce Commission, and the Bureau of Air Commerce. The Civil Aeronautics Act also abolished the old contract airmail system that had given the Post Office the power to determine both which airlines and which airports would handle the airmail. The contract system was replaced by a system of negotiated, noncompetitive certificates.[36] In order to operate in the United States, an airline had to be granted a certificate. That certificate allowed the airline to carry both passengers and the mail. Airlines no longer had to compete for airmail routes in order to carry the mail. Any certified airline could carry the mails. This did not completely eliminate the power of the Post Office, but it did increase the freedom of operation of the airlines. Thus, when New York City's new airport opened in 1939 it did not have to convince the Post Office to move, it primarily only had to lure the commercial operators.[37]

While still carrying on the fight for Floyd Bennett Field, in September, 1935, Mayor LaGuardia announced to the city's Committee on Airport Development's plans to build another airport in New York City. One suggested site was in the Bronx. In addition, the city was asking the WPA for $3 million to improve Floyd Bennett Field. And the mayor also reminded the committee that the city had an option on a third airport site. That was the former Glenn Curtiss Airport, known by the 1930s as the North Beach Airport, located in Queens. The chairman of the committee, Grover A. Whalen, emphasized the desirability of opening an airport in the city of New York. It would, he said, open up the opportunity to use air travel to the people in Brooklyn, Queens, and Long Island who "had little incentive to use air transportation while they had to make the long trip to Newark Airport to board an airplane."[38] Meanwhile, Newark had already asked the WPA for $4 million in order to make improvements to its airport.[39]

Within a year, both cities announced further plans guaranteed to keep the competition between the two cities alive. In August, 1935, New York City officials announced that the city had requested $2.5 million from the WPA for improvements to North Beach Airport. At that point, North Beach Airport—which the city planned to expand into "the second largest airplane terminal in the metropolitan area"—was viewed as an auxiliary to Floyd Bennett Field. The WPA money would be used "to cover the cost of filling in 38 additional acres of tidal flats, the laying out of 3,500 foot runways and the installation of a radio direction beam to meet the specifications of the Bureau of Air Commerce of the Department of Commerce for passenger transport flying." The city anticipated that the airport would be used heavily during the upcoming 1939 World's Fair. In addition, Pan American Airlines was looking for a site at which to locate a base for its transatlantic and Bermuda flying services. Floyd Bennett Field was not a good site for such a base, but the North Beach Airport, according to a *New York Times* editorial, might fit the bill. In the meantime the city of Newark hoped to lure Pan

American Airlines to its airport by building a new seaplane base there. By August, 1936, Newark had spent $30,000 (of which $20,000 came from the WPA) on the project, and the city planned to ask the WPA for an additional $100,000.[40]

Work began in earnest on the North Beach Airport in the fall of 1937. Until 1938 the city of Newark could continue to hope that the Post Office would simply refuse to move its operations to any new airport in New York. But as the midway point in the construction of the new, completely modern North Beach Airport approached, as noted, the rules changed. The Newark airport would have to compete with the new North Beach Airport without the power of the Post Office behind it. As early as September, 1938, Newark launched a campaign to keep the airlines at its airport. Mayor Ellenstein began by criticizing the safety of the new airport. Lieutenant Colonel Brehon B. Somervell, the WPA administrator for New York City, labeled the mayor's critique as "hysterical." He went on to declare: "It is a physical certainty that North Beach will be the finest airport in the United States and, so far as I know, in the world. . . . It will far surpass any metropolitan airport in this country." At that point Somervall estimated that over $21 million had been spent on the airport, $13.4 million coming from federal sources and nearly $7.8 million coming from the city.[41] On top of everything, North Beach Airport had better access to midtown Manhattan than either Floyd Bennett Field or the Newark airport.

Newark's worst fears were realized as North Beach Airport neared its dedication date in late 1939. In September, 1939, the CAA held hearings at which four major airlines asked to move their principal operations from the Newark airport to North Beach Airport. Three of the four major airlines operating out of the Newark airport already had signed leases with New York City in November, 1938, for space at the new airport once it opened.[42] Airline passengers, not the mail, meant the difference between long-term success and failure for the airlines by the late 1930s. Evidently three of the four airlines saw advantage in operating within, rather than simply near, the largest city in the United States. Those airlines, American Airlines, Transcontinental and Western Air (TWA), and United Air Lines, complained that the Newark airport was too congested and held that North Beach Airport was far more convenient to potential passengers. The airlines tried to reassure New Jersey officials that although centralizing their operations at the new airport, they would continue to offer service to Newark. Only Eddie Rickenbacker of Eastern Airlines had reservations about the plans, citing additional costs. However, if the other three airlines were moving, he concluded, Eastern would move as well.[43]

Of course Newark and New Jersey officials objected strongly. They tried unsuccessfully to question the safety of the new airport. They argued that the

"Newark airport had every advantage over the New York field." Evidently, though, most realized they were fighting a losing battle. One of New Jersey's senators lamented in a prepared statement: "It looks very much as if we were merely being allowed to go through the motions of protesting against a decision reached in advance of the hearing. . . . If this is so, we were only given a seat at our own funeral. I suppose we ought to be thankful for that." Given the fact that the airlines had signed leases with the city of New York almost a year earlier, there may have been some basis for the hopelessness felt by the New Jersey officials. The reference to a funeral also must have seemed very appropriate as the defenders of the Newark airport predicted that if the airlines were allowed to move their operations to North Beach, that decision would effectively kill the Newark airport.[44]

The CAA ruled in favor of the airlines' request on September 20, 1939. Newark officials continued to protest into early 1940, but to no avail. New York City dedicated its new airport on October 15, 1939. Soon after its opening, city officials voted to rename North Beach Airport after Mayor LaGuardia. More that $40 million had been spent creating the most modern, technologically advanced airport in the country.[45] It had the services of American Airlines, TWA, United Air Lines, and Eastern Airlines, as well as hosting the base for Pan American's transatlantic and Bermuda air services. The Newark airport, following the loss of the four airlines, closed in May, 1940. It reopened temporarily in June, 1941, after four airlines (American, TWA, United, and Eastern) agreed to resume service to the airport and prospects brightened. However, one year later, after the United States became involved in World War II, the U.S. Army took over the airport, and the airlines once again departed.[46]

New York City was not without its losses in the battle. Floyd Bennett Field never proved a commercial success. Just as in the case of Newark, however, the military played something of a rescue role. The Navy had shown an interest in Floyd Bennett Field throughout the 1930s. In 1931 it moved a naval reserve aviation unit there. In 1937 and again in 1939 the Navy expanded its operations. The following year the Navy began to negotiate with the city of New York for the purchase of Floyd Bennett Field in order to use the entire field as a naval air station. The city proved reluctant at first to lose complete control of the field. Therefore, the Navy agreed to a long-term lease on the property in May, 1941, and on June 2, 1941 the Navy commissioned New York Naval Air Station, Floyd Bennett Field. The Navy continued to push the city to sell the airport. In December, 1941, once the government agreed to pay the city $9.7 million for both the field property and some adjacent city-owned property, New York City agreed to sell. The deal was complete on February 18, 1942.[47]

The airmail battle between New York City and Newark demonstrated a number of things. First, both city boosterism and an enthusiasm for aviation were alive and well and very much a part of airport politics. City officials in New York could not accept the idea of an airport in Newark, New Jersey, being the primary facility serving the city and the region. Major cites had airports. The nation's largest city had to have an airport within its own boundaries worthy of the city's status. Second, as in the Tampa, Florida, and Philadelphia, Pennsylvania, examples, the enlarged federal role in airport funding and regulation made airport politics no longer primarily local in nature and far more complicated. And finally, the amount of money involved in the various airport projects in New York City and Newark demonstrated clearly just how expensive it was to build and maintain a modern airport. Only a little over a decade after early airport promoters such as Archibald Black asserted the minimal costs involved in establishing an airport, such facilities had evolved into complex, multi-million-dollar endeavors.

An Uncommon Model: Washington's National Airport

In many ways the nation's most unusual city, Washington, D.C., also went through a unique process in the construction of its "municipal" airport. In the 1920s and 1930s Washington was still a congressional city without the power of home rule. While most municipal airports in the United States and Europe came about as the result of actions taken by local politicians and local business leaders, provision of an airport adequate to serve the needs of the nation's capital required presidential and congressional action. This put Washington into roughly the same category as nationally supported airports in the European capital cities of London, Paris, and Berlin. Like New York's LaGuardia Airport, Washington's new airport was technologically up-to-date and presented as a model of the modern airport. The uniqueness of the situation did not prevent some familiar elements, particularly boosterism combined with aviation enthusiasm, from playing a part though. Washington's airport was unique in the nation, however, as the only federally owned and federally operated "municipal" airport when it opened.

The Washington area's first airport opened in 1926. Hoover Field, a small commercial airport, operated on a location near the present-day site of the Pentagon, along the banks of the Potomac River, across from the District of Columbia. The next year a second commercial airport, Washington Airport, opened literally across the street (Military Road) and for the next three years both airports operated from the Potomac River bottoms. Hoover Airport was managed by John S. Wynne, who served during the 1930s as the chief of the Airport Section of the Bureau of Air Commerce of the Department of Commerce. Washington Airport was operated by U.S. Air Transport, which ran a Washington-New York passenger line. Both airports attracted weekend and tourist crowds and both operated joy-hopping services. A 1929 *U.S. Air Services* article indicated that at both fields 95 percent of the passengers carried were tourists. Despite the brisk tourist business, as well as offering flight instruction, both fields felt the pinch of the Great Depression. In 1930 the two fields merged to form Washington-Hoover Airport.[48]

The newly merged field covered 143 acres. A 1930 *Airway Age* article painted a rosy picture of the airport, touting its fine facilities and the service offered passengers and pilots. In reality, about the only thing Washington-Hoover had going for it was the fact that it was located only two miles from the center of Washington—traditionally the U.S. Treasury Building. It was also the only game in town, and, as such, all airlines coming into and out of the city had to operate out of Washington-Hoover. More accurate than the 1930 *Airway Age* article were later assessments that declared that the airport "provided the national capital with probably the poorest aviation ground facilities of any important city in the United States or Europe." Not only was the field small and located in an area prone to fog, the Military Road that had separated the Washington Airport and the Hoover Airport still bisected the merged airport. The federal government refused to shut down or move Military Road. Washington-Hoover's longest runway ran right across the road. Special traffic lights had to be set up to halt automobile traffic in order to allow planes using that runway to land or take off.[49] Not surprisingly, the late 1920s saw the beginning of what became a long campaign to provide the nation's capital with better airport facilities.

In late 1926 the local chapter of the National Aeronautic Association (NAA) "launched a movement for the establishment at Washington of an airport, which should serve as a model for the national to follow."[50] To get the airport they wanted, the local members of the NAA had to get congressional approval. The lobbying effort begun in late 1926 would take more than a decade to bring a result.

By 1929 the effort to build a municipal airport for Washington had progressed to the point that Congress was considering a bill to authorize construction. The site chosen for the new airport was Gravelly Point on the Virginia side of the Potomac River, about a mile south of Washington and Hoover airports. That location had been favored by local airport supporters from the beginning. After a land reclamation effort, the Gravelly Point site would be large enough to house a Class A1A airport. The Stalker Bill proposed spending $1.5 million on the new airport. The District of Columbia Committee of the House of Representative reported favorably on the bill.[51]

The bill's supporters presented a number of arguments as to why the Gravelly Point airport was needed. First, the airport could be used by "various branches of the Federal Government having to do with civil aviation." It would also facilitate travel by officials of the federal government. Second, the backers produced an endorsement from Charles Lindbergh. He stated that European cities had airport facilities far superior to those provided by American cities and that "our lack of suitable airports . . . handicapped air transport companies in this country." The United States, the world's leader in terms of commercial aviation, certainly needed airports as good or better than those of European cities. And, third, Washington, D.C., needed a fully modern airport because, as the nation's capital, it would certainly attract air traffic from not just around the country but around the world. All the arguments came to naught. The measure ran up against the fact that the Air Commerce Act of 1926 forbade the federal government from developing airports.[52]

The issue of a new municipal airport for Washington, D.C., again came to a head in late 1935. At that time some members of Congress were working on a plan under which the federal government would take over Washington-Hoover Airport and then use PWA and WPA funds both to improve Washington-Hoover and to build a new Washington airport at Gravelly Point. The situation became especially critical in February, 1936, when the Post Office and the Department of Commerce threatened to close down Washington-Hoover Airport and move all airline and airmail operations to Baltimore. The Post Office and the Department of Commerce claimed that Military Road posed too great a hazard to airport operations. The road had to close and the airport had to be improved or else.[53] In the end the road wasn't closed and one local newspaper even suggested that the whole road issue was just a ploy to force the federal government to buy the airport. Washington-Hoover remained in private hands and no work was begun on an airport at Gravelly Point.

The breakthrough finally came in 1938. While Congress continued to battle over the appropriate solution to Washington, D.C.'s airport problem—the alternatives by that time were to build an airport at Gravelly Point or purchase land for a new airport at Camp Springs, Maryland[54]—President Roosevelt decided to take action. The Civil Aeronautics Act of 1938 had removed the ban on federal involvement in airport construction. When Congress went into recess in late 1938, Roosevelt turned to the Civil Aeronautics Authority and asked that agency to decide where the new airport should be built. It chose the Gravelly Point site. Despite the fact that Roosevelt personally favored the Camp Springs location, he approved CAA plans for construction of an airport on 750 acres at Gravelly Point.

The airport construction would be a joint project of the PWA, the WPA, and the Army Corps of Engineers.[55]

Of the 750 acres to be used for the new Gravelly Point airport, much was still under water in 1938. Therefore, construction of the airport began with a massive filling operation under the direction of the Army Corps of Engineers, involving the movement of almost 20 million cubic yards of sand and gravel. The process of dredging, filling, and draining the site was not complete until the spring of 1940. Once the site was prepared, construction began on the airport's four runways. The north-south runway was 6,875 feet long and 200 feet wide; the northwest-southeast, 5,300 feet long and 200 feet wide; the northeast-southwest, 4,820 feet long and 150 feet wide; and the east-west, 4,200 feet long and 150 feet wide. The new airport also included a 115,000-square-foot terminal building described as displaying "a pleasing blend of the modern with the colonial atmosphere which surrounds the country." Washington's National Airport opened on June 6, 1941.[56]

Construction of the new airport proceeded despite a number of controversies that arose almost immediately upon Roosevelt's approval of the project. First, Congress raised doubts as to whether the president had properly moved moneys from a restricted PWA fund into an unrestricted fund that would permit the expenditure of the moneys in the District of Columbia. Critics claimed that the president lacked the authority to authorize the spending of PWA and WPA funds in the District of Columbia on the airport project. Even *Aero Digest* opined that the methods which Roosevelt used to secure funding for the airport represented a "flagrant usurpation of congressional powers" even more disturbing that the recent "destroyers for bases" deal with Great Britain. Roosevelt had gambled that the project, once under way, would continue "under its own momentum" and he was proved correct.[57]

The second serious controversy involved a boundary dispute between the District of Columbia and the state of Virginia. As early as 1938 the CAA declared that the boundary question was "giving them a headache and that construction was rapidly reaching a point where no money could be spent without legal clarification." The dispute was not settled, however, until 1945. The problem stemmed from 1846 legislation that set the boundary of the District and the state of Virginia at "the mean high-water mark along the Virginia shore of the Potomac." The filling operation that altered the shoreline of the Potomac thus created a legal problem. Twice between 1941 and 1945 the boundary dispute raised jurisdictional issues. First, following a robbery at the airport, both the District of Columbia police and police in Virginia denied that they had jurisdiction.

Second, following the death of an airport guard on the airport property, neither the District coroner nor any coroner from Virginia would agree to sign the death certificate. Congress finally declared in October, 1945, that the airport was located in Virginia as the 1846 law set the boundary at the high-water mark regardless of any changes made to the shoreline. However, Congress also "asserted concurrent United States jurisdiction, which Virginia accepted." In practice, the airport, federally owned and federally operated, remained under federal jurisdiction well into the postwar period.[58]

Cities Push for a National Airport Plan

Even though federal aid meant meeting some federal guidelines, cities generally strove to take advantage of FERA, CWA, and WPA funding. By 1937, however, despite those programs, municipal airports were still lagging behind in terms of technology and they remained a burden on municipal budgets. All work relief project grants had to be matched by contributions at the local level, and airports seldom operated at a profit. By 1937 cities had begun to complain that they could no longer afford to finance their end of airport improvement projects. National organizations representing cities, such as the American Municipal Association and the United States Conference of Mayors, started to push for new and broader aid to municipal airports.

Organizations representing cities first took up the issue of municipal airports in early 1937. At a January meeting of the American Municipal Association (AMA) the group produced a report that called for a rethinking of federal aid to airports. The report pointed out that cities had invested large sums of money in airports. The benefits from those investments had gone not just to cities but to state and federal governments as well. The time had come, therefore, for "definite and complete Federal action . . . for a national system of civil airways and airports, in order that cities may know where they stand for the future."[59]

The report included a resolution passed by the executive committee of that organization that "[recommended] a complete projected national system of civil airways, including the establishment of financial responsibilities of the various agencies benefiting by such airports." It went on to assert that "rapid growth of air transportation [was] fast leaving most municipal terminal facilities in an obsolete condition," leaving most cities faced with the task of building new facilities. Because cities were not the only beneficiaries of the new facilities, the federal government should look at airports in the light of "their Federal value—as stops on the national airways or for national defense." And in that light, the federal government "should consider Federal responsibility for any projected federal airways program on a basis similar to the Federal responsibility in the national high-way system and rivers and harbors."[60]

When the AMA's executive committee met again in July, 1937, it reiterated the need "for a national program sharply defining the authority and responsibil-ity of city, state and Federal governments in the future airways program." It also stated again that airports functioned at several different levels: as part of the local transportation infrastructure; as part of interstate commerce; and as part of a sys-tem of national defense. In view of that, the committee again emphasized that each level of government benefiting from airports must pay its fair share in the maintenance and improvement of airports.[61] In late 1937 the AMA sponsored a conference involving municipal representatives and the Bureau of Air Com-merce. As a result of that meeting the bureau appointed a committee "to propose plans for future development of the aviation industry, and to allocate responsi-bility for [those] municipal projects which also benefit state and Federal govern-ments."[62]

The United States Conference of Mayors also took up the issue of munici-pal airports at its 1937 meeting. Four speakers addressed the issue at a session on "The Municipal Airport Problem." Colonel J. Monroe Johnson, assistant secre-tary of commerce, admitted that despite federal aid to airports from the FERA, CWA, and WPA, most of the financial burden for the construction, mainte-nance, and improvement of airports had fallen to cities. That burden was heavy and made heavier by the fact that few municipal airports returned any profits to their sponsoring cities. Johnson echoed the sentiments of the AMA when he stated that many felt that the burden of airport development must be not just borne by cities but shared between local, state, and federal governments. That was especially critical in light of the fact that many cities simply had no more money to devote to airport improvement; they could no longer contribute the lo-cal share required by the WPA.[63] Johnson concluded that all those factors ne-cessitated the creation of "some well-reasoned, comprehensive and coherent air-port plan, a plan that [would] be satisfactory to all the parties involved—the airline operators, the aircraft manufacturers, the municipalities, the Post Office Department, and the Department of Commerce."[64]

Harllee Branch, second assistant postmaster general, also pointed out that cities had reached their limits in terms of their ability to finance airport con-struction and improvement. He further described the frustration felt by many cities when, after paying for early improvements, they found themselves still lag-ging behind because of the extremely rapid development of aircraft and airport technologies. Branch offered few answers to those problems, however.[65]

The next two speakers, both mayors, had very strong suggestions as to what might be done. Frank Couzens, the mayor of Detroit, stated plainly "that the federal government should also share in the cost of providing a general national system of airports."[66] He believed that direct airport aid was no different than the federal aid afforded to highway construction and river and harbor improvements. The airport problem, he declared, was a national problem. The Congress should repeal that section of the Air Commerce Act of 1926 that forbade the spending of federal moneys specifically on airports and the federal government should begin to share in the cost of the improvement and maintenance of municipal airports.[67] R. E. Allen, the mayor of Augusta, Georgia, essentially echoed and reinforced the sentiments expressed by Couzens.[68]

At that 1937 meeting the United States Conference of Mayors adopted a resolution in favor of federal aid to airports. The resolution reiterated many of the points made by the speakers. It stated that cities had borne most of the financial burden involved in the development of the nation's airports, but that it was a burden cities could no longer bear. Since the federal government had aided in the development of other transportation systems (railroads, waterways, highways), aid to airports would not represent a radical departure from past practices. Therefore, the mayors resolved that Congress should pass legislation "to provide for and authorize a permanent program of Federal financial cooperation in the construction, improvement, development and expansion of publicly owned airports."[69]

In 1938 Congress passed a law, the Civil Aeronautics Act, which, as noted, greatly reformed the ways in which the federal government regulated civilian aviation.[70] Most of the act had little directly to do with municipal airports. Two sections, however, did address some of the concerns raised by cities. First, the act repealed the ban on federal aid to airports. Further, it also required the newly created CAA to conduct a survey of the nation's public airports and make recommendations to Congress "as to whether the federal government shall participate in the construction, improvement, development, operation, or maintenance of a national airport system, and if so, to what extent, and in what manner."[71] In preparing the report, the CAA consulted, among other groups, the United States Conference of Mayors and the American Municipal Association.[72]

The National Airport Plan of 1939

The CAA airport survey, completed in March, 1939, concluded that the United States did need to develop a planned system of airports and that "such a system should be regarded, under certain circumstances, as a proper object of Federal expenditure."[73] With that in mind, the CAA presented to Congress a complex proposal with three phases. If implemented, phase one required spending $128 million; phase two would increase total spending to $230 million; and phase three would result in spending a total of $435 million.[74]

City representatives and others voiced disapproval of the CAA program. It was not that the money was inadequate but that it was not exclusively for airports. Under the CAA proposal most of the money would go to the WPA for it to use to finance work relief airport projects.[75] As already noted, many believed that airports had already absorbed all the labor-intensive work that was possible and that the aid ought to be directed not at work relief but at airport upgrades and improvements. At a National Airport Conference held in June, 1939, supporters of federal aid to airports criticized the link to work relief and again called for more direct federal aid to airports.[76]

Timing, however, was against the proponents of a large program for the improvement of civilian airports. By 1939 the United States had begun a program of war preparedness. While airport supporters usually linked airports to the issue of national defense, Congress proved reluctant to act on a program aimed at civilian aviation and work relief. In late 1940, though, Congress did appropriate $40 million for airport work, separate from available work relief funds. The money would go to up to 250 airports as determined by a board composed of representatives from the departments of War, Navy, and Commerce and would fund improvements "'necessary to the national defense.'"[77] The appropriation was seen as a small but important first step in the creation of a national system of airports to serve both national defense and civilian aviation needs. Though far from what supporters had hoped for, the action in 1940 set an important principle. Congress had appropriated funds for airports within something of a national airport system.[78]

Conclusion

Though cities failed to get all they desired in the late 1930s, the precedents set by the end of 1940 established an important example for postwar federal action toward municipal airports. After a little more two decades of experimentation and innovation at both the local and the federal level, the now familiar, sometimes welcome and sometimes uncomfortable, relationships between cities and their airports and between municipal airports and the federal government had been established. The major airports in the United States would be owned and operated by cities (or by urban counties), and while the financing of municipal airports would continue to be largely a municipal responsibility, the federal government would provide aid and set standards for operations.

However, for the immediate future the improvement of airports in the name of civilian aviation would be put on hold and demonstrate the continuing reluctance of Congress to provide funding for civilian airport construction. National defense would provide the rationale for airport aid, and many cities received significant federal aid only when the United States began to prepare for and then engage in war. Before examining wartime airport policy, however, the relationship between cities, airports, and city planning will be explored in more depth. City planners demonstrated occasional interest in airports. Their interest generally coincided with two periods of airport enthusiasm—the late 1920s through the early 1930s and the late 1930s—as cities lobbied for a national airport plan. City planners generally viewed airports as very local, and while their ability to influence local airport planning was limited, they did provide an important tool in the form of airport zoning.

5

City Planning and Municipal Airports, 1927–40

Beginning in the mid-1920s and continuing through the 1930s, city planners periodically expressed an interest in airports as a developing bit of urban infrastructure. Attention to the issue seemed to come in bursts, periods
of concentrated interest that coincided, first, with the so-called Lindbergh
boom and, second, with the prospect of direct federal funding of airports in the
late 1930s. As the first solo nonstop flight across the Atlantic inspired civic action in airport construction, planners sought to gain influence in the matter.[1]
When the Lindbergh boom faded with the onset of the Great Depression, so too,
it seemed, did the interest of planners as articles about airports virtually disappeared from planning literature. Interest in airport planning reappeared in the
late 1930s as cities began to lobby strongly for more and more direct federal airport aid.

Between 1927 and 1930, especially, a number of prominent planners offered
their ideas on how to best plan for a municipal airport. Examination of their writings reveal much of how planners viewed airports at the dawn of modern commercial aviation. First, their ideas on airports reflected the contemporary debate

about the proper structure of the city. The early airport planners in many ways saw aviation and airports as instruments of urban decentralization. The group of planners involved in the Harvard airport study, in particular, viewed airports as parts of a local metropolitan system of transportation with a primary airport located in or near the central business district served by a variety of special purpose suburban airports. (Most planners, however, and to a certain extent the Harvard planners, came to realize that a CBD location for an airport may have been convenient, but it did not necessarily serve aviation safety.) The Harvard planners' ideas about airports reflected the views and theories of those involved with the development of the Regional Plan of New York and Its Environs. These urban planners held to a metropolitan vision of the city and believed that planning should act both to preserve and to strengthen the core city while allowing enough movement to promote the continued efficient operation of the city.[2] Planning groups in both New York and Philadelphia developed airport schemes that envisioned metropolitan systems of airports with a central terminal airport and a number of suburban airports. As will be shown, though, neither city built systems of airports, and, further, they constructed their primary municipal airports outside the influence of any regional planning.

The early writings also reveal that while the planners had certain fundamental ideas concerning airport location and the importance of good transportation links to airports, they did not necessarily have a clear grasp of the technology of aviation. For example, the most dangerous phases of flight are takeoff and landing. The Harvard study airport plan and its elaborate system of airports seemed to be designed to demand a maximization of the number of takeoffs and landings necessary for the people and airplanes using it. And planners, similar to many others at the time, bought into the most enduring great myth of aviation — the idea that the airplane would become as popular a form of personal transportation as the automobile. Planners also seemed not to have a firm grasp of the politics of technology either, as they made little or no mention of the role of the Post Office in shaping the route structure of the emerging American commercial airline system.

After 1937, planning thought generally evidenced a desire to focus on the coordination of local and regional plans with national airport planning. Despite the greater emphasis on national planning—which had also been touched on during the earlier period of airport planning enthusiasm—basically planners still viewed airports as essentially local in nature. Airports were primarily parts of a local, metropolitan transportation infrastructure and were ultimately a local responsibility.

Planners and their airport planning schemes had little influence during this formative period, aside from setting down within the planning literature and dialogue a certain number of very fundamental principles.[3] The planning profession, however, did make one very important contribution to the issue of airport planning at the local level and that was the idea of airport zoning. As Doug Karsner pointed out in his 1993 dissertation, zoning became an important tool local government could use to help protect their major airports from encroachments that might act as hazards to aerial navigation and to help shape land-use patterns around airports. Though used little in the 1930s through the mid-1940s, zoning was very important during the postwar years.[4] The justification for airport zoning and the earliest enabling acts date from this formative period.

Airports and City Planning: The Initial Enthusiasm, 1927–30

Just as Lindbergh's flight inspired cities across the country to plunge into the business of building airports, the sudden activity in that area inspired a number of the nation's most prominent city planners to present their ideas on the subject. George B. Ford, E. P. Goodrich, and John Nolan all published articles offering cities advice on how to plan for their new airports. The most extensive set of ideas and suggestions came with the publication of the Harvard airport study, conducted by a team led by Henry H. Hubbard and published in 1930. It aimed at a detailed and comprehensive look at all the issues involved in airport planning and administration. Some, if not most, of the advice offered by all planners seemed simply to reflect the existing, though limited, experience of local airport construction and planning. But their writings in some ways formalized many of the basic, fundamental, and commonsense ideas of airport planning.

George B. Ford served the War Department as a city planning advisor during the 1920s. As part of that work, Ford consulted with the Air Service, and its successor organization, the Air Corps, on the layout of military airfields. Ford drew on that experience to present himself as an early expert on the location, size, and layout of municipal airports. In a 1927 article in the *American City*, Ford offered cities advice on how best to plan for their municipal airports. Ford told his readers that "experience everywhere [showed] that an airfield of any importance must be on a large open tract of ground—the more nearly level, consistent with proper drainage, the better; unobstructed by buildings, wires, trees, rocks, marshes or water courses." Further, as much as possible, the potential airport site should be at a location where "there neither [were], nor [were] likely to be, high structures or even high trees or wires that would hamper low access in landing or create freak or gusty air currents." When one also took into consideration the problem posed by the noise created by aircraft, Ford concluded that the ideal location for an airport would be adjacent to "farm land, country clubs, playfields, cemeteries or bodies of water." The latter would be especially "desirable as they permit the access of amphibian planes."[5]

As to size and layout, Ford's recommendations basically followed those made by the Aeronautics Branch in its many airport bulletins.[6] Ford stated that airports must be of sufficient size to allow for a takeoff and landing area of at least 1,800 to 2,000 feet in each direction. Airports located at higher altitudes should plan for an area of at least 3,000 feet. With that in mind, Ford concluded that a "good minimum size for an all-round airport" would be 160 acres. However, certain layouts—such as an L-shaped or T-shaped field—could reduce the number of acres needed. Ford recommended, though, that when cities could afford to do so they should consider buying "anywhere up to a square mile" as such a site would allow for 3,000-to-5,000-foot runways in each direction.[7]

Ford joined the chorus of voices urging cities to take immediate action to establish a municipal airport. He noted that some cities might be disappointed to find that their new airports did not see much immediate use. He insisted, though, that cities must look beyond that to the future. Ford asserted that "around most cities there [were] only a very limited number of sites that [were] really desirable as airfields or that [could] be made practicable except at prohibitive expense." Good city planning dictated that cities "should determine early the most desirable sites and do everything possible to reserve them for eventual airfield use by making sure that no costly construction [was] placed upon them or near them that would eventually have to be removed when the field [was] wholly needed for aviation." Cities could economize somewhat by only constructing buildings on the airport as needed. Further, buildings should be added only after establishing a general layout for the completed airport.[8]

The following year two other prominent city planners, E. P. Goodrich and John Nolan, weighed in with their own advice for cities planning airport projects. Their recommendations were not that much different from Ford's and, again, they helped establish such ideas as where airports should be located and the importance of good transportation links.

The first point E. P. Goodrich made in his 1928 work, published as a supplement to the *National Municipal Review*, was to warn cities not to build their airports too far away in terms of travel time from the "business center of the community to be served." Such a mistake, according to Goodrich, had already been made in the New York metropolitan area and in Cleveland. Goodrich pointed out that the New York area airports had been built "so far away from the hotels of Manhattan that lately it took as long to motor from one of them to New York as it had taken to fly from Boston." (Goodrich's article appeared in March, 1928.

The Newark airport, convenient to midtown Manhattan, did not open until October, 1928.) Cleveland had also erred in building its airport thirty minutes' travel time from its downtown. As was recognized in Europe, Goodrich argued, American airports must be built as close to the city centers as possible.[9] To ensure that an airport, wherever located, was within reasonable travel time from the city, Goodrich emphasized that cities must plan to provide "ample means of access." He pointed out that when Lindbergh landed at LeBourget all roads from Paris to the airport were filled with traffic. Obviously, he concluded, Paris had not provided ample access to its airport. Goodrich defined ample access rather expansively as roads that extended "from the field in as many directions as possible and sufficient in capacity to carry away all the automobiles of all the inhabitants of the surrounding territory for a radius of at least fifty miles within a period of perhaps three hours." Goodrich stated that airports drew great automobile traffic at present owing to the fact that airplanes were still such a novelty. Once the novelty wore off, regular traffic to the airport would be much less. Therefore, given that "it [was] hardly to be expected that regular traffic [would] ever reach such figures as are now being attained," planning access roads based on "the present may, therefore, be expected to be ample for the future."[10]

John Nolan published a long article on "Civic Planning for Airports and Airways" in the *S.A.E. Journal* in April, 1928. He examined the locational issue from a little broader perspective than either Ford or Goodrich. First, he asked whether airports would determine the location of the nation's airways or would the airways dictate where airports would be built. Nolan answered by comparing air navigation to water navigation. He determined that the location of airports would shape the airways "just as water navigation [was] determined by the location of harbors." Nolan in particular seemed not to appreciate the role being played by the Post Office and its airmail contract system in establishing the route structure of the nation's infant airlines. Nolan, similar to the urban boosters promoting airports, seemed to evidence an "if you build it, they will come" attitude about airports. He concluded that "every place of importance" would eventually have an airport and would be connected to the airway system by being either on the main airway or on feeder or branch airways.[11]

Second, Nolan believed that airports would have to be located on the outskirts of cities except where cities might be able to create a large open field by filling in low-lying areas along a river or harbor. Nolan pointed out that the city of San Diego was building its airport on an in-city location on land recovered from the harbor.[12] Many planners came to realize that airports were probably best located in outlying areas (as such locations were more likely to allow for future expansion and were generally free of dangerous obstructions). Nonetheless,

Nolan, to some extent, and others, including the Harvard planners, held to the notion of a CBD or near-CBD location for airports. This was very much reflective of their view of airports as part of a metropolitan transportation system.

Nolan's article, though, also included a rather more elaborate diagram of a "Hypothetical AAA Airport with Seaplane Basin" of his own design and evidently conceived as being located in an outlying district. That plan included the location of a superhighway and railroad connection to the airport, areas for parking cars, for a farm belt, for airplane industry, for wholesale and retail businesses, for debarkation and embarkation buildings (with restaurant, waiting rooms, and sleeping quarters), for a satellite town (with apartments), and for future expansion. Nolan's airport built to the "highest standard" was also well equipped with hangars, repair shops, a weather tower, and fire-fighting and first aid equipment. The diagram did not indicate how many acres that particular airport would cover or how much it would cost.[13] Here Nolan reflected another hope of local airport proponents—that airports would become centers of economic development. That promise drove much of the airport enthusiasm of the time, though it was not realized to any great extent until after World War II.[14]

Nolan concluded with six major points. First, every city or town of any importance must build the best airport possible. Second, information on airport development must be constantly updated and published. Third, cities must act to chose a location for their airport as soon as possible and follow the highest standards of city planning and zoning. Fourth, airport sites should allow for future expansion. Fifth, airports must be located with due regard to available ground transportation facilities. And sixth, local planning boards as well as national organizations of planners should offer their advice and expertise to localities.[15] All of these rather basic ideas became fairly standard in the airport planning literature.

By far the most extensive publication dealing with city planning and airports was that prepared by a team at Harvard University. The team consisted of Henry V. Hubbard, Miller McClintock, Frank B. Williams, Paul Mahoney, and Howard K. Menhinick, and they published their findings in 1930. Harvard University had determined to publish a whole series of books on urban planning topics. This book, entitled *Airports: Their Location, Administration, and Legal Basis*, was the first. It contained a number of chapters, including "Physical Characteristics of Suitable Airport Sites," "Functional Relation of the Airport to the City and Region," "Relation of the Airport to the National Transportation Network," "Ownership," "Administration," and "Management." The study basically surveyed the existing airports in the United States and reported on the findings of that survey. More descriptive than analytical, its conclusions were not much different than those drawn by Goodrich, Ford, and Nolan, as they also based their work on existing airports. The book did, however, offer a far more detailed discussion of the issues involved in the siting and layout of airports. It also most clearly viewed airports as part of a metropolitan transportation system.

The Harvard study discussed in greater detail a theme that also appeared, though in a less elaborately articulated form, in the work of Goodrich and Nolan. Planning thought in the late 1920s included the idea that major cities would have to build not one airport but a system of airports, each designed for a specialized use. In the Harvard study's chapter entitled "Functional Relation of the Airport to the City and the Region," the authors suggested that there were many different uses for airports. They had outlined those uses in the previous chapter: airmail, transport, schools, air taxi service, sight-seeing and joyriding, use by private planes, and testing.[16] In the late 1920s single airports supported many, even most, of those uses. They argued that "it [would] soon become necessary to segregate these uses and to have different airports for different purposes." They then went on to discuss the various types of airports cities would have to provide for in their city plans.[17] Together the various types of airports formed a metropolitan aerial transportation system.

The chapter listed and described five different kinds of fields they believed had to be part of a planned system of airports. First was a "large intown [*sic*] municipal airport." Such an airport would serve air travelers in the same way a union railroad station served rail travelers. This airport needed to be as close to the center of the city as possible, certainly no more than fifteen minutes' travel time. A city might be able to provide for such an airport at up to seven miles from the center of the city if it planned to build or extend a rapid transit line of some sort connecting it with the downtown. Otherwise a location physically closer to the center of town was called for. The Harvard planners suggested that cities might find such a site by looking to tidal flats that could be filled, by electrifying their railway systems and building the airport on a platform covering the rail yards, or by clearing a blighted district. What cities must not do, they emphasized, was to convert a city park into an airport. Too much was lost to the city by such a conversion to be made up by any gain to the city from the airport. The in-town municipal airport would be closed to private planes and would cover the least amount of space consistent with safety and efficiency.[18]

The next type of airport listed was one that the planners called an "airplane garage." After an airplane had landed at the municipal airport and let off its passengers, it would then take off and travel to the airplane garage "for storage and repair facilities." These airports could be located at a great distance from the cities and did not have to be tied into the area's ground transportation system since passengers would not board there. The planners also listed another type of airplane garage, one that they referred to as an airplane parking field. This airport would be one to which suburban or rural peoples could fly to "by private airplane or taxi airplane" and then be transported to the municipal airport "quickly by mass transportation facilities." These airports would provide storage facilities for the private airplanes and air taxis.[19]

The last two types of airports discussed by the planners were local suburban airports, and private and special airports. The former would be located at "a very considerable distance from the heart of the big city" and would be used by suburbanites "in going to and from the big city by air."[20] The planners did not make it very clear exactly what types of planes would use this airport—private or air taxis. However, since they recommended that the in-town municipal airport be closed to private airplanes, one can assume that if the suburbanites were to use the local suburban airport to travel directly into the city by air, they would have to do so by an air taxi service. Apparently the difference between an airplane parking field and the local suburban airports was, first, the distance from the city and then the means by which passengers would travel to them and then from them to the municipal airport. People traveled to the close-in airplane parking field by airplane (private or air taxi) and then went on to the municipal airport via public ground transportation. On the other hand, it appears that people traveled to the more distant local suburban airports by private ground and then went on to the city's primary airport by air, most likely by air taxi. Or they could take their private planes from the local suburban field to the airplane parking field and then travel to the municipal airport via ground transportation. The bottom line was that this system required several takeoffs and landings for the people and planes involved, a situation that did not particularly promote safety.

The final type of airport listed, a private and special airport, was for the use of "airplane clubs, manufacturers' testing fields, and so on." Also falling into this category would be airport facilities that might make recreational areas that were difficult to travel to over land more accessible. All those small private and special use airports could also serve as emergency intermediate fields.[21] At the time, many concerned with air safety wanted to see airports, or at least emergency landing fields, located every ten miles.

The authors continued their discussion by emphasizing that airports of all kinds within the urban system of airports had to be carefully related to the regional plan, especially as it dealt with transportation. Most of the airport types the authors listed needed some kind of connection to the region's transportation system. It was also important, though, that the airports, like public parks, "be a continuous area, not cut through by public roads." That raised another issue involving airports and roads. Airports, through which no roads should be built, could be "an interruption to public traffic on the ground." Airports had to be sited carefully, therefore, in order that they have access to the transportation system without acting as a barrier.[22]

The authors concluded that they did not expect such a system of airports to be built anytime soon by all cities but only by "a few of our greater cities." Given that, the authors then concentrated the rest of their discussion on "the kind of airport that a city should provide at this time and which it would use for general purposes until such time as more specialization [was] justified."[23] The system of airports envisioned by the Harvard planners evidenced not only a view of airports as parts of a local, metropolitan transportation system but also a poor grasp of the technology and a uncritical acceptance of the future of private flying as promoted by the aviation enthusiasts of the day.

In fact, the degree of specialization the authors suggested in their study never really came about. Airports within metropolitan areas do tend to sort themselves out into general categories such as commercial airports—usually one large municipal airport serving the metropolitan area and, perhaps, a few suburban or county airports with freight, repair, or modification services available—and private airports. However, the complex system of highly specialized facilities including storage and repair, parking, and short-range commuter airports never really materialized. This prediction, which also seemed to be dependent upon a great increase in private flying, proved not very accurate. Commercial airlines located their repair facilities at the principal municipal airports they served, and private flying, despite the hopes and dreams of many, never became as common as travel by automobile. The general idea that a large metropolitan area might need to be serviced by more than one major airport, however, has proved closer to the mark. A number of the nation's largest metropolitan regions do benefit from the operation of more than one airport large enough to serve the major commercial carriers. Examples include New York City, Chicago, Washington, and the Los Angeles region. Although the exact predictions of the planners proved less than accurate, a number of cities did produce plans in the late 1920s that showed the influence of that thinking. As will be seen later, Philadelphia and New York City produced plans that envisioned either a regional system of airports or at least the existence of multiple airports to serve the metropolitan region.

Finally, perhaps reflecting somewhat the already waning enthusiasm for airports by the time of its publication in 1930, the Harvard study also included a short chapter in which the authors suggested that not every city needed to build an airport to serve commercial air transportation needs. At the height of the enthusiasm, airport boosters argued that every city of any size should build a municipal airport. The Harvard study suggested that cities needed to look carefully to determine whether or not it really needed a large airport facility. In this the Harvard planners did demonstrate a better understanding of the emerging route structure. They also demonstrated that while planners viewed airports primarily in local and metropolitan terms, they did have a sense that some national coordination or planning would be helpful. This emerged more strongly in the planning literature of the late 1930s.

The Harvard planners argued that cities needed to examine their relationship to the nation's airways, its railways, its highways, and its waterways in determining whether or not it needed to build an airport. John Nolan had suggested that the airways would go to where the airports were located. The Harvard planners reversed this. They suggested that cities should determine whether or not they were going to find themselves "on a regional or national airway route, existing or planned, or reasonably to be predicted." If a city was going to be located on an airway, then city officials needed to build an airport. If not, then city officials needed to think through the situation carefully. Could people from their city travel by road to a nearby city on an airway in a reasonable amount of time? If so, it might not make sense to build a municipal airport as it would likely only to serve local needs and not act as a feeder to airports on the airway.[24]

The Harvard planners further cautioned cities on the airways to look at where they fit on the airways, railways, highways, and waterways before completing plans for their airports. For example, cities on the airways should determine whether land planes or seaplanes or both would be likely to use their airports. They should also try and determine the type (passenger, express, or mail) and volume of traffic. Most important, the cities should determine what role their airport would play on the airway. The planners borrowed examples from the railroads and cautioned cities to ask whether any municipal airport they would construct would function as "a terminal, a junction point, a regular stop, a flag stop, or, although it [was] along the route, [would] it be so located that no stop could be profitably made by long-distance traffic except under extraordinary circumstances." Obviously the role played by the airport on the airway would determine to a great extent the size and complexity of the airport the city needed to provide. A terminal would need a large airport with storage facilities and close coordination with other forms of transportation. A regular stop would need to be able to expand with the growth of traffic on the airway. If, on the other hand, airplanes were likely to land only under extraordinary circumstances, then the city would probably only have to provide a relatively small, simple intermediate or emergency landing field.[25]

As to the other forms of transportation, cities also had to look closely at how their relationship to them might also influence the type of airport needed. A city on a railroad truck line might ask whether or not it could become part of a system of rail-air travel. The authors called such a system, by which passengers traveled "by train at night and [traveled] by airplane by day" as "not uncommon." (That was probably a bit of an exaggeration, although T.A.T.'s rail-air "Lindbergh Line" was in operation at the approximate time the authors conducted their study.) The authors also cautioned cities, though, that "we do not know how long this form of transfer from railway to air will remain effective and popular."[26] (Here the planners did seem to have a better sense of the future of air travel, as such systems went out of existence after only a short period of operation.) If cities were located on a spur line or not on any rail line, officials had to determine whether people could travel to an airport faster by rail or road than by air. If they could, then no local airport was really needed. Only if using a local airport to catch a flight to a major airport would save time and expense would it make sense to build a local airport. The planners argued that the same considerations were in place when it came to evaluating an airport's relationship to the nation's highway system.[27] Again, such an emphasis on harmonizing local airport plans with national transportation systems foreshadowed the arguments of planners in the late 1930s.

With the advent of the Lindbergh boom, when airports became a priority for cities, a number of pioneer city planners came forward to present themselves as experts on airport planning. The advice they offered was neither unique nor particularly influential. Their articles and books generally reflected common sense and the prevailing practices of the day. When they did present more elaborate ideas, they lacked the strong data needed to convince cities of the legitimacy of the plans and programs. Despite the general lack of influence, however, at least three cities produced what they called airport plans.[28] And the plans of two of those cities, Philadelphia and New York, definitely reflected at least some of the planning thought of the day.

The Philadelphia and New York Plans

A planning group in Philadelphia clearly produced a regional airport plan in 1930. While the plan was never fully realized, it did reflect some of the planning thought of the day—that planning should be done for metropolitan regions and that such regions would need systems of airports and airways. And although the plan was regional in nature, it clearly aimed at putting Philadelphia at the center of a national network of air transportation. Thus, old-fashioned boosterism as well as contemporary planning ideas shaped the Philadelphia regional airport plan. On the other hand, perhaps it could be said that some local airport boosters and planners had a better sense of their airports being part of the national transportation system than did the nationally prominent professional planners.

As early as 1923, Philadelphia's civic leaders had dreams of their city becoming a great center of air transportation. In that year, S. B. Eckert, the chairman of the Aviation Committee of the Philadelphia Chamber of Commerce, contributed an article to *Aeronautical Digest* in which he outlined the reasons that his city should soon become a "great airport." Eckert suggested that important air routes would soon develop along the Atlantic seaboard of the United States, especially a route or routes between Washington to the south and Boston to the north. He also stated that one of the cities along that path (either Washington, Baltimore, New York City, or Philadelphia) would become "the great air terminal of the Eastern coast." Boston, New York City, and Baltimore had already taken action to try and stake their claim upon the title. Philadelphia, though, was the most logical location for "the leading airport of the East." New York, Eckert asserted, was too far from Washington, while Baltimore was "not as convenient to New York as Philadelphia." Philadelphia, however, had not as "yet prepared to take advantage of the situation." Some progressive citizens, including members of the Aero Club of Pennsylvania and the Aviation Committee of the Chamber of Commerce, had been studying the issue. Eckert ended his article stating that he "hoped that the efforts of these citizens [would] soon bear fruit." Once they did, he was sure that Philadelphia would soon take "her rightful position in the very front rank of the aeronautical development."[29]

Philadelphia did acquire a local airport during the 1920s. The Ludington Philadelphia Flying Service, an aviation enterprise controlled by the wealthy Ludington brothers of Philadelphia—who, in late 1930, would establish the Ludington Line as a passenger carrying airline shuttling people between Philadelphia, New York City, and Washington—operated an airport.[30] The airport was adjacent to Hog Island, a site at which in 1929 the Philadelphia Business Progress Association proposed the city build an air-rail-marine terminal. The city already owned 239 acres. To build the larger facility as envisioned, the city needed to purchase an addition 911 acres owned by the U.S. Shipping Board. Following the Philadelphia Business Progress Association's recommendation, the city purchased the additional land for $3 million.[31]

The city of Philadelphia did not build the Hog Island airport until the late 1930s. The proposed airport site, though, appeared in the regional plan produced by the Regional Planning Federation of the Philadelphia Tri-State District, formally published in 1932.[32] The Regional Planning Federation of the Philadelphia Tri-State District included among its members business and civic leaders from Philadelphia, Delaware, and New Jersey. The group was "engaged in preparing a comprehensive Regional Plan to provide for the orderly development of all the major physical facilities necessary to the best interests of the social and economic life of the people living in the interdependent communities that compose the region." The list of facilities for which the organization hoped to create plans included "highways, railways, airways, ports and waterways; parks, parkways and recreational centers; use of land; and sanitation, drainage and water supply." The organization's Aviation Committee, in close coordination with its Technical Advisory Committee, produced the regional airport plan. The Aviation Committee included among its members S. B. Eckert (author of the 1923 article promoting Philadelphia's future as great center of air activity, he served as the chairman of the Aviation Committee), Charles Townsend Ludington (of the Ludington Line and other aviation endeavors), and Henry Du Pont (from Delaware and involved with aviation activities in that state).[33]

Before the publication of the entire plan in 1932, the Regional Planning Federation of the Philadelphia Tri-State Region published a separate document in 1930 dealing with airways and airports. "Regionally Planned Groundwork: Airways and Airports" began with a general survey of the growth of aviation since 1918. It pointed out the increased volume of both mail and passengers being carried by the airlines. It also highlighted the growth in the number of commercial planes being produced in the country as well as the burgeoning number of pilots. All of that growth and development had brought aviation to the point where coordinated planning, local and regional, was now necessary, they argued. Unfortunately, the local planners asserted, "there [had] been an almost total absence of coordinated planning for regional development." Such lack of coordination had resulted in unfortunate situations in which "too often the town airport has been misplaced or has been overdeveloped in relation to the needs of the community or the surrounding region." Instead, the local planners argued that "there [needed] to be a comprehensive viewing of the requirements of each town in relation to its neighbors, so that an entire district may develop as a homogeneous movement." The end product should be a regional "aerial plan" in which each town would have the aviation facilities most suited to its role within the region. The plan would also help create aviation facilities that would relate logically "to highways, railways, parks and other major factors of transportation and economic life."[34]

After asserting the need for both airways and airports, the Philadelphia planners then outlined their own vision of a system or hierarchy of airports. Like the Harvard study planners, the Philadelphia planners envisioned a day when airports would exist to serve specialized functions, as opposed to the many diversified uses present at most airports at that time and after. The system of airports they envisioned, however, was a bit less complex than that outlined by the Harvard study. They first described what they called transport terminals. Such airports were needed "at all points where concentration of population and industry [furnished] justification for a base of embarkation and debarkation of passengers and goods." Such airports would be specially designed to serve such needs. Student training, local air traffic, and casual air traffic (private recreational flying) would be excluded. Student pilots would receive their training at specialized training centers "located at such distance from built-up areas as to permit the carrying on of forced landing practice without danger of damage to surrounding property." It was also strongly suggested that those training airports be located far from the heavily traveled airways. Local and casual flying, as well as other general aviation activities (aerial photography, surveying, and advertising; sightseeing; and manufacturers' testing and experimentation) would require "numerous bases of operation spaced at convenient intervals." Finally, reflecting the thinking of the Aeronautics Branch and other aviation safety experts, the local plan called for the establishment of auxiliary fields "located at intervals of not more than ten or fifteen miles along all established airways."[35]

The next section of the plan discussed the location of the existing and planned airways in the Philadelphia region. The airways included those built or planned by both the federal government and the state of Pennsylvania. The local planners always couched their discussions in terms of regional planning. But it was clear from the language of the plan, as well as the language of an *Airports* article describing the plan, that a major purpose behind the regional planning initiative was to ensure a central role for Philadelphia in the emerging national airways network. The local planners envisioned a future in which their city would become, "as Chicago, Cleveland and Kansas City have already become, the center from which radiate a number of important air transport lines."[36]

As the local planners outlined suggested locations for various types of airports throughout the region, it was also clear that their planning reflected the state of the art of aircraft design and performance in 1930. They did not anticipate future improvements in the speed and range of commercial aircraft. The local planners based their ideas for a regional system of airports on the assumption that the average speed of a commercial airplane would be 95 miles per hour. According to the formula they used to determine the distances at which airplanes would offer a marked time advantage over trains and automobiles, air terminal facilities were needed every 35 miles along the major airways. Within three years, however, Boeing would introduce the Model 247, capable of cruising at 161 mph, and the following year Douglas would introduce its DC-2, capable of flying at 178 mph. The DC-3, introduced in 1936, could carry twenty-one passengers at 190 mph. The regional airport plan thus included a list of dozens of airports and proposed airports in the 4,000 square miles of the Philadelphia Tri-State District. The local planners did not suggest the exact locations for any of the proposed airports. Local authorities would have to determine exactly where the facilities would be located. The local planners emphasized, though, that airports needed to have good surface access roads. Certainly systems of rail-air travel (meaning in this case rail access to the airport from the city) were proving valuable, but the local planners believed that quick assess by motorbus and automobile would be even more important to the success of airports and air travel. Motorbuses and automobiles offered more flexible schedules and promised better to meet "the individual needs of air passengers." So while having rail access to the airport might prove a convenience, it was far more important "to establish air terminals and landing fields as close as possible to main highways of motor travel, so as to provide easy access by automobile, truck and motorbus."[37]

The local planners in Philadelphia also differed somewhat from the professional planners involved in the Harvard study when it came to the issue of ownership. The Harvard planners saw public ownership of airports as, perhaps, the most expedient way to get airports built at that time. They believed, however, that in the future, the trend would be toward private airports. The Philadelphia planners, on the other hand, believed that public ownership was the only means through which "to develop a permanent system of airports." Privately owned fields did not and could not meet the requirements of a permanent municipal airport. They were often too small and/or poorly equipped. The costs of equipping them to meet the needs of aviation, the planners held, were beyond the capabilities of private owners. Private owners could also close or sell their airports. And while a private airport had to make a profit, a publicly owned municipal airport would only need to break even. The local planners declared, therefore, that publicly owned airports were the best answer. Private airport companies could, however, manage those airports.[38]

By far the most important project presented in the plan was the construction of a new Philadelphia municipal airport at Hog Island. That airport, proposed by the Philadelphia Business Progress Association and, apparently, simply absorbed within the plan produced by the Regional Federation, stood at the center of the Philadelphia airport system outlined in the regional plan. The local planners urged Philadelphia to act quickly to build the needed airport. The city could no longer "afford to neglect its aviation development." The Hog Island airport promised to be "the natural air terminus for this populous, ever-growing social and economic unit forming the Tri-State District."[39]

Planning historian Mel Scott reported that the Regional Planning Federation went out of business shortly after the publication of its plan. He concluded that the main importance of the organization could be found in its education influence. Many people in the region at least came to see some value in planning as a result of the work of the Regional Planning Federation. The projects included in the plan that did come to fruition, Scott asserted, "would have been carried out in any event, as they were in the works, so to speak, before being incorporated into the plan."[40] So, though presented as an important component of a regional plan, Philadelphia's new airport would have been (and was) built with or without a regional plan.

Airports also appeared in the most noted regional plan of the late 1920s and early 1930s, the 1929 Regional Plan of New York and Its Environs. Here again while airports appeared in a regional plan, airport development largely came about outside the framework of the regional plan.

According to Mel Scott, the Regional Plan for New York and Its Environs grew out of the ideas and enthusiasm of Charles Dyer Norton. Norton, originally from Chicago, had been involved with the committee that sponsored Daniel Burnham's plan for that city. Relocated to New York City in 1911, Norton publicly advocated a regional plan for the city in 1915. Little developed initially, but in 1918 Norton became a trustee of the Russell Sage Foundation. The following year he presented his ideas to the foundation. His proposal was rejected, but he had stirred the interest of a fellow trustee, Alfred White. Eventually Norton and White persuaded the Russell Sage Foundation to reconsider the idea. Although White died suddenly just before the important meeting of the foundation board, the Russell Sage Foundation in 1921 agreed to employ a friend of White's, Nelson P. Lewis, for a year and also authorized the appointment of a committee (Charles Dyer Norton, John Glenn, and Robert W. De Forest) to begin preliminary work on a regional plan. Within a few months, foundation trustees formally named Norton as chairman of the group that became known as the Committee on the Regional Plan of New York and Its Environs. Two other members, Frederic A. Delano and Dwight Morrow, joined the committee at the same time. The committee hired noted British and Canadian planner Thomas Adams in 1923 as its general director of plans and surveys and also involved some of the most prominent planners in the United States in the process of preparing the plan. The Committee on the Regional Plan for New York and Its Environs began presenting the people of New York with its findings as early as 1927. It issued its first formal volume, *The Graphic Regional Plan,* in 1929. Two additional volumes, *The Building of the City* and *Buildings: Their Uses and the Spaces About Them* appeared in 1931.[41]

The first volume, *The Graphical Regional Plan,* included two short sections dealing with airports.[42] According to David A. Johnson's analysis of the plan, the sections of the regional plan dealing with airports represented not so much the work and ideas of the Committee on the Regional Plan of New York and Its Environs, but the work of the committee set up by then Secretary of Commerce Herbert Hoover in 1927 to study the airport needs of the New York metropolitan area. The regional plan essentially endorsed the work of the Hoover committee.[43]

There was a difference, however, between the Hoover recommendations and those of the 1929 regional plan. Whereas the Hoover commission called for the purchase of six airport sites, the 1929 plan called for the purchase of sixteen sites. The additional sites would help serve the needs of light aircraft.[44] This did not necessarily mean that the New York planners bought only into the idea of airplanes becoming as common as automobiles. Their call for additional sites also highlighted another planning issue concerning airports. As noted, professional planners debated, sometimes heatedly, whether airports could or did serve as open or recreational space. The longest section on airports in *The Graphic Regional Plan* appeared within the part of the plan dealing with open development areas. Open development areas included public parks, water supply reservations, and semi-public open spaces such as private golf and country clubs, military reservations and, according to the New York planners, airports. The planners involved with the New York plan believed that in some instances parts of landing fields could be used for recreation and that occasionally sites used for recreation could also be used for aircraft landings. They did conclude, however, that "no such interchangeability of use [was] now recognized as practical." How exactly they saw airports as ever serving as recreational open space—or how recreational open space might ever serve as an airport—was left hanging. The New York planners did state, though, that the additional airport sites they called for could be used as public parks until needed as airports. And, if in the future an airport site should prove "undesirable for airplane use," it "could be converted into a permanent public open space."[45] One could wonder if the New York planners' main concern was with the acquisition of airport sites or of park sites.

The second volume of the Regional Plan of New York and Its Environs, *The Building of the City,* also had a section on airports. Whereas the first volume of the regional plan focused on the location of airports, the section on airports in the second volume focused on the design of airports. Here again the New York planners relied not on their own studies but on airport design studies completed by others, namely the Lehigh Portland Cement Company's design contest held in 1929 and Archibald Black's critique of the winning entries in that contest. *The Building of the City* essentially noted the contest (and even reprinted copies of the winning design) and then summarized Black's critique as presented in the *American City* as a way of presenting the very basic design elements necessary for a successful airport—adequate landing area, clear approaches, well-designed buildings located on landscaped grounds, and connections to rail and land transportation. The rest of the section on airports in volume two reiterated what had been presented in volume one. It emphasized the importance of acquiring airport sites in advance of need and again noted that such sites could be used for recreational purposes until needed as airports. The second volume also briefly brought up the issue of airport zoning and suggested that zoning could be used to ensure good approaches to airports. The discussion of airports was very brief and a note at the end of the section suggested readers turn to the recently published Harvard study on airports for a "fuller discussion."[46]

As part of his analysis of the regional plan Johnson also asked whether or not many of the projects in the plan would have proceeded without the plan. His conclusion in relation to airports was unclear.[47] As has been shown, though, urban boosterism and aviation enthusiasm, as well as the availability of federal funds, drove the construction of both Floyd Bennett Field and LaGuardia Airport. Both were built on sites mentioned in the regional plan, but, as Johnson pointed out, the regional planners did not come up with the sites, the earlier Hoover commission did. So, as was the case in Philadelphia, it seems while airports played a role in the regional plan, the regional plan played little role in the development of airports.[48]

Airports and City Planning: Renewed Interest, 1937–40

As lobbying moved forward in the late 1930s to garner more and more direct federal funding for airport developments, airports seemed once again to spark the interest of professional planners. Not only did articles on airport planning begin to reappear in journals, but the American Society of Planning Officials and the American Municipal Association jointly produced a new study of the issue, *The Airport Dilemma: A Review of Local and National Factors in Airport Planning and Financing*. That document clearly reflected the experience of planners in the 1930s in that it focused not on local or regional planning of airports so much as it emphasized that local and regional airport planning must fit within national planning for airports. However, in the end, planners still viewed airports as very much part of the local infrastructure and, as such, a local responsibility.

As John Hancock has argued, during the 1930s many planners found themselves working within or in cooperation with one or another of the many agencies created as a result of New Deal policies. Their experiences with such organizations as the Public Works Administration, the Works Progress Administration, the Federal Emergency Housing Corporation, the Resettlement Administration, and the National Resources Planning Board convinced planners of the value and necessity of national planning. It also demonstrated to them the necessity of coordinating local, state, and national planning.[49] The airport study jointly produced in 1938 by the American Society of Planning Officials and the American Municipal Association reflected the emphasis on national planning and coordinated planning current in American planning thought by the late 1930s. While the earlier Harvard airport study also suggested that local airport planners think about their airport plans in relation to national ground transportation systems and plans for national airways systems, the 1938 airport study clearly demonstrated a greater emphasis and focus on national airport planning.

In their foreword to *The Airport Dilemma*, Walter H. Blucher (executive director, American Society of Planning Officials) and Clifford W. Ham (executive director, American Municipal Association) began by presenting, in the form of an eight-point list, the opinions expressed in late 1936 by the Executive Committee of the American Municipal Association. Points one and two emphasized *that while airports met important transportation needs of cities* (emphasis added), the transportation uses of airports were clearly "interstate in character." Point three asserted "an immediate need for uniform planning and development of airports." The fourth point in essence praised the contribution of Works Progress Administration relief projects to airport development and stated that planning "[would] allow for the continuance of such projects." In their fifth point, the executive committee raised the issue of airport revenue, concluding that cities had no way to "create and derive any revenue from the interstate business carried on through airports." Points six through eight brought up the issue of the importance of coordinating local and state airport planning with national planning. Point six asserted that airports had military value and thus were an "indispensable part of the system of state and national defense schemes." (Thus, planners also reflected the growing military preparedness mood of the late 1930s.) Point seven, while stating that state and local agencies still had important roles in supervising many aspects of airport design, construction maintenance, and operation, nonetheless stated it was "imperative that the federal government, with its licensing powers of aircraft, pilots, and airports for the national civil airways and interstate service, should first make more definite and complete plans to which the states and their municipalities may gear their plans." And finally, point eight declared that the "federal government should prescribe a system of national civil airways and airports" just as it had developed a system of national highways so that "states and cities may plan their state systems of airways and airports with reference to federal needs and requirements" and "that the federal government determine what [were] the federal values and the interstate values of airports coming within the national civil airways system." After listing the opinions of the American Municipal Association, Blucher and Ham expressed their own realization "that rational and economically sound airport programs [could] only be based upon national, state, and local planning." They closed their foreword by expressing their hope that the material in the report would be of use to planners at all levels of government.[50]

The joint report by the American Society of Planning Officials and the American Municipal Association differed from earlier airport planning literature. Most of the articles and reports created in the late 1920s and early 1930s focused on planning at the local or regional level. The end result was a plan for a municipal airport or a system of airports (often with one primary municipal airport at its center) for a metropolitan region. *The Airport Dilemma*, while outlining what cities had done in terms of airport planning, focused its attention on the importance of national planning and the need for local and state governments to adjust their airport planning to national planning.

After surveying the airport funding situation, authors of *The Airport Dilemma* examined the question of why cities should build airports. They immediately discounted two of the traditional reasons behind municipal airport construction. They argued that the "glamour of aviation" was not and never had been a sound reason for building an airport. They also pointed out that airports in general, and municipal airports in particular, had never been great revenue generators nor had they attracted much new industry or business to cities. They then noted that airports were a continual expense for cities as the rapid development of aviation, particularly in the 1930s with the introduction of larger planes needing a longer surface to reach takeoff speed, demanded nearly constant improvements. They concluded that the only reasons cities should build, maintain, and improve airports was that their airports might fit within either national air defense needs or national air transportation needs, or perhaps both.[51]

The authors then suggested that one of the major problems facing cities was the absence of a national airport plan. They did not see how a city could justify expenditures for airports without a clear grasp of how their airport might serve either national defense or national transportation needs. Cities needed the kind of information a national airways and airport plan could provide. The authors suggested that cities would find it increasingly difficult to raise the money needed to maintain and improve their airports in the absence of a national plan.[52]

The section of *The Airport Dilemma* that dealt specifically with local airport planning, while emphasizing the fact that cities would continue to have great responsibilities in terms of their airports, also reiterated the need for coordinating local, state, and national planning. The authors pointed out that city plan commissions or special airport commissions did most of the airport planning at the local level. They stated that such local agencies would be aided in their efforts by having available the kind of information a national airport and airways plan could provide. A national plan could help a city decide, first, if it really needed an airport and, second, if it did need an airport, what size and type of airport it needed.[53]

The section on local planning concluded with a discussion of airport financing. Here the authors seemed to suggest that even with a national airways and airport plan and national funding for airports, cities would continue to bear a significant share of the cost of building, maintaining, and improving the nation's airports. The authors turned toward an older idea when offering a suggestion on how cities might increase their airport revenues. They suggested that cities take greater advantage of service charges and fees. They pointed out, for example, that some European airports even charged admission fees. They also noted that European airports had been more aggressive in combining airport and recreational facilities ("hotels, restaurants, swimming pools, football fields, skating rinks, and the like") and charging fees for the leasing of those recreational facilities.[54] American airports had tried to raise revenue from such sources since the 1920s. A few airports did make some money from such activities, but how much such revenues could contribute in a time of rapidly increasing costs for airport improvements was not well developed by the authors.

Clearly, by the late 1930s when the interests of planners again turned toward the subject of airports, their ideas and suggestions reflected their experiences during the 1930s. They no longer focused primarily on individual or regional airport plans but on the importance of national planning. Yet, they continued to see airports as serving the transportation needs of cities and also saw cities as having the primary responsibility for planning, financing, and building airports. In addition, *The Airport Dilemma* brought up another issue connected with airport planning, one which captured the interests of planners perhaps more consistently than any other and one that proved the most important legacy of the formative period of airport planning. That issue was airport zoning.

Airports, City Planning, and Zoning

Zoning ranked, perhaps, as one of the most popular forms of city planning in the 1920s and 1930s. Cities that failed to produce city plans or to engage in much planning activity at all nonetheless passed zoning ordinances. Zoning, the division of cities into specified use districts (industrial, commercial, residential), promised to protect property values and to help guide the growth and development of cities.[55] In the late 1920s zoning proponents also examined how it might serve airports. While at least one author suggested how zoning might be used to prevent blighted districts from growing up around airports as they had around railroad stations,[56] most writing on the subject explored how zoning might prevent or eliminate hazards to aerial navigation. Most of the attention focused on preventing the construction of or eliminating the presence of tall buildings, towers, smokestacks, or other structures along the flight path of airplanes landing or taking off from airports.[57] The issues included whether zoning could be used at all, whether it could be used to protect both publicly and privately owned major commercial airports, whether it could be used to protect private landing fields, and whether laws should allow for zoning without compensation (regulation) or an equivalent of zoning with compensation (eminent domain). Those questions arose during the early period of interest in airport zoning (1928–32). By the end of the 1930s, attention centered primarily on zoning laws that regulated obstructions or hazards to the use of public and commercial airports. The issues were many, but generally this period saw the development of a strong argument in favor of the use of zoning to protect publicly owned, and the few privately owned, commercial airports.

For the July, 1929, issue of *City Planning*, Edward M. Bassett, an expert on zoning, presented a short zoning roundtable column based, in part, on zoning issues brought up at a conference on city planning held in Buffalo, New York. The first topic of the roundtable was zoning for airports. At that time, Bassett suggested a somewhat circumscribed use of zoning to protect airports. First, he asked, could an airport with a large amount of privately held land surrounding it be protected from "steeples, factory chimneys, or high buildings" through the use of zoning? Bassett answered no. In this case, however, when he referred to airports, he seemed to be thinking about privately owned commercial airports. He did not believe that zoning should be used in such a case as it would be discriminatory. He stated: "The surrounding land ought to be zoned as it would be zoned if the airports were not there." He suggested that the airport owners purchase the land surrounding their airports in order to control what would be built there. If that were not possible, he asserted that once private airports were determined to be public utilities—something he saw happening—then state laws could give the companies operating the commercial airports the power of eminent domain, "somewhat the same as waterworks companies and railroad companies have been granted it."[58]

On the other hand, Bassett presented a situation in which a publicly owned airport might use zoning to protect its surrounding area. He argued that if a public airport were established in a open area "suitable for low private residences, there would seem to be no reason why the surrounding private property belt should not be zoned for one-family detached houses of not more than two or two and one-half stories in height." Other buildings constructed in the zoning area could also be restricted as to height.[59] The short roundtable column did not suggest why the area around a private commercial airport, if suitable, might not also be zoned for single-family dwellings. It was also not clear what would happen if a public airport were located in an area in which the surrounding territory was not suitable for single-family dwellings. What was clear was that by the late 1920s and the early 1930s many people were concerned with how zoning might be used to protect airports from nearby uses that would pose as hazards to aerial navigation.

In 1930 the Aeronautics Branch of the Department of Commerce, citing great interest in the zoning issue on the part of city officials, airport managers, and others, formed a committee on airport zoning. It charged the committee with studying the issue, presenting its findings, and making recommendations. Clarence M. Young, the assistant secretary of commerce for aeronautics, stated that while most cities had recognized the need to build airports, it was also necessary for them to somehow use "suitable zoning ordinances" in order "to protect these air harbors against developments tending to jeopardize the safety of operations and otherwise reduce the effectiveness of the airport." Committee members were Harry H. Blee, director of aeronautics development, Aeronautics Branch, Department of Commerce, Chairman; Edward M. Bassett, Advisory Committee on City Planning and Zoning, Department of Commerce; W. M. Bishop, Air Transport Section, Aeronautical Chamber of Commerce; W. Irving Bullard, United States Chamber of Commerce; George B. Ford, Planning Foundation of America (who died in August, 1930); George B. Logan, Committee on Aeronautical Law, American Bar Association; A. Pendleton Taliaferro Jr., Airport Section, Aeronautical Branch, Department of Commerce, committee secretary; and James S. Taylor, Division of Building and Housing, Bureau of Standards, Department of Commerce.[60]

The committee issued their report and recommendations on December 18, 1930. The report first briefly surveyed the airport situation in the United States.

It noted that at the time ownership of airports in the United States was fairly evenly divided "between individual or corporate ownership, and ownership by some public authority." Further, the report suggested that airports might be grouped into three categories, regardless of ownership. First, there were terminal airports that served "as units in organized transportation including both scheduled and non-scheduled operations, where mail, merchandise, and passengers [were] taken on and discharged." Second were the service airports that "[catered] to general storage, repair and service business where airplanes [could] be purchased, stored, and repaired, and where miscellaneous activities, such as school, aerial photographing and mapping, crop dusting, air taxi service, etc., may be based." And finally there were the private airports "restricted to the service of their owners, such as the airplane manufacturers' airport, the airport belonging to a school and restricted to that school's activities, etc." This report, as with other planning literature that also attempted to divide airports into use categories, conceded that such classification was not "clearly in force today" and terminal airports especially still provided a base for a great variety of aerial activities.[61]

The report then took on the issue of why and how terminal airports— whether privately or publicly owned—might gain protection from encroaching hazards under the law. Airports, the report argued, were important to the community in which they were located and to the general flying public. Without the necessary terminal airports "our business and social life would doubtless be as badly crippled as it would be to-day were one of the older forms of transportation, which has become an integral part of our economic life, suddenly eliminated." Given the importance of airports, "it [was] evident that means must be determined upon to protect it in carrying out its responsibilities to the public and to continue it in effective use." Airports had to be free of surrounding hazards that would cause danger to arriving or departing airplanes and passengers. Terminal airports, both publicly and privately owned, the report concluded, should be granted the power of eminent domain "to condemn the additional area that may be required to meet the changing demands of larger flying equipment." They also needed the power "to condemn air easements over surrounding land and the power to condemn the right to air mark neighboring structures of a hazardous nature."[62]

Of the two forms of protection from hazards that airports might employ (zoning regulation or eminent domain), the authors of the report evidently favored the use of eminent domain (taking with compensation) over the use of zoning alone (taking without compensation) in providing for the protection of airports. Both eminent domain and zoning were forms of "taking." Under eminent domain, the original property owner received compensation when land was taken for public purpose. Under zoning, a land owner received no compensation when certain rights to the use of the land were taken away as a result of the zoning regulation. The authors of the report held that airports must first use eminent domain in dealing with the problem of hazards. The authors seemed to suggested that eminent domain was the best (and perhaps fairest) way to secure control of abutting territory as it offered a more permanent form of protection. Zoning regulations could be changed.[63]

The authors did not rule out the use of zoning regulation, though. In addition to arguing on behalf of terminal airports gaining the right of eminent domain, they also argued that zoning regulation could be used to protect them and the emergency intermediate fields operated by the Department of Commerce as well. Zoning could not be used simply to protect the interests of any airport. Zoning regulations, as with all uses of the police power of the state, had to serve the public welfare. Terminal airports, the authors asserted, served the public welfare by providing a base for "aircraft operating upon regular schedules in the transportation of commerce and passengers." The airlines operating at airports had to "be assured at all times of safe avenues of approach to the established terminals and intermediate fields." Intermediate fields also served the public interest as they provided a safe landing area in case of an in-flight emergency. Just as the authors argued that the power of eminent domain could be used by both publicly owned and privately owned terminal airports, both types of terminal airports could be protected by appropriate zoning ordinances.[64]

The authors specifically noted, though, that the use of zoning regulations to protect a service or private airport ("airports not in the public-service class") was more problematic. In such cases airports could "be considered only as one factor in connection with all the other interests and appropriate uses of land in the neighborhood." Any zoning regulation around a service or private airport, therefore, had to "be suited to the neighborhood." There were cases where the nature of the surrounding areas was such that zoning regulation might incidentally offer protection. For example, if the neighborhood surrounding an airport were somewhere that "the price of land [was] moderate, the existing buildings few and low, and the district suited to residential development," then it would be appropriate to zone the area in order to keep any buildings built within it at a low height. However, zoning regulation could not be used to restrict building heights around a private airport located in a district already containing taller residential, commercial, or industrial buildings. The establishment of a nonpublic airport in such an area "would not sufficiently change that character to make any other regulation reasonable and therefore valid."[65]

The report concluded with four recommendations. First, states must pass zoning enabling acts allowing political subdivisions other than municipalities to enact zoning ordinances. This recognized the fact that many airports, even those owned by municipalities, were located outside the city boundaries and, therefore, not necessarily covered by a municipal zoning law. Second, the authors held that municipalities and other political subdivisions enact zoning legislation in the interests of terminal airports (public and private) and intermediate fields. And the authors asserted that states must grant the power of eminent domain to terminal airports and intermediate landing fields in order for them to ensure safe approaches to the airport and the air marking of hazards and to allow for the expansion of the airport when necessary. Finally, the authors recommended that public utilities, such as electric companies, take actions to protect "airports and intermediate fields against the hazards of electrical supply and communication lines." The report, reflecting the associationalism of the time, also included a copy of a model act "under which counties, municipalities, and other political subdivisions may establish, develop, operate, maintain, regulate, and police airports and landing fields" as well as copies of existing laws that might also serve as examples.[66]

The report received attention in both city planning journals and journals addressing the aviation industry. And over the next several years a few states did pass zoning acts addressing the needs of airports. However, just as the enthusiasm for airports waned with the coming of the depression, interest in airport zoning also seemed to wane (although it never completely disappeared). As planners exhibited a renewed interest in airports at the end of the 1930s, they also exhibited a renewed interest in airport zoning.

In 1939 the Airport Section of the new Civil Aeronautics Authority conducted a survey of airport zoning legislation. Unlike earlier discussions of zoning and airports, this survey concentrated exclusively on the use of zoning as a means for protecting airport approaches. The report offered little analysis of the use of zoning. Instead, basically, it listed and described the types of state zoning laws in place as of late 1938. It also included copies of the twelve pieces of legislation, from nine states, on the books.

The same year as the publication of the CAA's airport survey, the state of Massachusetts enacted legislation "regulating the height of buildings and other structures within a certain distance of the Boston Airport, so called." Other cities included within their comprehensive zoning ordinances "restrictions on building heights in designated areas." By the time Charles S. Rhyne examined the issue of airport zoning in his work *Airports and the Courts*, published in 1944, the number of states with airport zoning legislation had increased from nine to thirty-one.[67] While comprehensive airport plans might have been few, cities clearly were ready to use zoning to direct and control land uses around their airports.

Rhyne offered several reasons why airport zoning had become such an accepted practice. First, he asserted that zoning itself had become a recognized exercise of the police power by cities in the United States. Second, airport zoning had become accepted because the law had come to realize a "compelling public interest" in airports. By 1944 all forty-eight states had passed laws "authorizing cities to acquire public airports." Further, airports were viewed "as essential to cities today as the highways and streets over which surface traffic [moved] in metropolitan areas." Therefore, Rhyne asserted, courts had come to view the zoning of areas around public airports as being in the public's interest. Airport zoning regulations, especially, benefited the public because, in protecting airport approaches from hazards, they proved "a most reasonable and necessary means to prevent aircraft accidents" and, therefore, were "designed for the promotion or protection of the public safety." While some local airport zoning ordinances had been declared invalid by courts as unreasonable, for the most part U.S. courts had accepted the validity of such zoning ordinances. Airport zoning regulations could not be retroactive, however. To remove existing hazards, cities could use the power of eminent domain. Zoning could then be used to prevent any further hazards. Rhyne concluded by asserting that airport zoning was "a reasonable exercise of the police power of states and local governments" and that "federal state and local policy [supported] such zoning."[68] Again, zoning, rather than comprehensive planning, proved the most popular means by which cities managed the land uses in the vicinity of their airports.

Conclusion

Examination of planning activity during the 1920s and 1930s supports and reinforces a conclusion drawn in an article in the *Journal of Urban History*. In that piece, Paul Barrett and Mark H. Rose concluded that city planners had very little influence in the area of airport planning. Especially when compared with highway planners, city planners were unsuccessful in presenting themselves as the experts with the answers to airport planning problems.[69] Planning articles dealing with airports generally reflected conventional wisdom and existing practices. Further, in a number of areas, such as where a city's major airport should be located or whether or not cities should build whole systems of airports, the advice was neither strong nor clearly reflective of the needs and/or limits of the technology. While planners, at times, certainly attempted to assert their influence, in the end, that influence was quite limited.

Planners did, however, establish within the literature a number of basic, fundamental, and commonsense ideas concerning airport planning. The most important contribution of planners turned out to be the idea of airport zoning. The ability to zone the areas around airports, especially the approaches, proved very important as cities worked to develop the potential of their airports as generators of economic development after World War II.

6

"For the Duration" and into the Postwar "Air Age"

Airports, World War II, and the
Federal Airport Act of 1946

The National Airport Plan, developed in response to the Civil Aeronautics Act of 1938, focused attention on the improvement and expansion of the nation's system of civilian airports. Very quickly, however, focus shifted from airport improvement in the name of commercial aviation to airport improvement in the name of national defense. So, while the government directed millions toward the nation's airports, the funds were spent on those airports that seemed most likely to contribute to national defense. That produced not so much a national airport program as one focused on a number of regions in the United States—the East Coast (to a certain extent New England, but especially Florida—an eastern as well as a southern state), the West Coast (California and Washington), and the South (particularly Texas). Some moneys did go to airport improvement elsewhere, but the bulk of the funds through the prewar and early war years (1940–42) concentrated on developing airports with locations that contributed to improved U.S. access to Europe and the Far East and that offered year-round flying for training purposes. Thus, as was the case with defense spending in general, the airport improvement program helped funnel federal dollars into the South and the West.[1]

During the war, the United States Army Air Forces (USAAF) further directed the spending of federal defense funds at municipal airports in many locations across the country. The USAAF, which grew dramatically in terms of manpower and material during World War II, needed to expand its base structure. To that end, the USAAF worked out several different levels of relationships with municipal airports across the country. In some cases, the USAAF entered lease agreements with cities for the use of part of their municipal airports for various military functions. In other cases, the USAAF leased entire airports and in many cases, though not all, took over their management. And a number of municipal airports, or parts thereof, were militarized during the war, becoming Army Air Bases "for the duration." The Navy participated in similar activities, but its involvement, in that it needed fewer continental land-based air facilities, was on a smaller scale than that of the USAAF. The Navy tended to concentrate on improving or constructing airports on island territories and possessions of the United States. Once the war ended, most of the U.S. airports drafted into military service reverted to their original civilian ownership and control. Again, the municipal airports benefiting from military spending were concentrated in the South (Florida and Texas) and the West (California), although they could be found in almost every state in the continental United States.

Even before the war was over, many aviation-minded individuals began looking forward to the postwar air age. The beliefs of the winged gospel were still in evidence, at least among a certain core of "true believers," as people predicted a rapid and substantial development of both commercial and general aviation. These visions led to renewed calls for federal aid to municipal airports and in some ways they shaped the initial federal airport aid package following World War II. The first postwar federal airport improvement program focused primarily on the nation's smaller municipal airports. These airports were needed if commercial aviation was to reach beyond and service more than the nation's largest cities and such airports also could facilitate the growth of general aviation or private flying. By 1947, however, the nation's larger airports began to share more in the new program. The Federal Airport Act, though, also demonstrated some of the limitations of the winged gospel as it seemed evident that beliefs about the future of aviation were held mainly by a significant but relatively small core of aviation leaders. Beyond the core of "true believers," support was weak. Most in congress, for example, never embraced airplanes and airports as they would automobiles and highways. Most important, the Federal Airport Act of 1946 set the pattern for aid to municipal airports—a program of federal aid, some sent directly to larger cities, some channeled to other cities through state aviation organizations—in the postwar period.

Those involved with influencing plans for airports at the local level also ranked among those still holding to certain tenets of the winged gospel. While some offered visions of elaborate airport systems and even more elaborate airports, much planning thought focused on the issue of airparks. These were small, often private, suburban airports designed for use by private pilots. Further reflecting at least some remaining influence of the winged gospel, the wartime cooperation of cities with the military and the postwar promises of federal airport aid also demonstrated the civic boosterism still attached to airport building and improvement. Many cities willingly turned the management and even ownership of their airports over to the military during the war. In exchange, the cities came into the postwar period with greatly expanded and improved airports at little or no direct expense to themselves. Then, hoping to benefit from the predicted expansion of aviation activities after the war, cities eagerly sought federal funds to enhance their ability to profit in the coming "air age."

Finally, the issue of federal airport aid highlighted the new, closer relationship between cities and the national government and suggested some tensions. Cities hoped to continue to build on the direct relationship they had forged with the national government during the New Deal. States, on the other hand, sought to reestablish their role as a mediator between the national government and local governments. The debate between local, state, and national governments over how the relationships should work colored the outcome of the Federal Airport Act of 1946.

The National Airport Plan: Shift in Focus

The National Airport Plan, sent to Congress in 1939, was both more and less than what cities had asked for in the way of airport aid. The ambitious plan, which potentially involved funding construction or improvements at up to 3,500 airport sites around the country, called ultimately for the spending of nearly a half billion dollars. As one observer noted, that plan "did little more than gather dust" as an economy-minded Congress stalled on appropriating the moneys. The nation's cities, while anxious to receive aid, objected to the fact that most of the funds would be funneled to airport projects through the WPA. Airport relief was still linked to work relief.[2] Within a few months, however, the country's expanding war preparedness activities led to a shift in the focus of airport aid from enhancing commercial and general aviation to enhancing the nation's defense.

In August, 1939, the War Department directed the Office of the Chief of the Air Corps (OCAC) to draw up a list of civil airports that, with improvements, could be put to military use. In mid-September, following the German invasion of Poland and the declaration of war in Europe, the Air Corps responded that, first, all civil airports "lying within 100 miles of the Atlantic coast from Maine to Mobile, Ala." should be "built up" for use by the military. Second, the Air Corps recommended that all of the nation's largest civil airports also be "developed to a point suitable for military use." Toward the end of September the OCAC, the CAA, and the WPA met to discuss the issue. The main stumbling block seemed to be the limitations imposed by WPA regulations. WPA funds had to be distributed in relation to the relief needs of the states and cities, not in relation to the degree to which a state's or a city's location made it important to a plan for national defense. Also, WPA funding required matching funds from the sponsoring agency—a city, county, or state. During the course of the conferences, the WPA agreed to take into account the priority assigned to the development of East Coast airports by the Air Corps and also stated it would do what it could to keep the local contribution requirement as low as possible. For its part, the CAA asserted it would help encourage localities to sponsor the needed projects. The Air Corps then started work on a list of airports.[3]

General Henry H. "Hap" Arnold, chief of the Air Corps, formed a committee to help develop the airport improvement list. Members were drawn from the War Plans Division, the Navy, and from his own office. The committee made recommendations for extensive airport improvements in the northeast, the southeast, and the northwest. The committee did not, apparently, recommend specific airports for improvements. One exception was the airport at Brownsville, Texas, seen as vital for ferrying men and material overland to Panama. Rather, the committee basically indicated how many airports required improvement in each region in order to meet Air Corps needs. The CAA and the WPA then designated which specific airports would be involved. The committee did recommended, however, that five-thousand-foot runways be constructed at each airport placed on the list. The WPA and CAA sent their recommendations to the War Department on December 11, 1939. The secretary of war forwarded his final revised list to the CAA on January 4, 1940. The Army, Navy, and CAA continued to work on the list throughout 1940. It eventually grew to include about four thousand airports, located throughout the continental United States, Alaska, Hawaii, and the South Pacific. The plan anticipated spending up to $560 million over six years.[4]

Even though the CAA and the WPA, working with the Air Corps, had clearly shifted their focus from a civilian-oriented airport improvement program to one focused on military needs, Congress hesitated to vote for such an extensive program. In 1940 the United States was not yet officially involved in the war in Europe, and many still believed that the country could and should stay out of the conflict. In the meantime, however, the WPA, in cooperation with the Air Corps and the Navy, helped sponsor improvements at military airfields across the country. The WPA had been involved in construction projects at military facilities since its founding in 1935. Between 1935 and 1940 a total of fifty-one Army, Navy, and National Guard airfields benefited from $17 million worth of state-sponsored WPA projects. In addition, the WPA transferred $15 million to the departments of the Army and Navy for them to use to hire WPA workers to work on military aviation construction projects.[5] By the time Congress appropriated $40 million for improvements at 250 airports deemed essential to national defense in October, 1940, several articles in aviation journals were already pointing out how WPA airport work was contributing to war preparedness.

In October, 1940, an *Aero Digest* article, which anticipated the passage of a defense-related airport improvement program, highlighted the work already completed by the WPA at military and civilian airports. Most of the projects mentioned in that article were located at airports or military airfields on either the East Coast or the West Coast or in the South. Of the twelve projects, only four were located elsewhere (Colorado, Minnesota, and two in Kansas). Most of the projects also involved improvements to civilian airports (nine), rather than military airfields (three). The article emphasized that all the projects contributed to enhanced national defense.[6] The WPA projects completed or under way by October, 1940, included new airports at Portland, Oregon, and Lake Charles, Louisiana; improvements to the municipal airports in Saint Paul, Minnesota; Wichita, Kansas; and Los Angeles, California; and expansion of military facilities at Lowry Field (Denver, Colorado) and McChord Field (Tacoma, Washington).[7]

After Congress appropriated the $40 million in October, 1940, for the improvement of up to 250 airports, the joint WPA-CAA-military airport program, known as the Development of Landing Areas for National Defense (DLAND), began in earnest.[8] The $40 million represented only half of what the CAA had requested, but it was the first time Congress had given the CAA money to use for airports. With the appropriation set, an airport approval board, consisting of the secretaries of War, Navy, and Commerce, worked to determine which 250 airports would receive funding. Also working with the committee were Major Lucius D. Clay, Army Corps of Engineers; Major A. B. McMullen, Federal Airways

Service; and, Lieutenant Colonel Donal H. Connolly, CAA administrator.[9] Clearly, this was now a military aviation program, not one aimed at civilian or commercial flying.

After receiving only half of the requested funds, the board initially pared down the number of airports to receive improvements to 200. The airports were located both in the United States and in its possessions. Further, reflecting the rules set for federal aid to airports under the WPA, every airport on the improvement list had to be "owned by a political subdivision of the Government." The political subdivision (most frequently a city or a county) had to agree to then "make it [the airport] available to the Federal Government without cost, and further pledge itself to maintain and operate the improved airport." Some of the airport improvements were constructed under contracts with private firms. The CAA also distributed funds to the WPA, which then provided labor for the projects.[10]

At the start of the next fiscal year (July 1, 1941), Congress proved a bit more generous to the DLAND program. It appropriated $95 million to the CAA. Of that, $33.5 million was to provide continued funding for airport improvements already under way (at the first 200 airports), while the rest of the money was to begin funding of improvements at an additional 149 sites. Also, Congress voted $42 million to fund WPA airport improvement projects. The construction projects involved improving the landing areas of the selected airports, particularly lengthening runways.[11] Further, the regional focus of the spending remained clear with the East Coast, the West Coast, and the South receiving the bulk of the funding.

In September, 1941, and again in December, 1941, *Aero Digest* surveyed the improvements made to airports under the DLAND program. The vast majority of the airports highlighted in those articles were located in one of the three regions deemed of strategic importance by the military. For example, the article mentioned fourteen of the airports in the New England state of Maine that received government-funded improvements. The articles also described improvements made at four Washington State airports, three in Connecticut, and two in California. The only airport mentioned in either article that did not fit the regional pattern was the municipal airport in Toledo, Ohio. A shorter *Aero Digest* article in October, 1941, listed by state the number of airport improvement projects in progress. While noting that the CAA program was active in all states but Delaware, Florida clearly led the nation in funding and number of projects. That state had $15 million worth of construction under way at 31 sites. California came in second with $8.3 million at 17 sites, and Maine ranked third with $7.2 million at 16 sites. Other states benefiting greatly from the program included Washington (12 projects), Texas (15 projects), and Massachusetts (10 projects).[12] Though several articles continued to refer to the DLAND program as "national," clearly certain regions of the country benefited far more than others.

Both small and large airports received improvement funding under the program. While most of the projects involved very basic runway extensions and paving, other more extensive or non-landing area improvements also received funding. At New York City's new airport, LaGuardia Field, the WPA funded construction of an additional gasoline bulk storage building enclosing eight tanks. The new tanks increased the field's reserve fuel storage capacity by 50 percent. Federal funds also transformed a 70-acre site at Moon Island, Washington, into "a first-class airport." The project involved a great deal of filling and draining in order to allow the construction of a paved, 5,170-foot-long landing area. Yakima County in Washington State spent $41,000 to buy the land necessary to expand its airport site from 116 acres to 357 acres. Federal funding then helped finance the construction of new runways and to provide adequate drainage. And, according to contemporary accounts, the city of San Diego worked with the federal government to improve its runways — extending, widening, and strengthening them — so that testing of the new 100,000-pound B-19 bomber might be completed.[13]

Congress voted the last funds to the DLAND program in May, 1942. At that time it appropriated $199.8 million, bringing the total spent on airports under DLAND to nearly $400 million. The funds approved in 1942 were expended over a three-year period, as Congress allowed unexpended funds to carry forward into next fiscal year. In 1943, Congress abolished the WPA. Upon its termination in February, 1943, the WPA transferred over $1 million in DLAND funds to the CAA. It also sent recommendations to the Army and Navy concerning a number of WPA airport projects under way, suggesting that the services complete them. The Army and the Navy rejected most of the WPA recommendations and work was suspended at a number of airports. Concurrently, the War Production Board moved to cancel forty-two CAA airport projects on the grounds of material and manpower shortages. The CAA and the military protested. In the end, only eleven projects remained uncompleted. Finally, in 1944, Congressman Karl Stefan of Nebraska sponsored an amendment to a war appropriation bill that would provide $9 million to complete suspended WPA airport projects. He called the proposed program Development of Civil Landing Areas (DCLA). Eventually Congress approved $9.7 million to complete twenty-nine airport projects begun under the WPA.[14] However, the DLAND program was not the only way in which federal dollars flowed to municipal airports during World War II.

Drafted: The Militarization of Municipal Airports

In addition to the money received under the DLAND program, the Army and Navy expended additional funds to improve a number of municipal airports around the country. The Army especially, with its air arm, the USAAF, was active in the leasing and management of a number of municipal airports. In some cases, when leasing arrangements failed, the Army purchased municipal airports. It leased or purchased a number of private, commercial airports as well. Further, the Army "drafted" a number of municipal airports into military service, transforming them, or at least large sections of them, into Army Air Bases "for the duration," with the promise that they would be returned to civilian service within six months of the end of hostilities. While the Army construction programs at municipal airports often provided cities with improved facilities, the program was not without a number of conflicts and controversies.

Following Pearl Harbor, the United States Army Air Forces (successor organization to the Air Corps, created June, 1941) began to disperse its pursuit— what today would be known as fighter—assets to municipal and private airports in the north and central Atlantic regions. Municipal airports involved in this initial deployment included those at Bendix, New Jersey; Philadelphia, Pennsylvania; Bridgeport, Connecticut; and, Norfolk, Virginia. By January, 1942, the USAAF had signed leases with those airports, and additional municipal airports in Newark, New Jersey; Dover, Delaware; Atlantic City, New Jersey; and Beltsville, Maryland, had construction projects under way. Throughout 1942 the USAAF continued to lease facilities at municipal airports across the country.[15]

Many of the airports utilized by the military during the war had been improved, meaning primarily that their runways had been extended, under the DLAND program. However, not all the airports needed by the USAAF had been improved. And making them fully functional for military use involved additional expenditures. For example, military housing was needed at airports hosting aviation units. Further, the USAAF also often required addition technical facilities (such as shop hangars). In March, 1941, the War Department received approval to spend over $17 million to build housing facilities, and additional funds were approved for runway improvement projects at seven municipal airports. Throughout the first half of 1941 Army construction projects were under way at over a dozen municipal airports.[16]

While many cities readily cooperated with the military plans to develop their airports for use, there were cases where conflicts or other complications resulted in the government having to purchase municipal airports. Such was the case in Bangor, Maine, where a dispute erupted over who would pay to maintain the new runways. The original lease signed by the Army and the city specified that the city of Bangor would be responsible for maintaining the runways. By April, 1941, however, the city expressed a reluctance to shoulder the burden of maintaining runways primarily used by military aircraft. The Air Corps asked to amend the lease so that it would take over the maintenance duties. However, both the quartermaster general of the Air Corps and the judge advocate general ruled against such an action, arguing that it "would incur new obligations for the government contrary to its interests." The city of Bangor then declared that it would no longer maintain the runways, and the Army aviation units at the field were prohibited from using Army funds for that purpose. The following year, the USAAF settled the conflict by purchasing the airport.[17]

Throughout the war military and civilian aviation authorities often found themselves in conflict. Such conflicts occurred at both the national and the local levels. At the national level, for example, the USAAF and the CAA often clashed over which organization would control flight activities (military and civilian) within the United States.[18] At the local level, as the military increased its flight and training activities at and around municipal airports, military and civilian air traffic often had difficulty sharing the increasingly crowded skies. The problems caused by trying to use municipal airports as both military and civilian airfields created many of the conditions that led to the USAAF seeking to lease entire municipal airports (rather than just space on them) or purchase fields for exclusive military use. Before the outbreak of war, the Air Corps suggested a number of potential answers to the problems. It recommended that civilian operations at airports being used by the military be limited "to scheduled air liners and aircraft equipped with two-way radio." The Air Corps also explored the idea of using CAA and WPA funds to develop alternative airports for use by civilian air traffic. In February, 1941, the Air Corps announced that "its tactical units would be located on municipal airports only when they could be leased in their entirety together with adjacent building area." Training fields and depots, it declared, should be government owned.[19] The military was not always able to follow its own policy recommendations, but what became clear was that the nation's municipal airports would play a significant role in the development of military airpower. In return, cities would receive for the wartime service of their airports a certain measure of benefits, at least in terms of infrastructure improvements.

Even at airports where the Air Corps/USAAF leased only a portion of the field, major improvements and expansion came in the wake of the increased military activity. For example, Atlanta's municipal airport had hosted Army Air Corps reserve training units since 1930. During the 1930s the Air Corps constructed hangars and other buildings to house the reserve flyers. As war approached, Atlanta's airport received DLAND funds to extend two runways and to build two new runways. In early 1941 the Air Corps also leased additional land adjacent to its facilities on the airport and undertook a major building project that included construction of a parking apron, taxiways, streets, and troop housing. During the war, the USAAF continued to lease a small section of the field. That section became the Atlanta Army Air Base. By 1944 Atlanta's municipal airport had benefited from $1.4 million in federal government spending on improvements. With the end of the war, the airport received possession of seven and a half acres of land that had been used by the military, the parking apron built by the military, as well as one of its metal hangars. That metal hangar, following a rather extensive conversion process, served as the municipal airport's first postwar terminal building. The airport also benefited from the "heavy-duty power station and water mains" the military had constructed on the field.[20]

Throughout 1942 the USAAF continued to lease all or portions of municipal airports for military use. As noted, it had also purchased a few airports. Beginning in late 1942 and primarily in 1943, the USAAF began to "draft" municipal airports into the military service, transforming them—or at least sections of them, as in the Atlanta example—into Army Air Bases "for the duration." Most of these wartime bases reverted to municipal control (and, hence, municipal financial responsibility) after the war. Not all did, however. A number of municipal airports ended up as "career" military air bases. These included Charleston Air Force Base, Davis-Monthan Air Force Base, Hanscom Air Force Base, McConnell Air Force Base, Myrtle Beach Air Force Base, Norton Air Force Base, Pease Air Force Base, and Richards-Gebaur Air Force Base.[21] Another example, this one involving the Navy, was Floyd Bennett Field. As noted in chapter 4, the Navy purchased New York City's first municipal airport in early 1942. Floyd Bennett Field, renamed Naval Air Station, New York, housed a variety of military units throughout the war. The Navy continued to use the field, redesignated Floyd Bennett Municipal Airport after 1946, as a naval air reserve training facility after the war. The field also housed commercial flight operations. In 1974, ownership transferred to the Department of the Interior and Floyd Bennett Field is currently a national park site.[22] Many municipal airports, however, served during the war as Army Air Fields and, like millions of soldiers, sailors and airmen, with the coming of peace reverted to civilian status.[23] Municipal airports drafted into military service as air bases included those in Los Angeles, Milwaukee, and Dayton, Ohio.

The city of Los Angeles embarked on a major airport expansion program in 1940. The coming of war, however, brought the projects, including the construction of a new administration building and terminal complex, to a halt. Military air activity soon dominated. In January, 1943, the government took over the management of the airport "for the duration." Both Army and Navy units operated out of Los Angeles Municipal Airport, and it became a major delivery point for aircraft produced by North American, Douglas, and other California-based manufacturers. The airport reverted to civilian control following the war and by December, 1946, Los Angeles Municipal Airport enjoyed the regularly scheduled service of five airlines—TWA, American, United, Pan American, and Western Airlines.[24]

The Milwaukee area's primary airport (owned by the county rather than the city)[25] was the Milwaukee County Airport, renamed General Mitchell Field in 1941. In 1940 the airport had became the home of a National Guard observation squadron. The location of the Guard unit brought the first of the military sponsored improvements to the airport. The military spent $450,000 to build a joint administration building/hangar for the unit. During 1940 the airport also received DLAND funds to extend the runways and to improve lighting and drainage. In April, 1942, by which time the guard unit had been called to active duty and had left General Mitchell Field, the USAAF selected the site as a training base for the 10th Troop Carrier Group. The following month the Milwaukee County Board authorized the use of General Mitchell Field by the USAAF. Later that same year, the military funded projects on the site, including the construction of barracks and additional runway improvements. The 10th Troop Carrier Group left Milwaukee in October, 1942, but by March, 1943, another Air Transport Command unit had moved to General Mitchell Field and began using it as its training base. The military continued to fund improvements, including the construction of more barracks and a wider airplane parking apron. The USAAF officially designated General Mitchell Field as an Army Air Base on June 15, 1943. Under USAAF use the facility was known as Billy Mitchell Field. By that time the airport-turned-air-base housed an officers' mess and club as well as a new seventy-five-bed hospital. Other Air Transport Command units, especially those from the Ferrying Division, used Billy Mitchell Field throughout 1943 and 1944, and the USAAF added to the list of improvements at the field a post exchange, a gymnasium, warehouses, and a cold storage plant. Military use of the field began to wind down in mid-1944. In August, 1944, the base was placed on inactive status, and the last of the military units left in January, 1945. Civilian commercial activity resumed at Billy Mitchell Field by later in 1945.[26] The Army, however, apparently did not return full control of Billy Mitchell Field to Milwaukee County until February, 1948, at which time the airport once again became General Mitchell Field.[27]

As early as May, 1941, the military began to work on plans to transform the Dayton Municipal Airport into a modification center. Modification centers served as important steps in the process of mass producing aircraft and getting them to battlefields around the world as quickly as possible.[28] Construction of the modification center at the Dayton airport began in November, 1942, and was completed in June, 1943. At that time, management of the airport transferred from the city to Northwest Airlines, which had the contract to operate the modification center. Under the contract Northwest was responsible for maintaining the airport facilities, servicing and repairing the aircraft used by the Accelerated Service Test Branch, which moved to the field in July, 1943, and modifying aircraft. In June, 1943, the Dayton Municipal Airport was renamed the Northwest-Vandalia Modification Center No. 11. Construction completed at the airport in order to transform it into a modification center included hangars, engineering shops, administration buildings, and a new CAA control tower, as a small number of commercial and private aircraft continued to use part of the field throughout the war. The modification center also boasted of a dispensary, firehouse, gasoline farm, and housing, first for civilian employees of the modification center and then for military personnel.[29]

Dayton Municipal Airport's service as a modification center was short-lived, however. Very quickly the USAAF expressed dissatisfaction with Northwest's management of the facilities. Also, the work of the Accelerated Service Test Branch soon became the chief activity at the field. As a result of both the dissatisfaction with Northwest and the activities of the Accelerated Service Test Branch, the USAAF decided in late 1943 to convert the modification center into a sub-base of nearby Wright Field. The conversion of the center into Dayton Army Air Field was complete by late February, 1944.[30]

In August, 1945, the USAAF began planning for the end of operations at Dayton Army Air Field. The Accelerated Service Test Branch moved to Wright and Patterson Fields[31] by the end of September. During October and November the remaining military units at the field prepared either to move or deactivate. On December 15, 1945, Dayton Army Air Field temporarily became part of the newly designated Army Air Forces Technical Base (consisting of Wright Field, Patterson Field, Clinton County Army Air Field, and Dayton Army Air Field). However, by January 18, 1946, the city of Dayton and the USAAF completed their negotiations and Dayton Army Air Field was transferred back to the city of Dayton. The last of the military and civilian personnel of Dayton Army Air Field left by January 22, 1946.[32]

Between DLAND funds and additional spending by the military, a large number of America's municipal airports had gained significant improvements from 1940 until the end of World War II. When these airports reverted to fully civilian use, cities (or in the case of Milwaukee, counties) found themselves in possession of much expanded and improved facilities. While many cities stood to benefit, a few—especially smaller cities—discovered that they had airport facilities far in excess of both their needs and their ability to afford even routine maintenance.[33] The return to local control meant that cities once again potentially faced full responsibility for the costs of maintaining, operating, and improving their airports. For the most part, though, cities looked forward to a return to commercial operations at their improved airports. In addition to those cities regaining their airports, a number of cities also acquired entirely new airports as many World War II bases, especially training bases, were declared surplus.

The Spoils of War

With the end of hostilities, cities across the country began to see what today might be called a "peace dividend" in the form of new and/or improved municipal airports. In nearly every state, military activity (USAAF or Navy/Marine Corps) had necessitated the construction of improvements at municipal airports or the construction of new air fields that, with the end of the war, were declared surplus and available to local communities. Just as Florida, Texas, and California had the largest number of military airfields during the war, so they also had the largest numbers of cities claiming or reclaiming airports and airfields no longer needed by the military. However, examples of cities benefiting from military air activity during the war could be found in nearly every state.

Like Los Angeles, Milwaukee, and Dayton, many cities reclaimed their municipal airports. Newark, New Jersey, lost the battle of the airports between it and New York City once LaGuardia opened for business in late 1939. During World War II, the Newark airport, which closed temporarily in both 1940 and 1941, became Newark Army Air Field. It served as a base of operations for East Coast defense and as an air depot. The USAAF expanded the facilities and once the war was over turned it back over to the city of Newark.[34] Shortly thereafter, Newark Airport came under the jurisdiction of the New York Port Authority. Municipal airports at a number of other cities, large and small, were also drafted into service during the war, returning to their municipal owners after the war much improved.[35]

Raleigh-Durham, North Carolina, was in the process of building a new municipal airport in 1941 when the USAAF took control of the unfinished airport and completed its construction. As Raleigh-Durham Army Air Base, it became operational in May, 1943. The USAAF used it for training but also allowed for the very limited use of the field for civilian commercial traffic. The city gained ownership of the now completed airport in 1948. In another example, even before the war, Niagara Falls Municipal Airport housed the facilities of the Bell Aircraft Corporation. After Pearl Harbor, the U.S. government closed the airport to civilian traffic, and Bell Aircraft used it exclusively as a test field throughout the war. It also housed a small military camp before reverting to civilian uses after 1945.[36]

While a number of cities regained their municipal airports in the postwar years, a number of other cities acquired new municipal airports in the form of military airfields built during the war and declared surplus after 1945.[37] Midland, Texas, and Spokane, Washington, offered examples of this pattern. Both the US-AAF and the Navy found uses for Midland's prewar municipal airport, Sloan Field, during the war, but both withdrew from the field in 1946. However, Sloan Field did not resume its earlier career as the city's airport. During the war the US-AAF built Midland Army Air Field, a training base for bombardiers and navigators while Sloan Field served as an auxiliary field for Midland AAF. When the Army declared Midland AAF surplus, it, rather than Sloan Field, was developed into the city's postwar municipal airport. Similarly, in Spokane, Washington, its prewar municipal airport, Felts Field, served as a bomber training base during the war. Six miles southwest of the city, however, the USAAF purchased a small airport known as Sunset Field and during the war built it up into a large air base known as Geiger Field. After the war Felts Field became Spokane's secondary airport as Geiger Field eventually evolved into Spokane International Airport.[38]

Pittsburgh, Pennsylvania, also gained a new airport in the postwar period as the result of leaving behind its old airport in favor of a field developed by the military. However, the field that Pittsburgh and Allegheny County developed into what is now the Pittsburgh International Airport was far less developed than Midland AAF or Geiger AAF.

Pittsburgh's original airport, Rogers Field, proved inadequate within a very short time. It was replaced in the mid-1920s by Bettis Field, which also quickly demonstrated its shortcomings. In 1928 the Aero Club of Pittsburgh, still a major player in airport development in that city, and the Chamber of Commerce invited Walter O. Snyder of the Department of Commerce's Aeronautics Branch to help them pick a new location for an airport. He selected a site in West Mifflin, eight miles southeast of downtown Pittsburgh. The voters of the city approved a bond issue, and, with matching funds from Allegheny County, the Allegheny County Airport was constructed. It served as Pittsburgh's major airport from its dedication in September, 1931, until the early 1950s. In the immediate postwar period, however, Allegheny County Airport proved incapable of handling the increased air traffic coming into the city. County commissioners spearheaded a plan to convert a military stopover field constructed near Moon Township (twelve miles west of downtown Pittsburgh) into a new, modern facility. Construction began in July, 1946, and Greater Pittsburgh Airport opened in 1952 with service provided by TWA, Capital, Northwest, All American, and Eastern airlines. Allegheny County Airport remained open and serves as a reliever field for Pittsburgh International Airport.[39]

Perhaps the best-known example of a city transforming a former military field into its major airport involved the city of Chicago. Just as in the Pittsburgh case, though, Chicago would have to wait several years before its new municipal airport would be fully ready for use. Chicago's existing municipal airport was used extensively during the war by the Army Air Forces and the Navy while remaining a municipal airport. Built originally in 1926, Chicago Municipal Airport, located only nine miles from the city's famed Loop, showed signs of being incapable of handling the projected increase in future air traffic as early as 1941, even after doubling in size. In 1944, Chicago Mayor Edward J. Kelly initiated a program to construct a second airport for the city, one that he hoped would allow Chicago to retain its position as a great air center of the nation, even the world. Chicago voters approved a $15 million bond issue in 1945. The following year the city selected Orchard Place Airport, built by the government in 1942 for use by the nearby Douglas Aircraft plant as the best site for its new airport. The government declared the airport surplus in 1946 and deeded one thousand acres to the city. A civilian airport then opened on the site known initially as both Douglas Field and Chicago Orchard Airfield. Over the next few years the city of Chicago purchased an additional six thousand acres. In 1949, Chicago renamed its original municipal airport Midway Airport, in honor of the Battle of Midway, and named its new airport O'Hare Field, in memory of Medal of Honor winner Edward "Butch" O'Hare, a Navy ace killed in action in the South Pacific. Activity at O'Hare remained low for a number of years, however. When Chicago first acquired the new field it lacked facilities for passengers and did not yet enjoy easy access to and from the city. Further, the military continued to use the field, especially during the Korean War. In addition, the city was busy building a third airport near the downtown and waterfront known as Meigs Field. The newly renamed Midway Airport remained the city's main airport well into the late 1950s. Gradually, though, the momentum shifted to the larger O'Hare. Following the election of Mayor Richard J. Daley in 1955, the airport witnessed the construction of new runways, access roads, and a new control tower. In 1955 only four airlines served O'Hare. By the following year, 17 operated out of the new airport. Then in 1959 United Airlines moved half its flights from Midway to O'Hare, and the following year the Northwest Expressway (now the Kennedy Expressway) opened between the city and the airport. By 1962 almost all of the major airlines had moved their operations from Midway to O'Hare.[40]

Whether the military used all or part of a municipal airport and whether the military or civilian authorities managed the airport during the war, municipal airports throughout the country benefited from wartime spending for infrastructure improvements. After the war, cities found themselves in possession of new or newly improved airports. Yet, one thing remained the same in the prewar as well as the postwar period: airports were expensive. Even though cities gained a number of improvements to their airports at little or no cost to them during the war, maintaining those airports and continuing to improve them in the wake of postwar demands would cost money. As early as 1943, cities across the country began to think about how to plan for their postwar airports, and they began to turn to Washington for a permanent postwar federal airport funding act to continue to help them shoulder the burden.

Boosterism and Planning for the Postwar "Air Age"

In January, 1943, the *American City* published an article looking at "Municipal Progress since 1909." One small section dealt with airports. It detailed the rapid growth of the number of municipal airports in the United States and stated that future growth in the aviation industry was "beyond serious exaggeration." The article encouraged cities to "awaken to their opportunity to develop further this new municipal utility after the war."[41] Cities, apparently, hardly needed to hear that advice as they continued to believe in the promise of the new "air age" suggested by the article. As noted above, cities very quickly took advantage of the opportunities provided by the war to build, expand, or otherwise improve their airports. In addition to the patriotism during the war evidenced in municipal participation in wartime programs and in the postwar airport planning, airport boosterism reminiscent of the 1920s, some of it expressed by CAA officials, helped support local demands for additional airport funding after the war. Given the experience cities had with airports in the 1920s and 1930s, it was interesting how quickly they returned to the optimistic boosterism of the past. Further, much of the planning focused on airports serving private flyers, demonstrating the continued hold of the winged gospel.

In June, 1945, the *American City* published an article strongly encouraging all cities to participate in the exciting world of air travel. The article was reminiscent of those from the early 1920s and seemed almost willfully to disregard the experience most cities had had with airports. All cities had a chance to benefit from "skyways of tomorrow." The only way the cities could take advantage of the opportunities, however, was to provide a municipal airport. The article suggested that the cost of constructing an airport was relatively low, "no more than [the cost] of a few miles of highway now serving your town." And the airport would link your city "with the skyways of the post-war world." Further, if cities planned their airports well, "future revenues from rentals and concessions [might] ultimately make the investment a profitable one." If nothing else, the article asserted that it would cost "nothing to organize an aviation committee of say 12 persons of rather diverse experience with a common determination to develop the facts and make recommendations toward the long-time welfare of their town." Then, if the committee determined the need for an airport or airpark, the city could draw on a number of sources for information, including the CAA, on how best to plan for their participation in the coming "air age."[42]

Robert W. F. Schmidt, superintendent of airports, Sixth Region, CAA, echoed the 1920s booster argument that a city which failed to provide for air travel in the postwar period would be like the nineteenth-century cities that failed to provide for rail traffic. He further stated that as each new form of transportation replaced the previous, cities that failed to adopt the new form of transportation found themselves bypassed, many becoming ghost towns. Airplanes, he suggested, had the potential to replace automobiles, at least for some kinds of travel, because the airplane promised to be a safer form of transportation than the automobile. While such a future might be hard to image, he nonetheless strongly urged cities at least to begin the process of studying their airport needs and, upon identifying a need for an airport, to begin the process of airport planning. In bold letters, the author asserted: "A community's future position may depend upon its airport planning today. Failure to provide airport facilities may not necessarily mean another ghost town, but it is too big a chance to take."[43]

Many of the articles focused on postwar planning echoed some of the planning ideas of the 1930s. Articles appeared in both aviation and planning-related journals promoting the idea that cities might have to build systems of specialized airports in order to handle the postwar air traffic. More commonly expressed, though, was the need to build small airports for private and general aviation traffic. Enthusiasm for the winged gospel may have often been in short supply among an urban electorate asked to vote for airport bond issues during the 1930s, but even into the 1940s many people (planners, engineers, civic leaders, and, significantly, postwar CAA administrator Theodore P. Wright) envisioning the future of aviation still held tight to the dream of the widespread use of small aircraft for personal travel. Much of the wartime and early postwar literature on airport planning focused on meeting the needs of the private pilot.

William Burden, special aviation assistant to the secretary of commerce, estimated that by 1950 there would be approximately 441,000 private aircraft operating in the United States. Major Albert Mayer, a New York architect who served in the Army Corps of Engineers, predicted a "large volume of private flying" owing to "the many thousands of returning pilots" after the end of hostilities. And planners in the Minneapolis-St. Paul metropolitan area, who produced a plan for an extensive system of airports for the Twin Cities, foresaw an even greater use of private aircraft. They argued that aviation authorities estimated that "10 percent of present automobile owners today will be future [aircraft] owners." If true, that meant their area soon would need airport and hangar space for 25,000 aircraft. Their plan for the Minneapolis-St. Paul area included the construction of "20 to 40 additional fields for private flying."[44] The hopeful and wildly optimistic dreams of those still holding to the winged gospel led to a concentration on planning for postwar airparks.

An airpark was basically a small airport, similar to what the CAA after 1944 termed Class 1 or Class 2,[45] serving primarily private flyers. Those developing plans for postwar airparks believed that private flying would expand dramatically after the war and that small, simple, and inexpensive airparks should be available in cities and towns all across the country. As Don Forbes of Cessna Aircraft, a manufacturer of personal aircraft, argued in an article in February, 1944, just as good roads allowed the widespread adoption of the automobile, airparks would allow personal aircraft to reach their "fullest utility." Forbes envisioned airparks serving everywhere from a small community, which might have one airpark, to a large city, which could have a number of airparks located in and around it, and from large industrial plants to pleasure resorts. And he believed that they could be built "at very little expense." The airparks he envisioned covered no more than twenty acres and had sod runways. He concluded that cities could "assure their place in the aerial world" by "establishing suitable landing areas close to the business and residential areas."[46]

The journal *Western Flying* took up the subject of airparks as part 6 of a whole series of articles it published on "Airports for the West" in 1944 and 1945. The airparks described in *Western Flying* were a bit more complex than those envisioned by Don Forbes. These airparks were either Class 1 or Class 2 airports. A Class 1 airport had runways from 1,800 to 2,700 feet in length; a Class 2, between 2,700 and 3,700 feet. The airparks could have either one or two runways. Runway surfaces would depend on soil conditions and the budget but ideally would be either sod or macadam. Those planning the facility should take care, the article noted, to ensure obstacle-free approaches and runways oriented to the most favorable wind directions. Use of the airpark would be limited to private fliers. Hangar space should be available on the field for both planes based at the airpark and transient traffic. The airparks could serve to beautify their areas if also provided with "well-planned landscaping." And, harkening back to the 1930s when ideas for transforming airports into social centers were current, airparks could additionally be of value to pilots and the local community if they also contained "badminton and tennis courts, lawn bowling greens, archery ranges and, of course, the ultimate swimming pool." While airparks could be developed by private interests, the *Western Flying* article suggested that they were best built and maintained by city governments. Airparks were not viewed "as the soundest investment for private capital."[47]

The *Western Flying* article on planning airparks in early 1945 seemingly put a damper on the enthusiasm of Forbes's earlier article by suggesting that airparks would be no more able to support themselves than any other type of airport. Another article in early 1946, however, suggested that airparks could be self-supporting. It told the story of Edwin Whiteman, a California manufacturer, and his effort to build a profit-making airpark at Pacoima in California's San Fernando Valley. Whiteman had made his money producing concrete finishing equipment. Unhappy with the service he received at small airports while traveling on business, Whiteman first attempted to enter the airport business in 1944. That first venture proved unsuccessful, but in June, 1945, Whiteman was ready to try again. With $200,000 to invest, he purchased 67 acres near the San Fernando Road in Pacoima. There he built an airpark with a 3,200-foot macadam-surfaced runway. In early 1946 he had under construction a large maintenance/storage hangar and sixteen hangars for personal aircraft storage. The airpark would generate revenue by charging for tie-down (outdoor parking space for aircraft affording anchors and ropes for holding the aircraft in place) or hangar space. The airpark also had its own flying school and charter service already in operation by early 1946. Whiteman also obtained dealerships "for Firestone aviation equipment and supplies and Stinson and Aeronca airplanes." He saw used plane sales as "one of the most important means of getting back the $200,000." Future plans included "an exclusive, high class Aerotel with cabins and all facilities" and a swimming pool. Riding horses could also be rented at the field.[48] The Whiteman Airpark had not yet been completed at the time of the article's publication, but it suggested that it, and other airparks like it, might thrive in the expected postwar "air age."

The numerous articles emphasizing the expected postwar expansion of private flying and suggesting plans for airparks to serve the large number of private pilots anxious to use their personal aircraft for a variety of purposes highlighted the continued hold of a certain romance about flying on the public's imagination. While there were limits as to how deeply and widely such ideas might have been held by Americans, the notion of a future in which personal aircraft would play a part was not quickly dismissed as completely impractical. Further, as will be shown, the idea of a future "air age" had enough legitimacy, at least among a core of influential aviation elites, that it helped shape the Federal Airport Act of 1946.

The Federal Airport Act

The Federal Airport Act of 1946 grew out of actions begun in the CAA and Congress in 1944. In that year the CAA submitted a report to Congress outlining a National Airport Plan. Support for some kind of federal airport funding grew through 1945 and 1946. The resulting act contained a number of interesting elements that demonstrated the many ideas shaping federal airport aid. First, the act placed great emphasis on providing for smaller airports, reflecting the anticipated postwar boom in private aviation and the strong support for private flying on the part of the CAA's administrator from 1944 until January, 1948, Theodore P. Wright. Second, the way airport aid was distributed under the act grew out of the debate over whether federal funds for airports should go directly to cities or should go to states that would then distribute the funds to cities. Cities preferred direct aid while states challenged the close link cities and the federal government forged during the New Deal. Third, although supporters of the act argued that it would create jobs—both in the construction of airports and in the manufacture of personal airplanes, the market for which would expand with the provision of a large number of smaller airports—the Federal Airport Act of 1946 did attempt to divorce airport aid from work relief and military needs. It was not entirely successful. And finally, the Congress developed the Federal Airport Act at the same time it also began to debate the need for a long-term postwar national aviation policy.

War preparedness efforts in the late 1930s had effectively shelved the civilian aviation-oriented airport plan developed by the CAA in 1939. The CAA, though, continued to provide the Congress with updated versions of that plan throughout the war years. In July, 1944, the CAA prepared its fifth annual revision of the 1939 plan. At the same time, though, one of the most vocal backers of federal aid to airports, West Virginia congressman Jennings Randolph, submitted a bill "calling for a 10-year, $100 million airport construction program." Following Randolph's action, another longtime supporter of airport aid, California congressman Clarence Lea, asked for formal recommendations from the CAA. After some delay, the CAA submitted its recommendations in November, 1944, for a ten-year, $1.25 billion program. The federal government would provide half the money with the other half coming from the states. Under the program a significant number of smaller airports would be built, benefiting private flyers, but over half the money would go toward larger Class 4 and Class 5 airports.[49]

The CAA justified the program on a number of grounds. First, it argued that "the airport construction projects met all the criteria of useful public works." In 1944 there was a fear that the end of hostilities might witness the return of depression conditions. In the long run, however, continuing in any way to tie airport aid to work relief, according to historian of the CAA John R. M. Wilson, worked against gaining the needed appropriations. Congressmen who favored the act because of its public works argument saw little need to fund the act fully when the postwar period brought prosperity rather than depression.[50]

Another argument presented in favor of federal funding continued to reflect the connection between civil airports and national defense. During the war, federal funding for airports had been justified on the grounds that they could be used for military aircraft and operations. The CAA plan, which called for the construction of a large number of small airports, too small for use by military aircraft, gave the national defense argument a new twist. Small airports supported national defense by helping protect the aircraft manufacturing industry. If private flying was truly going to boom after the war, private pilots needed airports out of which to operate their aircraft. Without the airports, the market for private aircraft might not be as great as anticipated. Aircraft manufacturing, in general, needed support going into the postwar period. By helping to create a market for private aircraft, the CAA's airport funding program was helping to support the future health of aircraft manufacturing firms. The CAA made that argument despite the fact that the firms building the larger planes that the military used or that could be converted from civilian to military use were not the same firms building small, private aircraft.[51]

Support for private flying reached the highest levels of the CAA. Administrator Theodore P. Wright, throughout his tenure from 1944 to early 1948, did what he could to support private flying. He was among those who envisioned a postwar world in which nearly a half-million small planes would fill the skies. He appointed a special assistant to deal with matters of concern to the private flyer. And when sales of personal aircraft declined dramatically in 1947, in direct contradiction to the optimistic predictions for the postwar airplane market, Wright had the CAA study the matter. He came to believe that safer, easier-to-operate aircraft, the provision of enough airports, and the eventual reduction in the price of aircraft would reverse the downward trend. However, the tensions between the needs of commercial operators—for example, more and more complex radio and navigation aids and more stringent air traffic control rules—and the interests of the private pilots proved too much for Wright to overcome. When he resigned in January, 1948, the CAA lost its most effective spokesman for the private flyer.[52] Wright, though, was able to ensure that the Federal Airport Act of 1946 looked out for the interests of the private flyer.

Congressman Jennings Randolph, who submitted the House version of what became the Federal Airport Act, also suggested other reasons for supporting a long-term federal airport funding program. He believed that such a program could and should be part of a larger program to create a formal national aviation policy dealing with "airpower as an instrument of national defense, international security, and the expansion of civil aviation." In 1945, he proposed the establishment of a commission to develop such a policy or set of policies.[53] While President Harry S Truman did not appoint his Air Policy Commission until 1947,[54] the Federal Airport Act, with its provisions for the long-term planning for a national system of airports, reflected the general feeling that the nation needed to have a coherent policy or set of policies, both on civilian and military aviation, to guide it into the future.

In addition to supporting private flying and the notion of developing a national aviation policy, the Federal Airport Act of 1946 also dealt with the way federal moneys would reach local governments for airport projects. As noted, during the 1930s, the federal government and cities forged a much closer relationship in a number of areas, including airport development. This close relationship represented a shift away from the traditional city-federal relationship in which state governments played a mediator role. After the war, in the area of airport funding, states attempted to shape the legislation so that it reflected the traditional mediator role of states. This would be in some ways an expansion of the state role in airport development. States, with few exceptions, through the enabling acts passed had given cities and/or counties the primary responsibility for constructing, operating, and maintaining airports. However, while usually not as directly active as cities in airport matters, states gradually developed a bureaucratic infrastructure for dealing with aviation matters. At first many states placed responsibility for aviation regulation and promotion within existing state bureaucracies, most usually highway, public works, or motor vehicle departments or with the secretary of state. Gradually, though, throughout the 1930s and into the 1940s, following the example of a pioneering few, more states began creating separate and independent aviation departments or commissions, and many appointed state directors of aviation. The creation of the regulatory and promotional bureaucracies, however, did not bring with it significant levels of state spending on aviation. Only a few states established separate aviation funds, though many states attempted at least to use gasoline tax revenues for aviation purposes. Nonetheless, by the time Congress began consideration of the Federal Airport Act, many state officials, based on what they saw as the growing role they were taking, believed that federal airport money, similar to federal highway money, should go to cities through the states. Cities objected citing the past lack of state aid for airports. Cities argued that federal aid should come directly to them as they, not states, had been responsible for airport development.[55]

Reflecting these opposing opinions on the role of states in airport funding, as the Federal Airport Act made its way through Congress, House and Senate versions of the final bill differed as to how airports grants would be negotiated and distributed. The Senate version favored sending the moneys "exclusively to state agencies, regardless of the state's interest in airports, financial or otherwise." The House version "neither [prohibited] nor [required] channeling the federal funds through state agencies, but [authorized] grants directly to the sponsoring government, state or local." Donoh W. Hanks Jr., the Washington representative of the American Municipal Association, saw the airport funding issue as yet another example of cities fighting to get the funding needed for a variety of tasks including housing and other public works, in addition to airports. He held that in all those areas state governments had generally shown indifference to the needs of the cities. He argued the cities found themselves with a whole array of responsibilities. In order to meet their obligations, cities needed outside help. Cities didn't care if that help came from the federal government or a state government as long as the help came. Hanks's article suggested that states generally had proved unwilling to provide cities with the needed aid while the federal government had proved increasingly willing to award the necessary grants. Therefore, he concluded, cities had to and would continue to turn to the federal government for aid.[56]

The final version of the Federal Airport Act, after difficult and drawn-out negotiations, was a compromise on the issue of how to distribute the funds. The process of arriving at the final version of the bill involved lengthy debate on two main issues. First, would the funds go to states only or could some funds go directly to cities? Second, how much funding would go to smaller airports (Class 1, Class 2, and Class 3) and how much would go to larger airports (Class 4 and Class 5)? The issues were in many ways intertwined, and efforts to resolve those differences took more than a year.

Bills creating a federal airport aid program appeared in Congress as early as 1944. Substantial movement on the issue, however, did not come until 1945 as the House and Senate held hearings to resolve the differences between the several bills introduced in each body. Most easily resolved was the issue of how large the program would be. Senator Pat McCarran of Nevada proposed a five-year,

$500 million program, and that version, the most modest of those put forth, won quick agreement. Much more difficult was deciding how much money would go to states for smaller airports and how much would go directly to sponsoring agencies (usually cities, but possibly counties or states) for larger airports. CAA administrator Wright favored giving 75 percent of the annual funds to states and 25 percent to cities. The Senate version of the bill favored a 50–50 split. Fifty percent of the funds would go to state agencies for Class 1 and Class 2 airports; 50 percent would go to sponsoring agencies for Class 3 (under this version considered a large urban airport), Class 4, and Class 5 airports. The CAA objected to the addition of Class 3 airports to those that might receive direct funding. It argued that the addition of that class of airports would require the CAA to have to deal with far too many governmental units at the local level. A version of the bill worked out in April, 1945, dictated that 65 percent of the funds would go to state agencies for Class 1, Class 2, and Class 3 airports and 35 percent would go to sponsoring agencies of Class 4 and Class 5 airports. After overcoming objections from private flyers, the railroad industry, and the military, the conference committee sent the bill to the House and Senate in late June.[57]

The conference committee had expected quick action. Neither house, however, took up the bill until September. The Senate voted on the bill on September 11, 1945, and added an amendment, sponsored by Owen Brewster, that required all funding to go through state agencies. The House passed a different version of the bill, specifically without the Brewster amendment. The Senate and the House again had to reach agreement. That proved very difficult. The Senate version dictated that all moneys go to airport projects though state agencies, unless no state agencies existed, in which case cities could apply directly for aid. The House version called for 75 percent of the funding to be set aside for states, the amount going to each state based on area and population. However, any governmental unit within a state could apply for a portion of the funding allocated to that state. The CAA administrator held 25 percent of the funds in a discretionary account that could be used "to assure that a balanced national system resulted rather than a hodgepodge of state and local fragments." The United States Conference of Mayors attended the hearings to argue in favor of aid to cities. State aviation officials argued for aid to states. The CAA favored the compromise worked out in April, 1945. Unable to come to any agreement, the hearings stretched into early 1946. Finally, Senator Pat McCarran led an effort to resolve the issues in March, 1946. With Brewster still vowing to oppose any compromise, the conferees settled on the House version of the bill and sent it to Congress. The House voted in favor of the bill in April; the Senate, in May. The act created a seven-year, $500 million program.[58]

The Federal Airport Act of 1946, though it did allow for cities to apply directly for aid, still favored smaller airports. The act allowed for a 50 percent match of federal funds for local funds in the construction of Class 1, Class 2, and Class 3 airports. Class 4 and Class 5 airport projects could also receive matching funds, but the rules developed concerning larger airports imposed important limitations. In airport projects at Class 4 or Class 5 airports costing up to $5 million, a 50 percent matching of funds would be available. However, the larger the project, the smaller the match available. The percentage of matching funds decreased by 5 percent for every $1 million in cost over $5 million and up to $11 million. Thus, for very large airport projects, costing $11 million or more, the matching funds available would be limited to 20 percent. Under certain conditions, though, the CAA administrator might be able to help fund such an airport project out of the discretionary fund.[59] In addition, the act required that "two months prior to the close of each fiscal year, the [CAA] Administrator . . . submit to the Congress a request for authority to undertake during the next fiscal year those of the projects for the development of class 4 and larger airports."[60] The Federal Airport Act of 1946 did not pass in time for the CAA to meet that requirement for fiscal year 1947. Therefore, all the money appropriated for 1947 went to smaller airports.[61]

Not only did cities find themselves at a disadvantage when it came to their share of federal funding, but states refused to surrender on the issue of whether cities had to go through a state agency in order to get funding. When the act passed in 1946 only a few states had laws mandating that cities go through state agencies. Not only did Owen Brewster continue to fight the issue in Congress, but in 1947 the Council of State Governments developed a "model bill" that "[prohibited] direct federal grants to municipalities for airports and [required] the channeling of all such grants through state agencies." That action met with strong opposition from the American Municipal Association. As it saw the situation, state governments, having lost the battle in Congress, were now trying to find another way to gain some control over federal funding going to cities. The American Municipal Association especially objected to the creation of a situation where the states would try to gain control over federal-municipal airport projects without providing any share of the total cost.[62] Despite strong municipal opposition, twenty-one states had passed such legislation by 1949.[63]

Both the long struggle behind its passage and Congress's actions concerning appropriations for carrying out the act in the late 1940s and well into the 1950s indicated the limits of the winged gospel. Certainly, a core of "true believers," especially CAA administrator Wright, had managed to shape the act to fit some of the visions of the winged gospel. The fact that the act favored small airports over larger airports was a clear example of that. However, Congress's reluctant approach to airport aid in the first place and its subsequent reluctance fully to fund the act demonstrated that while many in the nation may have been "airminded," a majority of congressmen were not necessarily among them. When you compare federal aid to airports to federal aid to road construction, it was clear that most in Washington were far more "auto-minded" than they were "airminded."

With the Federal Airport Act of 1946 cities received some, but certainly not all, of what they desired. Under certain conditions cities could apply directly for federal matching funds for airport construction. The total amount of aid they could receive, however, was limited. Further, Congress never appropriated full funding for the act. From the beginning the amount appropriated was lower than that called for under the act, and the amount appropriated per year continued to fall below the amount of spending authorized well into the 1950s. For fiscal year 1947, Congress appropriated $42.75 million. Under the act, which called for spending $500 million over seven years, approximately $71 million was authorized per year. In 1948 the total appropriated dropped to $30.4 million. Congress increased spending somewhat in 1949 and 1950, but appropriations dropped significantly during the Korean War, falling to only $10.2 million in 1953. (In 1950, Congress did extend the life of the act from seven to twelve years.) Defense spending during the Korean War, though, included $500 million for airports with military usefulness. As during the late 1930s through the mid-1940s, military utility seemed to be a very important factor in acquiring large-scale funding for airport aid.[64]

Finally, airports, though important, did not rank as the top priority of the CAA in the postwar era. In 1946, William A. Burden, then assistant secretary of commerce, addressed the Third New England Conference for Aviation on the role and responsibilities of the CAA. He gave the speech in May, 1946, the same month Congress passed the Federal Airport Act. He hardly mentioned airports. Instead, he noted that the CAA's "largest activity [was] the design, operation, and construction of the basic network of radio navigation facilities known as the Federal airways system." In the late 1940s and early 1950s, the CAA had to ensure the upgrading of the nation's airways in light of the development of new and advanced communication and navigation technology. Burden also mentioned the issue of safety, particularly on the nation's airlines. An issue throughout the history of commercial aviation, aircraft accidents in the late 1940s and early 1950s, especially a cluster of accidents around the Newark Airport in 1951, forced the CAA to concentrate a great deal of time and energy on assuring the American public that airline flight was safe. The CAA also had to regulate and inspect the products of the nation's aircraft manufacturers.[65] Airport construction was only one of many responsibilities of the CAA. However, the Federal Airport Act of 1946, extended several times and generally in effect until 1970, authorized the CAA and then its successor organization, the Federal Aviation Administration, to help cities construct and improve their airports and set the pattern for federal airport aid to cities.

Conclusion

The coming of World War II brought with it the first direct federal aid to cities for airports. The temporary DLAND program, initiated in 1940, provided moneys for airport improvements and created a precedent for future airport aid. The Federal Airport Act of 1946 created a more permanent structure for federal aid for airports. It, however, turned out to be much less than what cities had desired. The funding was limited, and states managed to assert themselves, to a certain extent, as mediators between the national government and local governments. What was clearly established by 1946, though, was the idea that local governments, especially cities (but sometimes counties) would be responsible for the nation's airports. Yet they would not have to bear the burden alone, as the national government would provide a certain level of aid. It was an outcome that had been worked out over nearly a generation. It has remained the pattern for airport construction and development to the present.

Conclusion

Between 1919 and 1947 a number of factors came together to produce the working definition of municipal airports in the United States as locally and publicly owned and managed facilities. Their maintenance, improvement, and operation, though, also involved federal funding and regulation. The final sense of what municipal airports were and how they would work and be funded came about because of the interaction of local and federal actions and policies, urban boosterism and aviation enthusiasm, and the basic economics of airport operations. This early period in airport history was an important formative time.

Having traced the significant trends and developments between 1919 and 1947, one can draw a few additional conclusions. First, throughout this formative period airports must be viewed as peripheral. Though they occasionally, but briefly, captured center stage at both the local and national level of politics, they did not rank as a major overriding concern of government at any level during this period. As both Brodherson and Karsner suggested, airports did not became a major part of the lives of Americans or a truly vital part of the urban infrastructure until the post-World War II period. Second, as a result of the formative period, the general airport landscape of the United States was in place. For the most part, by the late 1940s, cities had developed those airports that serve as their primary airports today or they had available to them surplus military airfield sites they used as a base for building their postwar primary airports. And finally, just as the relationships between cities, their airports, and the federal government evolved during the years up to 1947, they would continue to evolve to the present.

Until relatively recently historians failed to pay much attention to airports. One might argue that airports paled beside pilots and planes in their ability to inspire the historical imagination. That, though not without some truth, provides a very unsatisfactory explanation for the relative lack of airport studies. Perhaps more to the point, historians and the questions they ask tend to reflect the major concerns and issues of their times. Airports did not play a major role in the lives of most Americans until very recently. It was only after the introduction of the jet aircraft and, more important, the deregulation of aviation in the late 1970s that travel by airplane and, thus, trips to the airport became parts of the lives of a broad segment of the American public. With the explosion of air travel over the past two decades, air travel and airports became truly familiar. Further, as Karsner in particular pointed out, airports really did not have a significant economic impact on their cities until the 1950s.

During the 1920s and through the 1940s airport boosters promised great economic benefits from airport development, but their great expectations were seldom met. Air travel, though exciting in theory to many, in reality was limited to the few. Those who flew as passengers early on in the Ford Tri-Motor and later in the ubiquitous DC-3 were for the most part well-to-do people traveling for business purposes. Air travel and airports were not significant to the lives of the vast majority of Americans during this formative period.

Many cities had their aviation champions for whom airport development was personally quite important. In most cases they were able to ensure enough attention from local governments to promote airport projects successfully. They were aided in this by both urban boosterism and the significant aviation enthusiasm of the day. At times of crucial council votes or bond elections and at both groundbreaking and dedication ceremonies, airports could capture the headlines. Any major controversies during the construction process could also bring an airport to the attention of the public. For the most part, though, the development of an airport simply did not rank among the most significant and ongoing concerns or issues facing cities at this time. Accommodating the automobile through road and bridge construction, providing other basic services such as water, electricity, and sewers, struggling with the housing problem, and assuring adequate police and fire protection all proved of far greater and more lasting significance to city leaders than the issues surrounding airports and air travel. At the national level, the Great Depression and World War II took center stage. Airports only figured in national politics to the extent that they first offered an outlet for relief funds and second were viewed as important to national defense and war-preparedness. Today, with the more important transportation and economic development roles played by airports, they are more likely to capture a greater and more sustained share of the attention of city leaders, federal officials, and the general public. Until the postwar period, though, airports must be viewed as peripheral.[1]

In addition, during the formative period the airport landscape was established both locally and nationally. A large number of the major municipal airports today date back to the 1920s and 1930s. Examples covered in this study include airports in the New York City area (Newark and LaGuardia), Boston, Philadelphia, Washington, D.C., Atlanta, Cleveland, Dallas, Dayton, Omaha, Los Angeles, San Diego, and Oakland. A number of other cities used surplus military fields after World War II. These include Cincinnati, Pittsburgh, Chicago, and Spokane. New York's third airport, Idlewild (now JFK) was under construction by the early 1940s and completed in 1948. Very few completely new airports were built at the nation's major cities after the late 1940s. Important exceptions include Washington, D.C.'s Dulles Airport, the Dallas-Fort Worth Airport, Kansas City's International Airport, and Denver's new airport. For the most part, the land that would be used for the nation's primary airports had been identified as land for airport use by the late 1940s.

Finally, just as the relationships between cities and their airports and the federal government evolved between 1918 and 1947, so they would continue to evolve and change in the postwar period. In 1947, Springfield, Illinois, received attention in the *American City* for its new airport authority. Created as a result of an Illinois law passed in 1945, the Springfield Airport Authority had the responsibility to build and operate an airport. It had the power "to levy an annual tax for operation and maintenance and to issue bonds secured by the taxes and bonds secured by operating revenue."[2] In the postwar period, cities, following state action, increasingly turned their airports over to special authorities created specifically to operate and maintain airports. In some cases, airports were turned over to other existing extra-governmental bodies. For example, the Port Authority of New York took responsibility for that area's airports in the late 1940s. As airports became increasingly important to cities, they moved away from direct control of their airports and toward control by special extra-governmental bodies.

Federal regulation of airports increased in the postwar period. Regulations involved safety in the skies around airports as well as on the airport grounds. Airport funding also saw changes. In 1970 Congress passed the Airport and Airway Development and Revenue Acts. Until 1970, funding for airports depended on congressional appropriations. The 1970 acts created an airport trust fund. The fund was fed by taxes on airline tickets, air cargo, fuel, and the airlines. As air travel grew, the fund would grow. While the creation of the fund did not result in the construction of many new major airports, it did allow for the upgrading of the air traffic control systems at airports with the aim of improving safety.[3] However, creation of the fund did not guarantee increased or even steady spending because Congress often refused to release moneys, as the surplus in the trust fund could be used to "balance the budget." Airport politics changed, yet remained interesting and contentious.

Though airports did not become significant to the lives of a broad segment of Americans until after 1947, the formative period was important nonetheless. As a result of the interaction between cities, states, and the federal government, the way the nation's airports would be built, operated, and maintained was basically worked out. Where the nation's major airports would be both within the local landscape and within the national system of transportation was established. Many of the basic ideas city planners would use to help cities plan for and make use of their airports were articulated. And airports gained a role in national defense, one that they continue to play to this day. As the centennial of manned, powered flight approaches, it is clear that airports will play an increasingly important role in the lives of Americans and in the economies of their cities and their nation.

Notes

Introduction

1. Two recent dissertations in particular included a discussion of the Air Commerce Act of 1926. Both focused on the debate at the federal level over the funding of airports and the adoption of the dock concept that essentially made localities wanting airports responsible for their construction. Both also emphasized that the adoption of the dock concept meant that local governments would be responsible for building airports. As will be shown, however, while local governments did play an increasing role in financing airports, local private interests proved important as well. Local governments did not become to a great extent exclusively responsible for airport construction until the 1930s. See David Phillip Brodherson, "What Can't Go Up Can't Come Down: The History of American Airport Policy, Planning, and Design," Ph.D. diss., Cornell University, 1993, pp. 28–68, and Deborah Gwen Douglas, "The Invention of Airports: A Political, Economic, and Technical History of Airports in the United States, 1919–1939," Ph.D. diss, University of Pennsylvania, 1996, pp. 16–56.

2. See Brodherson, "What Can't Go Up Can't Come Down."

3. See Douglas, "Invention of Airports," pp. 316–477. See also Deborah G. Douglas, "Airports as Systems and Systems of Airports: Airports and Urban Development in America before World War II," in *From Airships to Airbus: The History of Civil and Commercial Aviation, Volume 1: Infrastructure and Environment*, ed. William M. Leary (Washington, D.C.: Smithsonian Institution Press, 1995), pp. 55–84.

4. See John Zukowsky, ed., *Building for Air Travel: Architecture and Design for Commercial Aviation* (Munich and New York: The Art Institute of Chicago and Prestel-Verlag, 1996). This work also has an essay by Brodherson. See David Brodherson, "'An Airport in Every City': The History of American Airport Design," pp. 67–95.

5. See Marc Dierikx and Bram Bouwens, *Building Castles of the Air: Schiphol Amsterdam and the Development of Airport Infrastructure in Europe, 1916–1996* (The Hague: Sdu Publishers, 1997).

6. See Marcus Binney, *Airport Builders* (London: John Wiley & Son Ltd., Academy Editions, 1999).

7. See Frank Robert van der Linden, "Progressives and the Post Office: Air Mail and the Creation of U.S. Air Transportation, 1926–1934," Ph.D. diss., George Washington University, 1997. See also F. Robert van der Linden, "Progressives and the Post Office: Walter Folger Brown and the Creation of United States Transportation," in *From Airships to Airbus: The History of Civil and Commercial Aviation, Volume 2: Pioneers and Operations*, ed. William F. Trimble (Washington, D.C.: Smithsonian Institution Press, 1995), 245–60. Paul Barrett also wrote an important article on federal aviation policy. His focus was on demonstrating how federal policies failed to result in effective land-use planning for airports. See Paul Barrett, "Cities and Their Airports: Policy Formation, 1926–1952," *Journal of Urban History* 14 (Nov., 1987).

8. Van der Linden, "Progressives and the Post Office: Air Mail and the Creation of U.S. Air Transportation," pp. 16–17.

9. See Richard Paul Doherty, "The Origin and Development of Chicago-O'Hare International Airport," Ph.D. diss., Ball State University, 1970, and Charles Clifton Bonwell, "Technology and the Terminal: St. Louis's Lambert Field, 1925–1974," Ph.D. diss., Kansas State University, 1975.

10. See Betsy Braden and Paul Hagan, *A Dream Takes Flight: Hartsfield Atlanta International Airport and Aviation in Atlanta* (Atlanta: Atlanta Historical Society; and Athens and London: University of Georgia Press, 1989).

11. Douglas George Karsner, "'Leaving on a Jet Plane': Commercial Aviation, Airports, and Post-industrial American Society, 1933–1970," Ph.D. diss., Temple University, 1993. See also Douglas Karsner, "Aviation and Airports: The Impact on the Economic and Geographic Structure of American Cities, 1940s–1980s," *Journal of Urban History* 23 (May, 1997): 406–36.

12. Robert P. Olislagers, *Fields of Flying: An Illustrated History of Airports in the Southwest* (Encinitas, Calif.: Heritage Media Corp., 1996).

13. In addition to the Brodherson and Douglas dissertations, for a brief official history of the adoption of the dock concept, see Ellmore A. Champie, "The Federal Turnaround on Aid to Airports, 1926–38," (Washington, D.C.: Department of Transportation, Federal Aviation Administration, Office of Management Systems, Agency Historical Staff, 1973), pp. 2–4.

14. Eric H. Monkkonen, *America Becomes Urban: The Development of U.S. Cities and Towns, 1780–1980* (Berkeley and Los Angeles: University of California Press, 1988), 158.

15. For Monkkonen's full discussion on the relationship between cities and transportation technologies see ibid., 158–81.

16. See Joseph Corn, *The Winged Gospel: America's Romance with Aviation, 1900–1950* (New York: Oxford University Press, 1983).

17. Ibid., pp. 98–102.

18. See Dominick A. Pisano, *To Fill the Sky with Pilots: The Civilian Pilot Training Program, 1939–1946* (Urbana and Chicago: University of Illinois Press, 1993).

19. For a discussion of the changing relationship between cities and the national government see Mark I. Gelfand, *A Nation of Cities: The Federal Government and Urban America, 1933–1965* (New York: Oxford University Press, 1975).

Chapter 1. Pioneer Efforts

1. See John Wood, *Airports: Some Design Elements and Future Developments* (New York: Coward-McCann, Inc., 1940).

2. Lois E. Walker and Shelby E. Wickam, *From Huffman Prairie to the Moon: The History of Wright-Patterson Air Force Base* (Washington, D.C.: Government Printing Office, 1986), pp. 3–5, 10–14, 17–54.

3. While airports were built from the beginning for both land-based and water-based aircraft, in the interests of simplicity this work will concentrate almost exclusively on facilities built for land-based craft.

4. "First Air Port in World Established at Atlantic City," *Aerial Age Weekly* 9 (Apr. 14, 1919): 235. Tucson also lays claim to the nation's first airport. In Olislager, *Fields of Flying*, Tucson's airport, known as Fisburn Field, is noted as being founded in 1915 (see p. 35). However, the official history of Tucson's Airport Authority (see n. 8) as well as War Department Documents (see ns. 5–7) indicate Tucson's city government did not take action to build a municipal airport until late 1919.

5. War Department, Air Service, Division of Military Aeronautics, *Weekly News Letter—Week Ending Saturday November 9, 1918*, Washington, D.C.: 1. [Bound copies of the *Weekly News Letter* are available in the Air Force Command History Office Library located on the Bolling AFB-Anacostia NAS complex in Washington, D.C.]

6. U.S. Air Service, *Weekly News Letter—Week Ending Saturday, November 23, 1918*, Washington, D.C.: 2.

7. U.S. Air Service, *Weekly Newsletter—Week Ending Saturday December 14, 1918*, Washington, D.C.: 3.

8. Quoted in "The Story of Tucson Airport Authority, 1948–1966, Tucson, Arizona," prepared under the direction of Charles H. Broman, A.A.E., General Manager T.A.A., Dec. 31, 1966, p. 5.

9. The municipal airport-military connection remained strong in Tucson. That first municipal field was eventually replaced in 1927 by Davis-Monthan Field, then the largest municipal airport in the country, jointly used by the city and the military until after World War II. Ibid., pp. 5–6.

10. U.S. Air Service, *Air Service News Letter* 5, no. 4 (Jan. 28, 1921): 2–3.

11. U.S. Air Service, *Air Service News Letter* 5, no. 5 (Feb. 3, 1921): 1.

12. Ibid., 1–2; Chief of Air Service, *Report of the Chief of Air Service for the Fiscal Year Ending June 30, 1921* (Washington, D.C.: Office of the Chief of Air Service, 1921), p. 44.

13. Chief of Air Service, *Annual Report of the Chief of Air Service for the Fiscal Year July 1, 1922 to June 30, 1923* (Washington, D.C.: Office of the Chief of Air Service, 1923), p. 61.

14. U.S. Air Service, *Air Service News Letter* 5, no. 5 (Feb. 3, 1921): 3.

15. Chief of U.S. Air Service, *Annual Report of the Chief of Air Service, 1921*, pp. 43–44.

16. Untitled, undated, typewritten manuscript, pp. 1–2, National Air and Space Museum Technical Files, Air Transport Series, Airports, U.S., Pennsylvania, Pittsburgh. (This document appears to be a copy of a petition or resolution drawn up by the members of the Pittsburgh Aero Club in support of their actions in establishing Rogers Field. An approximate date for the document would be late 1924.)

17. Director of Air Service, *Report of the Director of Air Service to the Secretary of War, 1920* (Washington, D.C.: Government Printing Office, 1920), pp. 48–49.

18. Chief of Air Service, *Annual Report of the Chief of Air Service for the Fiscal Year Ending June 30, 1922* (Washington, D.C.: Office of the Chief of Air Service, 1922), p. 31.

19. Untitled, undated, typewritten manuscript, pp. 1–2, National Air and Space Museum Technical Files, Air Transport Series, Airports, U.S., Pennsylvania, Pittsburgh.

20. Ibid., pp. 2–4.

21. Chief of Air Service, *Annual Report of the Chief of Air Service*, 1922, p. 31.

22. Chief of Air Corps, *Annual Report of the Chief of the Air Corps for the Fiscal Year Ending June 30, 1927* (Washington, D.C.: Office of the Chief of Air Corps, 1927), p. 35.

23. Airways Section, Training and War Plans Division, Office of the Chief of Air Service, "Airways and Landing Facilities," *Air Service Information Circular* 5, no. 404 (Mar. 1, 1923): 1–3.

24. Ibid., p. 3.

25. Ibid., pp. 3–4.

26. Ibid., p. 3.

27. Major H. C. K. Muhlenberg, "Seattle's Fine Flying Field at Sand Point," *U.S. Air Services* 9 (Feb., 1924): 33.

28. Ibid.

29. Henry Ladd Smith, *Airways: The History of Commercial Aviation in the United States* (Washington, D.C.: Smithsonian Institution Press, 1991), pp. 50–63.

30. Braden and Hagan, *Dream Takes Flight*, pp. 16–17.

31. Ibid., p. 17.

32. Ibid., pp. 23–26, 45.

33. David Young and Neal Callahan, *Fill the Heavens with Commerce: Chicago Aviation, 1855–1926* (Chicago: Chicago Review Press, 1981), pp. 83–84, 145.

34. Ibid., pp. 149–51.

35. Smith, *Airways*, p. 66.

36. Ibid., pp. 3–5; "New Landing Field at Pittsburgh," *U.S. Air Services* 10 (May, 1925): 45.

37. Arnold Knauth et al., eds., *U.S. Aviation Reports, 1928* (Baltimore: United States Aviation Reports, Inc., 1928), p. 484.

38. Joseph H. Wenneman, *Municipal Airports* (Cleveland, Ohio: Flying Review, 1931), pp. 336, 346–47, 355, 357.

39. The first of those enabling acts referred to the facilities to be allowed under them as municipal flying fields, aviation fields, or airdromes. In 1926 both the Ohio and Kentucky laws called them airports. (The Kentucky law included two different spellings—airport and air port.)

40. Knauth, *1928 United States Aviation Reports*, pp. 484–89, 495, 545, 557, 564–67, 575–77.

41. Ibid., pp. 537–39.

42. Ibid., pp. 496–98.

43. Offprint copy of "An Act Authorizing the Department of Public Works to Construct and Lease to the United States Government an Airplane Landing Field on the Property of the Commonwealth in East Boston." House No. 831, The Commonwealth of Massachusetts, 1922, National Air and Space Museum Technical Files, Air Transport, Airports, U.S., Massachusetts.

44. William P. Long, "The Development of the Boston Airport," *American City* 48 (Apr., 1933): 51–52; Wood, *Airports*, p. 43; "Report of the Committee on Post Office & Postal Facilities on the Airplane Landing Field Situation in Boston," Jan. 9, 1922, National Air and Space Museum Technical Files, Air Transport, Airports, U.S., Massachusetts.

45. Robert E. Adwers, *Rudder, Stick, and Throttle: Research and Reminiscences on Flying in Nebraska* (Omaha, Nebr.: Making History, Inc., 1994), p. 216.

46. *Annual Report of the Postmaster General for the Fiscal Year ended June 30, 1920* (Washington, D.C.: Government Printing Office, 1920), p. 58; James J. Horgan, *City of Flight: The History of Aviation in St. Louis* (Gerald, Mo.: Patrice Press, 1984), pp. 6–7; Major Albert Bond Lambert, "St. Louis Has an Aeronautical History," *U.S. Air Service* 8 (Sept., 1923): 34.

47. Horgan, *City of Flight*, pp. 8–10.

48. Ibid., pp. 11–14.

49. Smith, *Airways*, p. 66; Braden and Hagan, *Dream Takes Flight*, p. 10.

50. William M. Leary, *Aerial Pioneers: The U.S. Air Mail Service, 1918–1927* (Washington, D.C.: Smithsonian Institution Press, 1985), pp. 21–22, 25, 51, 58.

51. Committee on the Post Office and Post Roads, *Hearings before a Subcommittee of the Committee on the Post Office and Post Roads, House of Representatives, Sixty-Ninth Congress, First Session, on H.R. 4326 and H.R. 4642* (Washington, D.C.: Government Printing Office, 1926), pp. 1–9, 12–14, 27–33.

52. See, for example, Leary, *Aerial Pioneers*, pp. 113–15, 133–36, 156–57, 183–85.

53. Jerold E. Brown, *Where Eagles Land: Planning and Development of U.S. Army Airfields, 1910–1941* (New York: Greenwood Press, 1990), pp. 36–40.

54. Robert Fairbanks, "A Clash of Priorities: The Federal Government and Dallas Airport Development, 1917–1964," in *American Cities and Towns: Historical Perspectives*, ed. Joseph F. Rishel (Pittsburgh, Pa.: Duquesne University Press, 1992), p. 165.

55. See Walker and Wickam, *From Huffman Prairie to the Moon*.

56. "Municipal Landing Fields for Air Service," *American City* 21 (July, 1919): 22–23.

57. U.S. Air Service, *Air Service News Letter* 5, no. 5 (Feb. 3, 1921): 1.

58. Ibid; U.S. Air Service, *Air Service News Letter* 5, no. 6 (Feb. 15, 1921): 1–2.

59. Major-General Charles T. Menoher, Chief of the Army Air Service, "The Need for Landing Fields," in *Municipal Landing Fields and Air Ports*, ed. George Seay Wheat (New York and London: G. P. Putnam's Sons, Knickerbocker Press, 1920), pp. 1–3.

60. R. Preston Wentworth, "Have You a Little Landing Field in Your Community?" *U.S. Air Service* 4 (Aug., 1920): 12–14.

61. Archibald Black, "Air Terminal Engineering," *Landscape Architecture* 13 (July, 1923): 226–27.

62. Ibid., p. 228; Archibald Black, "Have You a Landing Field in Your Town?" *Aero Digest* 6 (Apr., 1925): 186–87.

63. For a discussion of this issue see M. Christine Boyer, *Dreaming the Rational City: The Myth of American City Planning* (Cambridge, Mass., and London: MIT Press, 1983), pp. 118–21. For an example of a city stepping in and taking over a privately provided public service once profitability became problematic see Clifton Hood, *722 Miles: The Building of the Subways and How They Transformed New York* (Baltimore and London: Johns Hopkins University Press, 1993).

64. Charles Whitnall, "Municipal Airports," *National Municipal Review* 15 (Feb., 1926): 107.

65. James M. Curley, "Boston: The Northeastern Airport," *Aeronautical Digest* 2 (Apr., 1923): 237.

66. Charles Rieman, "Chicago: The Nation's Airport," *U.S. Air Service* 8 (Feb., 1923): 27–28.

67. S. B. Eckert, "Philadelphia as a Great Airport," *Aeronautical Digest* 2 (Apr., 1923): 241.

68. Hiram Bingham, "The Most Precious Thing in the World," *U.S. Air Services* 10 (Aug., 1925): 11–14.

69. Henry Woodhouse, ed., *Textbook of Aerial Laws and Regulations for Aerial Navigation, International, National and Municipal, Civil and Military* (New York: Frederick A. Stokes Company, 1920), pp. 89, 96.

70. National Advisory Committee for Aeronautics, *Sixth Annual Report of the National Advisory Committee for Aeronautics, 1920* (Washington, D.C.: Government Printing Office, 1921), pp. 54–56.

71. Knauth, *1928 U.S. Aviation Reports*, p. 490.

72. Ibid., pp. 494–95.

73. "Connecticut's New Laws of the Air," *U.S. Air Service* 5 (June, 1921): 25–26.

74. Garland W. Powell, "The Maryland State Aviation Commission," *U.S. Air Service* 5 (Apr., 1921): 31–32.

75. Airplanes and pilots were not facing a unique situation. At about the same time states were still debating whether automobiles had to be registered in each state in which they were operated and whether drivers needed to be licensed in each state in which they drove.

76. "What Will Your Town Do?" *U.S. Air Service* 4 (Nov., 1920): 31.

77. City of Omaha, "Ordinance No. 11170," Oct. 11, 1921 [Copy in City of-Omaha Recorder's Office, City-County Building, Omaha, Nebraska].

78. Ibid.

79. Ibid. This part of the ordinance made a very early reference to zoning or regulating the height of structures of obstructions around the airport. The subject of airport zoning will be taken up in more detail in chapter 5.

80. Whitnall, "Municipal Airports," p. 105.

Chapter 2. The Era of Airport Enthusiasm, 1926–33

1. Within urban history there has been debate over whether and/or to what degree region (geographic and/or cultural) shapes urban growth, development, character, and so on. One of the most prominent proponents of a strong influence of region on cities is Carl Abbott. For a sense of his argument see Abbott, *The Metropolitan Frontier: Cities in the Modern American West* (Tucson: University of Arizona Press, 1985), and his most recent work, *Political Terrain: Washington, D.C., from Tidewater Town to Global Metropolis* (Chapel Hill and London: University of North Carolina Press, 1999), esp. 8–17. Arguing against a shaping role for region is Robert B. Fairbanks. For a sense of his argument see Fairbanks, *For the City as a Whole: Planning, Politics, and the Public Interest in Dallas, Texas, 1900–1965* (Columbus: Ohio State University Press, Urban Life and Landscape Series, 1998). Falling in between is the argument of Amy Bridges. See Bridges, *Morning Glories: Municipal Reform in the Southwest* (Princeton, N.J.: Princeton University Press, 1997).

2. See Wenneman, *Municipal Airports*, pp. 319–58.

3. Knauth, *Aviation Reports*, 1928, pp. 496–97, 535.

4. "Virginia Realizing Plan for System of Airports," *American City* 41 (July, 1929): 86; Address by Harry F. Guggenheim before the Governor's Conference, New London, Conn. July 17, 1929, (unpublished manuscript), Harry F. Guggenheim Papers (hereafter referred to as HRG Papers), Library of Congress, Box 285; Harry F. Guggenheim, "Safety in the Air" (print

of Radio Address, July 22, 1929), HFG Papers, Library of Congress, Box 285. For more detailed information on the Daniel Guggenheim Fund for the Promotion of Aeronautics see Richard P. Hallion, *Legacy of Flight: The Guggenheim Contribution of American Aviation* (Seattle and London: University of Washington Press, 1977).

5. Robert L. O'Brien, "State Control of Airports: How Massachusetts Does It," *Airports* 4 (Jan., 1930): 25–26, 55.

6. A. H. Heermance, "Miami Has an Organized System of Airports," *American City* 48 (Jan., 1933): 64.

7. U.S. Department of Commerce, Aeronautics Branch, "Construction of Airports," *Aeronautics Bulletin*, no. 2 (Apr., 1928): 2.

8. Ibid. The argument presented in this chapter suggesting a limited ability of the federal government to regulate airports stands somewhat at variance with the argument presented in Deborah Douglas's dissertation. She suggested that with the passage of the Air Commerce Act and the creation of the Aeronautics Branch the federal government immediately began asserting its role in shaping airport development to a significant degree. See Douglas, "Inventing Airports," 56–71, 76–81.

9. Wenneman, *Municipal Airports*, pp. 377–81. For another, briefer, description and discussion of the airport rating system see also Charles C. Rohlfing, *National Regulation of Aeronautics* (Philadelphia: University of Pennsylvania Press, 1931), pp. 133–38.

10. Wenneman, *Municipal Airports*, pp. 381–96.

11. Ibid., p. 375.

12. Department of Commerce, *Air Commerce Bulletin* 1, no. 16 (Feb. 15, 1930): 3–4.

13. "Why Not Compulsory Ratings for Airports?" *U.S. Air Services* 17 (Dec., 1932): 19.

14. Department of Commerce, "Airports: Types of Management, Rentals, Concessions, Field Rules," *Information Bulletin* 21, 2nd ed. (Mar. 31, 1928).

15. Department of Commerce, Aeronautics Branch, "Suggested City or County Aeronautics Ordinance and Uniform Rules for Airports," *Aeronautics Bulletin*, no. 20 (Oct. 1, 1929).

16. City of Omaha, Ordinance No. 13508, June 19, 1928 [Copy in City of Omaha Recorder's Office, City-County Building, Omaha, Nebr.]; City of Omaha, Ordinance No. 13581, Dec. 26, 1928 [Copy in City of Omaha Recorder's Office, City-County Building, Omaha, Nebr.].

17. Rohlfing, *National Regulation of Aeronautics*, pp. 129–30.

18. Charles H. Gale, "The First National Airport Conference," *Aviation* 26 (June 1, 1929): 1879.

19. Charles H. Gale, "The Second National Airport Conference," *Aviation* 28 (May 24, 1930): 1037–40.

20. Ibid., p. 1040.

21. A. T. Stewart, "Regional Aviation Conferences," *Journal of Air Law* 2 (Jan., 1931): 29–34.

22. Frank Joseph Rowe and Craig Miner, *Borne on the South Wind: A Century of Kansas Aviation* (Wichita, Kans.: Wichita Eagle and Beacon Publishing Company, 1994), pp. 57–62; O. J. Swander, "Exceptional Site, Landscaping, Lighting, and Buildings Characterize Wichita Airport," *American City* 44 (Apr., 1931): 109.

23. Swander, "Exceptional Site," p. 109; Wenneman, *Municipal Airports*, p. 330.

24. Swander, "Exceptional Site," pp. 109–10; Edwin W. Pryor, "Wichita's Municipal Airport," *Aero Digest* 18 (Apr., 1931): 192–93.

25. J. W. Brennan, "Lindbergh Field," *Aero Digest* 21 (Sept., 1932): 40–41; "City and Federal Government Cooperate in Creating Extensive Airport," *American City* 38 (Feb., 1928): 148.

26. Ibid.

27. The Board of Port Commissioners, City of Oakland, "Oakland Municipal Authority," (pamphlet, Aug., 1928), pp. 5–7, National Air and Space Museum, Air Transport Series, Airport, U.S., California.

28. Ibid., pp. 7–8.

29. G. B. Hegardt, "Development and Management of Oakland Municipal Port," *Airports* 3 (July, 1929): 17–18, 42.

30. Much of this argument was first expressed by Gerald D. Nash in *The American West in the Twentieth Century: A Short History of an Urban Oasis* (Englewood Cliffs, N.J.: Prentice-Hall, Inc., 1973). It was reiterated in large part in Roger Bilstein, "Aviation and the Changing West," *Journal of the West* 30 (Jan., 1991): 5–17. The West's embrace of military aviation before World War II is covered in Roger D. Launius, "A New Way of War: The Development of Military Aviation in the American West, 1908–1945," *American Aviation Historical Society Journal* 41 (fall, 1996): 221–33.

31. "Tulsa's Air Terminal," *Airports* 1 (Nov., 1928): 35.

32. Ibid., pp. 36, 39.

33. Frank E. Bernsen, "Tulsa's Airport Is Tops," *Southern Flight* 13 (May, 1940): 23.

34. Jeff Miller, *Stapleton International Airport: The First Fifty Years* (Boulder, Colo.: Pruett Publishing Company, 1983), pp. 5, 9.

35. Ibid., pp. 13–15.

36. Ibid., pp. 16–18.

37. Ibid., pp. 18, 20, 24.

38. "Choose Your Coast and Air-Rail to It," *U.S. Air Services* 13 (June, 1928): 19–20.

39. "Transcontinental Air-Rail Service Becomes a Fact," *U.S. Air Services* 14 (July, 1929): 22–23.

40. D. R. Lane, "A New Air Harbor in Central Ohio," *Airports* 3 (Aug., 1929): 25–26, 48–49.

41. "Where Plane and Train Meet," *U.S. Air Services* 14 (July, 1929): 24.

42. Braden and Hagan, *Dream Takes Flight*, pp. 26, 53; Wenneman, *Municipal Airports*, pp. 324–25.

43. Janet R. Daly Bednarek, "False Beacon: Regional Planning and the Location of Dayton's Municipal Airport," *Ohio History* 106 (summer/autumn, 1997): 126–30.

44. Ibid., pp. 131–32.

45. Paul D. Friedman, "Birth of an Airport: From Mines Field to Los Angeles International, L. A. Celebrates the 50th Anniversary of Its Airport," *Journal of the American Aviation Historical Society* 23 (winter, 1978): 286–88; George N. Kramer, "From Beans to Planes in One Year: The Story of Metropolitan Airport, Lost Angeles, One of the Busiest Western Air Terminals," *Airway Age* 11 (Apr., 1930): 525; Wenneman, *Municipal Airports*, pp. 320–21.

46. Friedman, "Birth of an Airport," pp. 288–89.

47. Henry V. Hubbard et al., *Airports: Their Location, Administration, and Legal Basis* (Cambridge, Mass.: Harvard University Press, 1930), pp. 169–70.

48. U.S. Department of Commerce, Aeronautics Branch, "Airports: Types of Management, Rentals, Concessions, Field Rules," *Information Bulletin* 21, 2nd ed. (Mar. 31, 1928): 1.

49. Hubbard et al., *Airports*, pp. 59–60.

50. Ibid., pp. 55, 62.

51. Lieutenant Colonel U.S. Grant III, "Airports and Public Parks," *City Planning* 6 (Jan., 1930): 33–34.

52. L. H. Weir, "The Airport as Transportation Terminal," *City Planning* 6 (Apr., 1930): 119–20.

53. Gilmore D. Clarke, "The Airport Is Specialized Commercial Space," *City Planning* 6 (Apr., 1930): 123–24.

54. John Nolen, "Under What Jurisdiction Should Public Airports Be Placed?" *City Planning* 6 (Apr., 1930): 125–27.

55. "Editorial: Airports," *City Planning* 6 (Jan., 1930): 28–29.

56. "New Jersey Governor Opposes Leasing Park Lands for Airport," *American City* 40 (Feb., 1929): 129.

57. The material in this paragraph and in the following discussion of municipal airports is drawn from a number of the most prominent examples of published arguments in favor of municipally owned airports. These included: Archibald Black, *Civil Airports and Airways* (New York: Simmons-Boardman Publishing Company, 1929), pp. 3–5; Donald Duke, *Airports and Airways: Cost, Operation, and Maintenance* (New York: Ronald Press, 1927), pp. 5–8; Hubbard et al., *Airports*, pp. 46–53; Austin F. MacDonald, "Airport Problems of American Cities," *Annals of the American Society of Political and Social Sciences* 151 (Sept., 1930): 225–83.

58. Hubbard et al., *Airports*, p. 53.

59. MacDonald, "Airport Problems," p. 265.

60. Ibid.

61. For a general overview of the legal arguments supporting public ownership of airports in addition to the other sources cited in this chapter, see Oscar L. Pond, *A Treatise on the Law of Public Utilities Including Motor Vehicle Transportation, Airports, and Radio Service*, 4th ed., revised and enlarged, vol. 1 (Indianapolis, Ind.: Bobbs-Merrill Company, 1932), pp. 113–46.

62. Harry J. Freeman, "Establishment of Municipal Airports as a 'Public Purpose,'" *National Municipal Review* 18 (Apr., 1929): 263–64.

63. Ibid., p. 265.

64. Ibid.

65. Ibid., p. 266.

66. "Chamber of Commerce Finds Deep Interest in Aeronautics," *U.S. Air Services* 12 (June, 1927): 29. More on zoning will be offered in chapter 5.

67. W. Gordon Kuster, "The Civic Organization's Part in Local Airport Programs," *Aero Digest* 15 (Nov., 1929): 74.

68. Ibid., pp. 270, 272.

69. Ibid., p. 274.

70. Black, *Civic Airports and Airways*, pp. 3, 7.

Chapter 3. Depression and Reality

1. See Airways Section, *Air Service Information Circular*, Mar. 1, 1923.

2. Hallion, *Legacy of Flight*, p. 101.

3. Ibid., pp. 103–105; see also Public Works Association, *History of Public Works in the United States, 1776–1976* (Chicago: American Public Works Association), pp. 210–11.

4. Hallion, *Legacy of Flight*, pp. 105–106.

5. Ibid., pp. 111–24.

6. Ibid.

7. Leary, *Aerial Pioneers*, pp. 140–44; Nick A. Komons, *Bonfires to Beacons: Federal Civil Aviation Policy Under the Air Commerce Act, 1926–1938* (Washington, D.C.: Smithsonian Institution Press, 1989), pp. 129–30.

8. Komons, *Bonfires to Beacons*, pp. 130–31.

9. While cities had built airports to attract airmail service, the Post Office frequently flew the mail using military fields. For example, the landing field in Omaha was located at Fort Crook, south of the city near the small town of Bellevue. Omaha's original airport had been destroyed by a tornado, and airmail operations moved to the Army field. The airmail landed in San Francisco at the Army's Crissy Field. Leary, *Aerial Pioneers*, pp. 180–81.

10. Komons, *Bonfires to Beacons*, pp. 131–32; Leary, *Aerial Pioneers*, pp. 178–83

11. Komons, *Bonfires to Beacons*, p. 144.

12. Hubbard et al., *Airports*, pp. 90–93.

13. "Henry Ford's Concrete Airport Runway Dedicated," *U.S. Air Services* 14 (Apr., 1929): 92; Public Works Association, *History of Public Works*, p. 211.

14. B. Russell Shaw, "What Is an Airport?" *Airports* 1 (Dec., 1928): 17.

15. MacDonald, "Airport Problems of American Cities," p. 251.

16. Shaw, "What Is an Airport?" p. 17.

17. Ibid., pp. 17, 30.

18. Ibid.

19. Hugh J. Kneer, "Airports Must Improve Service," *U.S. Air Services* 13 (Oct., 1928): 21.

20. Ibid., p. 22.

21. Wyatt Brummitt, "The Airport Snaps Out of It," *Aero Digest* 17 (Dec., 1930): 88.

22. Ibid.

23. Ibid.

24. MacDonald, "Airport Problems of American Cities," pp. 226–27.

25. Ibid., pp. 234–44.

26. Ibid., pp. 244–45.

27. Ibid., pp. 244–48.

28. Ibid., pp. 248–51.

29. Ibid., pp. 252–56.

30. Ibid., pp. 256–60.

31. Ibid., pp. 260–63.

32. Charles H. Gale, "America's Airport Problem To Date," *Aviation* 29 (Dec., 1930): 330–31.

33. Ibid., p. 331.

34. The Douglas dissertation also focused a section on financing the nation's airports. It detailed the growing expense associated with airport construction. The argument, though, was shaped by a certain bias. Douglas seemed to suggest with her argument that both the federal government and local governments both could have and should have spent more on airports. In this she suggests that airports should have been a much higher priority for both the federal government and local governments. While acknowledging some of the political realities of the time, she still seems to suggest that there could have and should have been more public money available. See Douglas, "Inventing Airports," 186–94.

35. J. E. Bullard, "Financing the Municipal Airport Site," *Airports* 3 (Nov., 1929): 24.

36. Ibid., p. 25.

37. Ibid.

38. J. E. Bullard and Avery E. Lord, "Making the Airport Pay for Itself," *Aviation* 27 (Nov. 9, 1929): 932–33.

39. Ibid.

40. Ibid., pp. 933–34.

41. Ibid., pp. 934–35.

42. Ibid., p. 935.

43. James P. Wines, "The Airport on a Paying Basis," *Aviation* 28 (June 21, 1930): 1217.

44. Ibid., p. 1218.

45. Richard Lincoln West, "Making an Airport Pay," *Airway Age* 11 (Sept., 1930): 1211–12.

46. Ibid., p. 1212.

47. Gale, "Second National Airport Conference," p. 1039.

48. Ibid.

49. Preston Sneed, "The Problem of Revenues at a Municipal Airport," *Southern Aviation* 2 (July, 1931): 10.

50. Ibid., pp. 10–11.

51. Ibid., p. 11.

52. Ibid., pp. 11–12.

53. The Harvard Airport Study asked the subject airports to report how many people visited the airport on a average summer day and on an average summer weekend. It also asked them to report the largest single-day crowd at the airport. The results were published in a chart in the appendix to the study. Hubbard et al., *Airports*, pp. 146–47.

54. Stratton Coyner, "The Job of the Airport Manager," *American City* 42 (Mar., 1930): 126–28.

55. Major C. C. Moseley, "Hitch Your Airport to the Stars," *Aviation* 34 (Nov., 1935): 16.

56. Ibid., pp. 16–18.

57. William D. Strohmeier, "More Fun at the Airport," *Aviation* 39 (Nov., 1940): 38–39, 106. Only a few airport country clubs were ever constructed. One of the most prominent and successful was the Aviation Country Club in Long Island. Opened in 1929, the club catered to the rich, well-born, and famous. But even this club proved short-lived. It closed in 1948 after William Levitt offer $2,200 per acre and made it part of his Levittown housing development. John Fleischman, "High Society," *Air & Space* 13 (Feb./Mar., 1999): 32–39.

58. "Quarterly Review of Decisions: Aeronautics," *Air Law Review* 10 (July, 1939): 310.

59. Ibid.; Solomon Rothfeld, "The Law May Get You . . . ," *Aviation* 39 (June, 1940): 38.

60. "Quarterly Review," p. 311; Rothfeld, "Law," p. 38.

61. "Municipal Airports—Liability for Negligence in Operation," *National Municipal Review* 21 (May, 1932): 330.

62. David Schlang, "Notes, Aeronautics: Airports-Operation as a Nuisance-Injunctions," *Air Law Review* 4 (Jan., 1933): 64–70.

63. Solomon Rothfeld, "To Sue or Not to Sue," *Aviation* 39 (Nov., 1940): 43.

64. Ibid.

65. Lehigh Portland Cement Company, *American Airport Designs* (New York: American Institute of Architects Press, 1990), pp. 5–9. [Originally published: New York: Published for the Lehigh Portland Cement Company, Allentown, Pa., by Taylor, Rogers & Bliss, 1930.]

66. See ibid; for a discussion of the contest see Brodherson, "What Can't Go Up Can't Come Down," 409–504, and Douglas, "Inventing Airports," 401–409.

67. See Leslie Valentine, "The Development of the Omaha Municipal Airfield, 1924–1930," *Nebraska History* 62 (winter, 1981).

68. Ibid., pp. 403–404.

69. Ibid., pp. 403–407.

70. Ibid., pp. 407–13.

71. Carrolyle M. Frank, "Who Governed Middletown? Community Power in Muncie, Indiana, in the 1930s," *Indiana Magazine of History* 75 (Dec., 1979): 325–26.

72. Ibid., pp. 327–28.

73. Ibid., p. 329.

Chapter 4. We Have to Have a Plan (And Money to Pay for It)

1. For additional discussions of federal relief programs and airport development in the 1930s see Douglas, "Inventing Airports," pp. 103–14, 125–33, and Karsner, "'Leaving on a Jet Plane,'" pp. 12–51. Kasner looked at the programs in general and then offered examples of the use of those programs by the cities he examined as his case studies—Detroit, Tucson, and Tampa.

2. For a discussion of the development of the Boeing 247 and the DC series of aircraft see Roger Bilstein, *Flight in America: From the Wrights to the Astronauts*, rev. ed. (Baltimore and London: Johns Hopkins University Press, 1994), pp. 85–96.

3. For a more detailed discussion of the Civil Aeronautics Act of 1938 see Clinton M. Hester, "The Civil Aeronautics Act of 1938," *Journal of Air Law* 9 (July, 1938): 451–59; and Robert J. Pritchard, "The Civil Aeronautics Act," *Western Flying* 18 (July, 1938): 14–15, 22–23.

4. See Gelfand, *Nation of Cities*, pp. 3–70.

5. That airports played such a role was pointed out in Fairbanks, "Clash of Priorities," p. 164.

6. For information on European airports, including those in capital cities, see Dierikx and Bouwens, *Building Castles of the Air*, pp. 19–69; Hans-Joachim Braun, "The Airport as Symbol: Air Transport and Politics at Berlin-Templehof, 1923–1948," in *From Airships to Airbus: The History of Civil and Commercial Aviation, Vol. 1: Infrastructure and Environment*, ed. William M. Leary (Washington, D.C.: Smithsonian Institution Press, 1995), pp. 45–54; Wolfgang Voigt, "From the Hippodrome to the Aerodrome, from the Air Station to the Terminal: European Airports, 1909–1945," in *Building for Air Travel: Architecture and Design for Commercial Aviation*, ed. John Zukowsky (Munich and New York: Art Institute of Chicago and Prestel-Verlag, 1996), pp. 27–49.

7. Speech, Major V. C. Burnett (Manager, Detroit City Airport; President, Association of Airport Executives), "Minutes of Annual Convention, National Aeronautic Association, January 1940," National Air and Space Museum Archives, National Aeronautic Association Archives, Acc. XXXX-0209, Box 3803.

8. "PWA to Finance 2,000 New Aircraft Landing Fields Throughout the United States," *American City* 49 (Jan., 1934): 72.

9. Ibid.

10. "Airport Construction Under the CWA Program," *American City* 49 (Aug., 1934): 9.

11. Bednarek, "False Beacon," pp. 134–36.

12. "$45,000,000 Airport Program Launched," *National Aeronautics Association Magazine* 14 (July, 1936): 20–23.

13. Works Projects Administration, *America Spreads Her Wings* (Washington, D.C.: Government Printing Office, 1937), p. 10.

14. Friedman, "Birth of an Airport," p. 291; "What About the Los Angeles Airport?" *Western Flying* 18 (Nov., 1938): 18.

15. Bednarek, "False Beacon," pp. 136–37.

16. Ibid., pp. 133–38; George F. Baker, "Dayton Improves Its Municipal Airport," *Aero Digest* 29 (Dec., 1936): 28–29.

17. Rohlfing, *National Regulation of Aeronautics*, pp. 133–38.

18. "City Should End Deadlock by Canceling Airport Lease," *Daily Times*, July 22, 1936, p. 4; and "A Happy Outcome for the Airport Situation," *Daily Times*, July 30, 1936, p. 6; Box 83; Florida; Work Projects Administration Division of Information Newspaper Clipping File, 1935–42; Records of the Work Projects Administration, Record Group 69; National Archives, Washington, D.C. [hereafter WPA Newspaper File].

19. "Board Accepts Pan-Am Offer to Cancel Airport Deal," *Tribune*, July 31, 1936, p. 1; Box 83; Florida; WPA Newspaper File.

20. The Philadelphia Business Progress Association, "A Plan for the Development of the Philadelphia Terminal Air-Marine-Rail," Sept. 6, 1929, National Air and Space Museum Technical Files, Air Transport Series, Airports, Pennsylvania, Philadelphia; "Mayor to Continue Work on Airport With City Funds," *Philadelphia Record*, Dec. 29, 1938; Box 86; Pennsylvania; WPA Newspaper Files; "City Congressmen Promise Fight to Save New Airport," *Philadelphia Record*, Dec. 30, 1938; Box 86; Pennsylvania; WPA Newspaper Files.

21. "City Congressmen Promise Fight to Save New Airport," *Philadelphia Record*, Dec. 30, 1938; Box 86; Pennsylvania; WPA Newspaper Files; "$2,000,000 Tied Up in Runway Dispute with U.S. Agencies," *Philadelphia Record*, Dec. 31, 1938; Box 86; Pennsylvania; WPA Newspaper Files.

22. "Navy May Make Fort Plane-Proof to Save Airport," *Philadelphia Record*, Jan. 7, 1939; Box 86; Pennsylvania; WPA Newspaper Files; "Solution Is Held Near in Airport Controversy," *Philadelphia Inquirer*, Jan. 7, 1939; Box 86; Pennsylvania; WPA Newspaper Files; "Compromise Urged in Airport Dispute," *Philadelphia Record*, Jan. 29, 1939; Box 86; Pennsylvania; WPA Newspaper Files; "Neeson Forecasts Accord on Airport," *Philadelphia Inquirer*, Feb. 17, 1939; Box 86; Pennsylvania; WPA Newspaper Files; "Airport Row Ends, Work Will Resume in About 10 Days," *Philadelphia Inquirer*, Mar. 2, 1939; Box 86; Pennsylvania; WPA Newspaper Files; "Map Plan to End Airport Hazard," *Philadelphia Inquirer*, Mar. 21, 1939; Box 86; Pennsylvania; WPA Newspaper Files; "W.P.A. to Abandon All Further Work on City's Airport," *Philadelphia Record*, Apr. 21, 1939; Box 86; Pennsylvania; WPA Newspaper Files.

23. "Will Philadelphia 'Save' $115,000—and Lose Its Airport?" *Philadelphia Record*, Apr. 24, 1939; "WPA Again Refuses to Finance Airport," *Philadelphia Record*, May 3, 1939; "Resumption of Plans for Airport Sought," *Philadelphia Evening Bulletin*, May 3, 1939; "Vote for Full PWA Allotment Urged," *Philadelphia Inquirer*, May 27, 1939; "WPA Accord Near on City Airport," *Philadelphia Inquirer*, July 7, 1939; "Municipal Airport Will Be Ready For Use By End Of Year," *Philadelphia Record*, Aug. 6, 1939; "U.S. Clears Way for City Airport," *Philadelphia Record*, Aug. 31, 1939; "WPA Paves Way For Final Work on City Airport," *Philadelphia Inquirer*, Aug. 31, 1939; "WPA Awaits Word on Airport Job," *Philadelphia Bulletin*, Aug. 31, 1939, all in Box 86; Pennsylvania; WPA Newspaper Files.

24. "$45,000,000 Airport Program Launched," pp. 20–23; W. Sumpter Smith, "The WPA Airport Program," *Journal of Air Law* 7 (Oct., 1936): 495–99.

25. Porter R. Blakemore and Dana C. Linck, *Historic Structures Report, Historical Data Section, Archeological Data Section, Floyd Bennett Field, Gateway National Recreation Area, Volume I* (Denver, Colo.: United States Department of the Interior, National Park Service, Denver Service Center, Mid-Atlantic/North Atlantic Team, Branch of Historic Preservation, n.d.), pp. 4–5; John C. Holme Jr., "Surveying the Airport Problem in New York City, Part I" *Aviation* 28 (Jan. 11, 1930): 56–58.

26. Blakemore and Linck, "Historic Structures Report," pp. 5, 9–10.

27. John C. Holme Jr., "Surveying the Airport Problem in New York City, Part II," *Aviation* 28 (Jan. 25, 1930): 158; Blakemore and Linck, "Historic Structures Report," p. 33; Press Release, "News from the Port of New York Authority," Oct. 1, 1968, pp. 3–4, National Air and Space Museum Technical Files, Air Transport Series, Airports, U.S., New Jersey, Newark.

28. Blakemore and Linck, "Historic Structures Report," p. 34; "Municipal Airport at New York," *Airway Age* 12 (June, 1931): 581.

29. Blakemore and Linck, "Historic Structures Report," pp. 36–37.

30. Ibid., pp. 38–40; "New York City Dedicates Its Airport," *Aviation* 30 (June, 1931): 343.

31. Blakemore and Linck, "Historic Structures Report," pp. 43–44.

32. "Brief Prepared by Meyer C. Ellenstein of Newark, N.J. in support of the retention of the Newark Metropolitan Airport as the Eastern Airmail Terminal," printed and distributed by Fidelity Union Trust Company, June 20, 1935, pp. 3–11.

33. Ibid., p. 7.

34. Ibid., pp. 13–14.

35. Ibid., pp. 4, 14–16.

36. For more detailed discussions of the changes in the airmail system brought by the Civil Aeronautics Act, see Ellis W. Hawley, *The New Deal and the Problem of Monopoly: A Study in Economic Ambivalence* (Princeton, N.J.: Princeton University Press, 1966, 1969), pp. 240–44, and Richard H. K. Vietor, *Contrived Competition: Regulation and Deregulation in America* (Cambridge and London: Belknap Press of Harvard University Press, 1994), pp. 24–30.

37. Smith, *Airways*, p. 306; Komons, *Bonfires to Beacons*, pp. 355–56, 378–79.

38. "LaGuardia Plans New Airport in Bronx and $3,000,000 Outlay on Bennett Field," *New York Times*, Sept. 12, 1935; Box 85; New York; WPA Newspaper Files; "Mayor Reveals Plan for New Bronx Airport," *New York Herald Tribune*, September 12, 1935; Box 85; New York; WPA Newspaper Files; "Glenn Curtiss Airport, *Aero Digest* 20 (May, 1921): 30.

39. "WPA Speeding City's Bid for Airport Funds," *Newark Evening News*, Aug. 26, 1935; Box 85; New Jersey; WPA Newspaper Files.

40. "2,500,000 Asked for North Beach Plan Terminal," *North Shore Journal*, Aug. 3, 1936; "New York as an Air Terminal," *New York Times*, Aug. 28, 1936; "City Pushes Bid to Sea Air Line," *Newark Evening News*, Aug. 19, 1936, all in Box 85; New Jersey; WPA Newspaper Files.

41. "Replies to Ellenstein," *New York Times*, Sept. 29, 1938; Box 85; New York; WPA Newspaper Files.

42. "Leases Signed by 3 Air Lines at North Beach," *New York Herald Tribune*, Nov. 17, 1938; Box 85; New York; WPA Newspaper Files.

43. "Airlines' Experts Back North Beach," *New York Times*, Sept. 13, 1939; "Third Airline Assures Newark of Full Service," *New York Herald Tribune*, Sept. 14, 1939; "Newark Favored

by Rickenbacker," *New York Times*, Sept. 15, 1939, all in Box 85; New York; WPA Newspaper Files.

44. "Airlines' Experts Back North Beach," *New York Times*, Sept. 13, 1939; "Newark Airport End Seen If 4 Lines Leave," *New York Times*, Sept. 22, 1939; "Newark Airport Failure Feared If Lines Move," *New York Herald Tribune*, Sept. 22, 1939, all in Box 85; New York; WPA Newspaper Files.

45. Douglas, "Invention of Airports," pp. 467–77.

46. "North Beach Plea by Newark Denied," *New York Times*, Sept. 20, 1939; "Newark Plans Court Appeal on Airport Ruling," *New York Herald Tribune*, Nov., 9, 1939; "Newark Appeals in Airport Fight," *New York Times*, Jan. 5, 1940, all in Box 85; New York; WPA Newspaper Files; "New York City Municipal Airport," *Aero Digest* 35 (Nov., 1939): pp. 33–36; Brehon B. Somervall, "New York Municipal Airport," *Civil Engineering* 10 (Apr., 1940): 201–204; Brehon B. Somervall, "Servicing a Modern Airport," *Civil Engineering* 10 (May, 1940): pp. 295–98; "News from the Port of New York Authority," Oct. 1, 1968, press release, National Air and Space Museum Technical Files, Air Transport Series, Airports, U.S., New York.

47. Blakemore and Linck, "Historic Structures Report," pp. 44, 52–54, 59–60.

48. "The Building of Washington National Airport," reprinted from *FAA World*, Apr., 1979, National Air and Space Museum Technical Files, Air Transport Series, Airports, U.S., District of Columbia; "Commercial Airports Near the Capital," *U.S. Air Services* 14 (May, 1929): 48.

49. "New Airport at National Capital," *Airway Age* 11 (Aug., 1930): 1077–79; Wood, *Airports*, p. 141.

50. Nation's Capital Working for Ideal Airport," *U.S. Air Services* 12 (Jan., 1927): 28.

51. Ibid; Allen M. Smythe, "A Municipal Airport for Washington," *Aeronautic Review* 7 (Jan., 1929): 12.

52. Smythe, "Municipal Airport for Washington," pp. 12–14; "The Building of Washington National Airport," p. 1.

53. "Move to Give City Modern Airports Told by Officials," *Evening Star*, Dec. 10, 1935; "U.S. May Move Air Center Here from Capital," *Evening Sun*, Feb. 5, 1936; "Capital to Lost Air-Mail Line If Port Closes," *New York Herald Tribune*, Feb. 6, 1936; "The Airport Rumpus," *Washington Herald*, Feb. 6, 1936; "Arlington Offers a Plan to Save D.C.'s Airport," *Washington Daily News*, Feb. 6, 1936; "Bill Prepared to Close Road, Save Airport," *Washington Herald*, Feb. 8, 1936; "Emergency Airport Action," *Evening Star*, Feb. 8, 1936, all in Box 83; District of Columbia; WPA Newspaper Files.

54. No municipal airport was ever constructed at the Camp Springs site. Instead, it is the location of Andrews Air Force Base, which saw its construction begin (as Camp Springs Air Base) on Sept. 16, 1942. Robert Mueller, *Air Force Bases, Volume I: Active Air Force Bases Within the United States of America on 17 September 1982* (Washington, D.C.: Office of Air Force History, 1989), p. 5.

55. "Gravelly Pt. Airport Will Begin Soon," *Washington Post*, Sept. 28, 1938; "Capital Airport Plan Approved by Roosevelt," *New York Herald Tribune*, Sept. 28, 1938, both in Box 83; District of Columbia; WPA Newspaper Files; "The Building of Washington National Airport," pp. 1–2.

56. "Building of Washington National Airport," pp. 2–3; "Washington National Airport," *Aero Digest* 38 (June, 1941): 48–52.

57. "Building of Washington National Airport," pp. 2–3.

58. Ibid.

59. "Municipal Airports and Federal Responsibility," *American City* 52 (Mar., 1937): 15.

60. Ibid.

61. "Cities Seek National Airport Program," *American City* 52 (Aug., 1937): 13.

62. "A Year-End Message from the American Municipal Association," *American City* 58 (Jan., 1938): 5.

63. Col. J. Monroe Johnson, "Airports and the Bureau of Air Commerce," in *Federal-City Relations in the 1930s* (New York: Arno Press, 1978), pp. 26–29.

64. Ibid., p. 29.

65. Harllee Branch, "Airmail Service and Municipal Airports," in *Federal-City Relations in the 1930s*, pp. 31–38.

66. Frank Couzens, "The Municipal Airport Problem from the Viewpoint of the Larger Cities," in *Federal-City Relations in the 1930s*, p. 42.

67. Ibid., pp. 42–43.

68. See R. E. Allen, "The Municipal Airport Problem from the Viewpoint of the Smaller Cities," in *Federal-City Relations in the 1930s*, pp. 44–52.

69. "Federal Aid for Airports," *American City* 53 (Jan., 1938): 11.

70. For more on the debate at the federal level over the Civil Aeronautics Act see Douglas, "Inventing Airports," 140–46, 304–15.

71. A. B. McMullen, "Airports: Development and Problems," *Journal of Air Law* 9 (Oct., 1938): 651.

72. Civil Aeronautics Authority, "Airport Survey: Letter from the Civil Aeronautics Authority transmitting recommendations as to the desirability of federal participation in the construction, improvement, development, operation, and maintenance of a national system of airports," (Washington, D.C.: Government Printing Office, 1939), p. xiii.

73. Ibid., p. 129.

74. "CAA Suggests Adoption of New Airport System," *Shreveport Times*, Apr. 23, 1939, 21; Box 87; Misc.; WPA Newspaper File.

75. Cy Caldwell, "Putting Our Airports on Relief," *Aero Digest* 35 (Apr., 1939): 56.

76. "The Problem of the Airport," *National Aeronautics* 17 (July, 1939): 20.

77. Quoted in "$40,000,000 Program to Improve Nation's Airports Announced," *Washington Star*, Dec. 12, 1940, p. B-4; Box 87; Misc.; WPA Newspaper File.

78. Kendall K. Hoyt, "The Airport Program Makes a Start," *National Aeronautics* 18 (Nov., 1940): 10.

Chapter 5. City Planning and Municipal Airports, 1927–40

1. Brodherson also identified this period as one of intense planning activity, although he dated it from 1926 to 1929 and focused primarily on architects and their response to the emergence of airports. See Brodherson, "What Can't Go Up Can't Come Down," 19–117.

2. Much has been written on the "Regional Plan of New York and Its Environs." For a basic understanding of the background and history see Harvey A. Kantor, "Charles Dyer Norton and the Origins of the Regional Plan of New York," in Donald A. Krueckeberg, ed., *The American Planner: Biographies and Recollections*, 2nd ed. (New Brunswick, N.J.: Center for Urban Policy Research, 1994), pp. 163–81; David A Johnson, "Regional Planning for the Great American Metropolis: New York between the World Wars," in *Two Centuries of American Planning,*

ed. Daniel Schaffer (Baltimore: Johns Hopkins University Press, 1988), pp. 167–96; Mel Scott, *American City Planning Since 1890* (Berkeley and Los Angeles: University of California Press, 1969), pp. 261–65.

3. This is very similar to the role architects in the 1920s and 1930s played in determining the basic principles involved in the design of airport terminals as described by Brodherson, "What Can't Go Up Can't Come Down," 206–408. The limited influence of planners, especially in regard to land-use planning around airports was also dealt with in Barrett, "Cities and Their Airports," pp. 112–37.

4. See Karsner, "'Leaving on a Jet Plane,'" pp. 343–434. Barrett, however, emphasized the limits to zoning, at least through 1952. See Barrett, "Cities and Their Airports," 126–28.

5. George B. Ford, "Location, Size, and Layout of Airports," *American City* 37 (Sept., 1927): 301.

6. The Aeronautics Branch, created in 1926 as part of the Department of Commerce, issued a number of bulletins in the late 1920s aimed at providing cities with information on how to finance, design, and build airports. Examples include Department of Commerce, "Airports: Types of Management, Rentals, Concessions, Field Rules," *Information Bulletin* 21, 2nd ed. (Mar. 31, 1928), and Department of Commerce, Aeronautics Branch, "Suggested City or County Aeronautics Ordinance and Uniform Rules for Airports," *Aeronautics Bulletin*, no. 20 (Oct. 1, 1929).

7. Ford, "Location, Size, and Layout," pp. 301, 303.

8. Ibid., p. 303.

9. E. P. Goodrich, "Airports as a Factor in City Planning," Supplement to *National Municipal Review* 17 (Mar., 1928): 181.

10. Ibid., pp. 182–83. In their article, "Street Smarts: The Politics of Transportation Statistics in the American City, 1900–1990," Paul Barrett and Mark Rose argued that one of the reasons planners were unable to gain influence in the area of airport planning was the fact that they did not have the well-developed statistical tools available to highway planners. In fact, airport planning often borrowed models from highway planning. The result was that airport planners never gained the legitimacy of highway engineers. The rather "off the cuff" estimation of airport traffic needs by Goodrich would seem to support the conclusions drawn in "Street Smarts." Paul Barrett and Mark H. Rose, "Street Smarts: The Politics of Transportation Statistics in the American City, 1900–1990," *Journal of Urban History* 25 (Mar., 1999): 418–27.

11. John Nolan, "Civic Planning for Airports and Airways," *S.A.E. Journal* 22 (Apr., 1928): 411–13.

12. Ibid. John Nolan prepared a plan for the city of San Diego in 1926 that included the location for what became Lindbergh Field, the city's municipal airport. In a book chapter entitled "'Smokestacks and Geraniums': Planning and Politics in San Diego," John Hancock strongly criticized Nolan for the airport site, which the author felt had left the city with a very poor airport. His judgment of Nolan was, perhaps, a bit harsh. The San Diego Chamber of Commerce had suggested the waterfront site near the city's downtown in 1922. Nolan himself did not return to San Diego until 1924 to begin work on the plan he produced in 1926. Therefore, it is reasonable to assume that Nolan simply incorporated into his plan the chamber's airport project, location and all. And, given the Lindbergh boom the following year, it is also reasonable to assume that the airport would have been built with or without the Nolan plan. See John Hancock, "'Smokestacks and Geraniums': Planning and Politics in San Diego," in *Plan-*

ning the Twentieth-Century American City, ed. Mary Corbin Sies and Christopher Silver (Baltimore and London: Johns Hopkins University Press, 1966), pp. 161–86.

13. Nolen, "Civic Planning," pp. 415–16.

14. For a discussion of how airports finally came to be economic development generators see Karsner, "'Leaving on a Jet Plane,'" 435–505.

15. Nolen, "Civil Planning," pp. 416–17.

16. Interestingly, even though many of the airport maps included in the report clearly indicated use of the airports by the Army Air Corps Reserves and the Naval Air Reserves, the authors made no mention of the military uses of these civilian airports.

17. Hubbard et al., *Airports*, pp. 5, 20.

18. Ibid., pp. 20, 22.

19. Ibid., pp. 22–23.

20. Ibid., p. 23.

21. Ibid.

22. Ibid., p. 23–24.

23. Ibid., p. 24.

24. Ibid., p. 37.

25. Ibid., pp. 37–38.

26. Ibid., p. 38.

27. Ibid., pp. 38–39.

28. The third city with an airport plan receiving attention in the planning literature was Buffalo, New York. That plan primarily concerned itself with the internal layout of the Buffalo airport. For more on the Buffalo plan see *Buffalo Airport: Its Conception and Construction From the Original Plan to the Finished Product as of the Month of April 1927* (Buffalo, N.Y.: Grosvenor Library, 1927), found in the National Air and Space Museum Technical Files, Air Transport Series, Airports, U.S., New York, and "Developing the Buffalo Municipal Airport," *Airway Age* 12 (Oct., 1931): 583–84.

29. Eckert, "Philadelphia as a Great Airport," p. 241.

30. The Ludington Line began as the New York, Philadelphia, & Washington Airway Corporation, which had terminal facilities in Newark and Camden, New Jersey, and Washington, D.C. (Hoover Airport). The Ludington brothers, Charles and Nicholas, became the airline's principal backers, and the name was changed. Charles Townsend Ludington was especially involved in aviation as he had been involved in the building of the Camden, New Jersey, airport and "was also a director in several other aviation enterprises." Eugene Vidal, later the director of the Bureau of Air Commerce, managed the airline. Ludington Line service began in September, 1930, and the airline showed a net profit in its first year of operation. Upon failing to gain a contract to carry express airmail in order to promote continued profitability, the Ludington line was sold to Eastern Air Transport in 1933. R. E. Lenton, "Airways and Airports for the Philadelphia Region," *Airports* 4 (June, 1930): 22; Smith, *Airways*, pp. 215–24.

31. Lenton, "Airways and Airports," p. 22; see also the Philadelphia Business Progress Association, "A Plan for the Development of the Philadelphia Terminal Air-Marine-Rail," Sept. 6, 1929, National Air and Space Museum Technical Files, Air Transport Series, Airports, U.S., Pennsylvania, Philadelphia.

32. The Regional Planning Federation of the Tri-State District traced its origins to an organization created in 1924, the Regional Planning Federation of the Tri-State Metropolitan Area of Philadelphia. This group conducted a number of preliminary planning studies be-

tween 1924 and 1927. In 1927, the group presented its preliminary findings to "the leading business and civic interests of the region." The initial report found enough favor that it led to the incorporation of the Regional Planning Federation of the Philadelphia Tri-State District in May, 1928. That group had a budget of "$600,000 to cover the cost of survey, studies and preparation of a comprehensive plan." Regional Planning Federation of the Philadelphia Tri-State District, *The Regional Plan of the Philadelphia Tri-State District* (Philadelphia: Press of William F. Fell Co., 1932), p. 2.

33. Regional Planning Federation of the Philadelphia Tri-State District, "Regionally Planned Groundwork: Airways and Airport," Philadelphia, Pa., Apr., 1930, pp. 12, 32, National Air and Space Museum Technical Files, Air Transport Series, Airports, U.S., Pennsylvania, Philadelphia.

34. Ibid., pp. 7–9.

35. Ibid., pp. 10–11.

36. Ibid., pp. 12–15; see also Lenton, "Airways and Airports for the Philadelphia Region."

37. Regional Planning Federation, "Regionally Planned Groundwork," pp. 15–21.

38. Ibid., p. 22. It should be noted that the planners received help in developing their plan from the Airport Development and Construction Company, presumably a local firm involved in the airport business. Also, Charles Ludington served on the airport committee. His company, Ludington Philadelphia Flying Service, operated the existing Philadelphia Municipal Airport for the city. See Lenton, "Airways and Airports."

39. Regional Planning Federation, "Regionally Planned Groundwork," p. 23.

40. Scott, *American City Planning Since 1890*, pp. 219–20.

41. Ibid., pp. 102, 176–78, 199–204, 261–65.

42. Committee on the Regional Plan of New York and Its Environs, *The Graphic Regional Plan: Atlas and Description, Regional Plan, Volume One* (New York: Regional Plan of New York and Its Environs, 1929), pp. 305–307, 366–75.

43. David A. Johnson, *Planning the Great Metropolis: The 1929 Regional Plan of New York and Its Environs* (London: E&FN Spon, 1996), p. 166.

44. Ibid., pp. 166–67.

45. Committee on the Regional Plan of New York and Its Environs, *The Graphic Regional Plan*, pp. 336–75.

46. Thomas Adams, *The Building of the City: The Regional Plan*, vol. 2 (New York: Regional Plan of New York and Its Environs, 1931), pp. 265–73.

47. Johnson, *Planning the Great Metropolis*, p. 250.

48. For an example of a case in which airport planning proceeded in the absence of regional planning see Bednarek, "False Beacon," pp. 125–45.

49. See John Hancock, "The New Deal and American Planning: the 1930s," in *Two Centuries of American Planning*, ed. Daniel Schaffer (Baltimore: Johns Hopkins University Press, 1988), pp. 197–224.

50. American Society of Planning Officials and the American Municipal Association, *The Airport Dilemma: A Review of Local and National Factors in Airport Planning and Financing* (Chicago: Public Administration Service, 1938), pp. v–vi. The opinions expressed also reflected a general trend in thinking about airports the late 1930s. While the military had early on played a role in the establishment of municipal airports, its role had diminished by the early 1930s. In the late 1930s, however, the military utility of airports came to the forefront.

51. Ibid., pp. 19–21.

52. Ibid., pp. 21–24.

53. Ibid., pp. 39–42.

54. Ibid., p. 43.

55. For a basic history of zoning see Seymour Toll, *Zoned American* (New York: Grossman Publishers, 1969).

56. Robert Kingerly, "Zoning for Airports," *Airport Construction and Management* 2 (July, 1930): 14–15.

57. Omaha's 1921 municipal ordinance outlining the powers of its Air Board granted to the board the authority "to regulate the height of structures or obstructions in the vicinity of flying fields that tend to make the use of the field unsafe." Omaha's city government enacted its first zoning ordinance the year before, so such regulation was known to city leaders. This appears to be a very early application of zoning regulations to airports. The city, however, took no action to remove any obstructions until 1929, when it sought to cut down some willow trees believed to make approach to the airport dangerous. The effort became very controversial as some of the trees were located on park property. The family that had donated the park land and many others strongly objected to removing any trees from Carter Lake Park, located adjacent to the airport. Eventually, only trees located on adjacent private property were removed. This took place after Omaha had repealed its 1921 ordinance with the passage of a revised 1928 ordinance. The 1928 ordinance removed control of the airport from the appointed Air Board and transferred it to the city's Department of Street Cleaning and Maintenance. It also replaced the Air Board with an appointed Aviation and Airport Commission. Neither the city department nor the new commission were granted the authority to regulate the height of structures or other obstructions near the airport. Leslie Valentine, "The Development of the Omaha Municipal Airfield, 1924–1930," M.A. thesis, University of Nebraska at Omaha, May, 1980, pp. 136–42; City of Omaha, Ordinance No. 11170, Oct. 11, 1921 (copy in City of Omaha Recorder's Office, City-County Building, Omaha, Nebr.); City of Omaha Ordinance No. 13581, Dec. 26, 1928 (copy in City of Omaha Recorder's Office, City-County Building, Omaha, Nebr.).

58. Edward M. Bassett, "Zoning Roundtable," *City Planning* 5 (July, 1929): 194.

59. Ibid.

60. "Cooperative Committee on Airport Zoning Organized," *American City* 42 (Apr., 1930): 167.

61. U.S. Department of Commerce, Aeronautics Branch, *Report of Committee on Airport Zoning and Eminent Domain* (Washington, D.C.: United States Government Printing Office, 1930), pp. 2–3.

62. Ibid., pp. 3–4.

63. Ibid., pp. 4–9.

64. Ibid.

65. Ibid., pp. 6–7.

66. Ibid., pp. 9–14.

67. "An Act regulating the height of buildings and other structures within a certain distance of the Boston Airport, so called," in *1939 United States Aviation Reports, with English and Canadian Statutes and Decisions*, ed. Arnold Knauth et al. (Baltimore: United States Aviation Reports, 1939), pp. 440–44; "Zoning Laws to Regulate Buildings Near Airports," *American City* 55 (May, 1940): 13; Charles S. Rhyne, *Airports and the Courts* (Washington, D.C.: National Institute of Municipal Law Officers, 1944), pp. 171–72.

68. See Rhyne, *Airports and the Courts*, pp. 177–90.

69. Barrett and Rose, "Street Smarts," pp. 418–27.

Chapter 6. "For the Duration" and into the Postwar "Air Age"

1. The rise of the so-called Sunbelt or Gunbelt, particularly the role of federal defense spending, has been well documented in the literature over the last quarter century. For examples of the literature documenting this phenomenon see Carl Abbott, *The New Urban America: Growth Politics in Sunbelt Cities* (Chapel Hill: North Carolina University Press, 1981); Richard M. Bernard and Bradley Robert Rice, eds., *Sunbelt Cities: Politics and Growth Since World War II* (Austin: University of Texas Press, 1983); Robert B. Fairbanks and Kathleen Underwood, eds., *Essays on Sunbelt Cities and Recent Urban History* (College Station: Texas A&M University Press, 1990); Roger Lotchin, *Fortress California, 1910–1961: From Warfare to Welfare* (New York: Oxford University Press, 1992); Gerald Nash, *The American West Transformed: The Impact of the Second World War* (Bloomington: Indiana University Press, 1985); David C. Perry and Alfred J. Watkins, eds., *The Rise of Sunbelt Cities* (Beverly Hills, Calif.: Sage, 1977); and Kirkpatrick Sale, *Power Shift: The Rise of the Southern Rim and Its Challenge to the Eastern Establishment* (New York: Random House, 1975).

2. Caldwell, "Putting Our Airports on Relief," p. 56; "Problem of the Airport," p. 20; Brigadier General Donal H. Connolly, "The Airport Program Takes Shape," *Aero Digest* 39 (Aug., 1941): 57.

3. Frank Futrell, "Development of AAF Base Facilities in the United States, 1939–1945," U.S. Air Force Historical Study No. 69, USAF Historical Division, Air University, 1951, pp. 20–21.

4. Ibid., pp. 21–22; "4000 Airports for U.S. Visioned Under New Plan," *Aero Digest* 37 (Oct., 1940): 161.

5. "200,000,000 Worth of Airports," *Western Flying* 20 (Sept., 1940): 18–20.

6. "Expansion and Improvements to Military and Commercial Airports," *Aero Digest* 37 (Oct., 1940): 57–66.

7. Ibid; Mueller, *Air Force Bases*, p. 391.

8. Karsner's dissertation also includes a discussion of federal spending during World War II, particularly the impact of the DLAND program. His dissertation provides a brief overview of the DLAND program and then focuses on the importance of federal spending on airports in his case study cities—Detroit, Tampa, and Tucson. He also pointed out that many surplus military airfields were turned over to civilian uses following the war. See Karsner, "'Leaving on a Jet Plane,'" pp. 61–91.

9. "CAA Forging Ahead on Airport Program," *Aero Digest* 37 (Dec., 1940): 74. Lieutenant Colonel Connolly, a West Point graduate, left active military service in the Army Corps of Engineers when he was confirmed as CAA administrator. The post of CAA administrator was created in the same reorganization in 1940 that transformed the Civil Aeronautics Authority into the Civil Aeronautics Administration.

10. "200 Airports in New CAA Program," *Aero Digest* 38 (Jan., 1941).

11. Connolly, "Airport Program Takes Shape," p. 57.

12. "Large-Scale Improvement Program Modernizes Strategic Airports," *Aero Digest* 39 (Sept., 1941): 88, 90, 94, 98, 260; "Recent Improvements in Airports Vital to Defense," *Aero*

Digest 39 (Dec., 1941): 77–78, 81–82, 166; "278 Defense Airports Under Construction," *Aero Digest* 39 (Oct., 1941): 87.

13. "Large-Scale Improvement Program," pp. 88, 90, 94; "Recent Improvements," pp. 81–82, 166.

14. John R. M. Wilson, *Turbulence Aloft: The Civil Aeronautics Administration Amid Wars and Rumors of War, 1938–1953* (Washington, D.C.: United States Department of Transportation, Federal Aviation Administration, 1979), pp. 110–13.

15. Futrell, "Development of AAF Base Facilities," pp. 78–86.

16. Ibid., pp. 39–43.

17. Ibid., pp. 43–44.

18. For a more detailed discussion the military-civilian conflict, particularly that between the CAA and the AAF, see Wilson, *Turbulence Aloft,* pp. 65–129.

19. Futrell, "Development of AAF Base Facilities," pp. 45–47.

20. "History of the Atlanta Army Air Base Army Airport, Atlanta, Georgia, 1930 to Dec. 7, 1941 (Compiled in 1944)," pp. 2–11 [microfilm copy available at United States Air Force, History Support Office, Bolling AFB, Washington, D.C.]; "History of the Atlanta Army Air Base Army Airport, Atlanta, Georgia, Part II (Covering the Period 1939 to 7 December 1941)" (July 13, 1942), pp. 2–12 [microfilm copy available at United States Air Force, History Support Office, Bolling AFB, Washington, D.C.]; Braden and Hagan, *Dream Takes Flight,* pp. 112, 114.

21. See Mueller, *Air Force Bases.*

22. Richard E. Osborne, *World War II Sites in the United States: A Tour Guide and Directory* (Indianapolis, Ind.: Riebel-Roque Publishing, 1996), p. 176.

23. Apparently, the USAAF did not have to take over control of a municipal airport in all cases in order to designate it an Army Air Field. Portland's municipal airport, for example, served as an Army Air Field during the war while remaining under civilian management. This allowed civilian operations to continue at the base throughout the war. Osborne, *World War II Sites,* p. 209.

24. Friedman, "Birth of an Airport," p. 292.

25. The city of Milwaukee developed two small airports near its downtown lakefront. The first, Maitland, opened in 1927. That same year Milwaukee's city planners developed a plan to replace Maitland with a more elaborate airport featuring facilities for both land and, primarily, sea planes. The Air Marine Terminal (later known as the Seadrome) opened in 1932. However, within two years, the airport had lost its only commercial service when the airline serving it merged with Pennsylvania Air Lines and all its amphibious planes were replaced with Ford Tri-Motors and Boeing 247s. The small downtown airport remained open through World War II but following the war became first a site for Nike anti-aircraft missiles and then the location for the city's annual Summerfest event. Michael J. Goc, *Forward in Flight: The History of Aviation in Wisconsin* (Friendship, Wis.: Wisconsin Aviation Hall of Fame and New Past Press, Inc., 1998), pp. 142–43.

26. "Brief History of Billy Mitchell Field, Milwaukee, Wisconsin" (compiled by Historical Officer, CWO Roland L. Beck-W-2111052, Billy Mitchell Field, Milwaukee, Wisconsin, to 31 August 1944), pp. 4–10, 18–21 [microfilm copy available at USAF Historical Support Office, Bolling AFB, Washington, D.C.]; "History of Billy Mitchell Field, Milwaukee, Wisconsin, 1 January 1945 to 16 January 1945" (compiled by Harold Moffett, 1st Lt, Air Corps, Adjutant), pp. 30–31 [microfilm copy available at USAF Historical Support Office, Bolling AFB, Washington, D.C.]; Goc, *Forward in Flight,* p. 266.

27. George A. Hardie Jr., *Milwaukee County's General Mitchell International Airport* (Milwaukee, Wis.: Friends of the Mitchell Gallery of Flight, 1996), p. 45.

28. For a more detailed discussion of modification centers see Alfred Goldberg, "Expansion of Aircraft Production," in *The Army Air Forces in World War II, Volume 6: Men and Planes*, ed. Wesley Frank Craven and James Lea Cate (Washington, D.C.: Office of Air Force History, New Imprint, 1983), pp. 316, 332, 335–36.

29. "A History of the Dayton Army Air Field, Vandalia, Ohio, for the Year 1944," Headquarters, Dayton Army Air Field, Vandalia, Ohio, 1 July 1945, pp. 2, 7 [microfilm copy available at USAF Historical Support Office, Bolling AFB, Washington, D.C.].

30. Ibid., pp. 4, 14–17.

31. Wright Field and Patterson Field were adjacent to one another. In December, 1945, the two fields, along with Dayton Army Air Field and Clinton County Army Air Field, were combined to form the Army Air Forces Technical Base. Dayton Army Air Field and Clinton County Army Air Field were both returned to civilian use in early 1946. In 1947, the Army Air Forces Technical Base (consisting of Wright Field and Patterson Field) was renamed HQ Air Force Technical Base. In January, 1948, Wright Field and Patterson Field were merged and renamed Wright-Patterson AFB. Mueller, *Air Force Bases*, pp. 597–606.

32. Appendix to "A History of the Dayton Army Air Field, Vandalia, Ohio, for the Year 1944," dated July 1, 1945 (Headquarters, Dayton Army Air Field, Vandalia, Ohio, Jan. 28, 1946), pp. 1–2 [microfilm copy available at USAF Historical Support Office, Bolling AFB, Washington, D.C.]. Obviously, whoever wrote the base history completed it several days after the deactivation of the base. Even though the historian noted that the base itself transferred to the city of Dayton on January 18, 1946, and that all personnel had departed by January 22, 1946, in the tradition of the Air Force history function this historian was the person left behind "to close the door and turn off the lights."

33. Wilson, *Turbulence Aloft*, p. 112.

34. Osborne, *World War II Sites*, p. 161.

35. Ibid., pp. 36, 58, 138, 152, 230, 270, 284. Examples include Birmingham, Alabama; Oakland, California; Jacksonville, Florida; Gulfport, Mississippi; Lincoln, Nebraska; Fargo, North Dakota; Memphis, Tennessee; Richmond, Virginia; and Walla Walla, Washington.

36. Ibid., pp. 171, 188.

37. Ibid., pp. 5, 44, 62, 66, 149, 156, 229, 291. Examples include Kingman, Arizona; La Junta, Colorado; Kissimmee and St. Petersburg-Clearwater, Florida; Lewiston, Montana; Reno, Nevada; Sioux Falls, South Dakota; and Casper, Wyoming.

38. Ibid., pp. 248, 281–82.

39. Frank Kingston Smith and James P. Harrington, *Aviation and Pennsylvania* (Philadelphia: Franklin Institute Press, 1981), pp. 89–90; William F. Trimbel, *High Frontier: A History of Aeronautics in Pennsylvania* (Pittsburgh: University of Pittsburgh Press), pp. 195–96.

40. Osborne, *World War II Sites*, pp. 76–78; Stanley Ziemba, "Late Bloomer: Slow to Embrace Commercial Aviation, Chicago Soars," *Chicago Tribune*, Oct. 26, 1997.

41. "Municipal Progress Since 1909," *American City* 58 (Jan., 1943): 39.

42. "Your New Airport—Why, Where and How," *American City* 60 (June, 1945): 107–108.

43. Robert W. Schmidt, "Preventing Ghost Towns of the Air," *Western Flying* 26 (Jan., 1946): 38–39, 54.

44. William A. Burden, "Air Traffic and Airports in Relation to Urban Planning," *American City* 58 (Nov., 1943): 35; Major Albert Mayer, "Will Cities Come of Air Age?" (part 1),

American City 59 (Aug., 1944): 81; "Airport Planning for the Future," *Western Flying* 23 (May, 1943): 73.

45. The CAA's classification system, published in 1944, sorted out airports primarily based on runway length. A Class 1 airport had runways 1,800–2,700 feet in length; Class 2, 2,700–3,700; Class 3, 3,700–4,700; Class 4, 4,700–5,700; and Class 5, 5,700 or longer.

46. Don Forbes, "Airparks for Tomorrow," *Western Flying* 24 (Feb., 1944): 52–53. Forbes's airparks were actually a little smaller than a CAA Class 1 airport. He called for only 1,500-foot-long runways. Aircraft builders were not the only types of companies promoting small airports and airparks in order to promote private flying. The oil industry, which produced aviation oils and fuels, was also involved. See Standard Oil Company, "Community Airports and Air Parks," Aviation Division, Esso Aviation Products, 1945.

47. "Airports for the West, Part 6: Airparks," *Western Flying* 25 (Feb., 1945): 54, 88.

48. George Stromme, "$200,000 Airpark," *Western Flying* 26 (Jan., 1946): 32–33, 54.

49. Wilson, *Turbulence Aloft*, pp. 171–74.

50. Ibid, p. 174.

51. Ibid., pp. 174–75.

52. Ibid, pp. 164–68, 268.

53. Jennings Randolph, "Congress and the Challenge of Aviation," *Aero Digest* 48 (Jan. 15, 1945): 56–57.

54. For a discussion of the work of the Air Policy Commission and others formed in the late 1940s to work on some type of national aviation policy see Wilson, *Turbulence Aloft*, pp. 193–216.

55. Most of the information on state actions concerning aviation and airports was drawn from the editions of *U.S. Aviation Reports* between 1928 and 1945, especially 1928–39, 1941, and 1945. These *Reports* contained reprints of state laws dealing with aviation. Other information was drawn from Committee on Interstate and Foreign Commerce, *Hearings Before the Committee on Interstate and Foreign Commerce, House of Representatives, Seventy-Ninth Congress, First Session on H.R. 3170: A Bill to Provide Aid for the Development of Public Airports and to Amend Existing Laws Relating to Air Navigation Facilities, May 15, 16, 22, 23, 24, 25, 29, 30, 31 and June 1 and 5, 1945* (Washington, D.C.: Government Printing Office, 1945), pp. 44–47, 66–69, 156–73, 262–73, 326–29, 385–97.

56. Donoh W. Hanks Jr., "Neglected Cities Turn to U.S.," *National Municipal Review* 35 (Apr., 1946): 172–76.

57. Wilson, *Turbulence Aloft*, pp. 175–80.

58. Ibid., pp. 180–84.

59. J. Kirk Baldwin, "Analysis of Rules for Federal Airport Aid," *Airports* 11 (Feb., 1947): 19.

60. Arnold Knauth et al., eds., *1946 U.S. Aviation Reports, with English and Canadian Statutes and Decisions* (Baltimore: United States Aviation Reports, Inc., 1946), p. 340.

61. "T. P. Wright Announces 1947 Airport Allotments," *Airports* 11 (Feb., 1947): 20–21.

62. "States Would Control Federal Airport Grants," *National Municipal Review* 36 (Jan., 1947): 35–36.

63. Wilson, *Turbulence Aloft*, p. 184.

64. Ibid., pp. 186–87, 191.

65. William A. M. Burden, "The Civil Aeronautics Administration: What It Is and What It Does," *U.S. Services* 31 (May, 1946): 24–26, 28, 35; Wilson, *Turbulence Aloft*, pp. 217–65.

Conclusion

1. Another indication of the peripheral nature of airports can be found in Charles S. Rhyne, *The Civil Aeronautics Act Annotated* (Washington, D.C.: National Law Book Company, 1939). In this lengthy work, which devotes 188 pages to the explanation of the various provisions of the Civil Aeronautics Act, Rhyne's entire discussion of airports covers only a few paragraphs at the end of the last chapter before the conclusion. See Rhyne, *Civil Aeronautics Act*, pp. 182–85. (And the discussion is even more limited than the page numbers would indicate, as the book was printed with footnotes and they cover most of the pages devoted to the airport discussion.)

2. "The Springfield Airport Authority," *American City* 62 (Feb., 1947): 73.

3. T. A. Heppenheimer, *Turbulent Skies: A History of Commercial Aviation* (New York: John Wiley & Sons, Inc., 1998), p. 271.

Bibliography

Books and Articles

Abbott, Carl. *The Metropolitan Frontier: Cities in the Modern American West*. Tucson: University of Arizona Press, 1985.

———. *The New Urban America: Growth Politics in Sunbelt Cities*. Chapel Hill: University of North Carolina Press, 1981.

———. *Political Terrain: Washington, D.C., From Tidewater Town to Global Metropolis*. Chapel Hill and London: University of North Carolina Press, 1999.

Adams, Thomas. *The Building of the City: The Regional Plan, Volume 2*. New York: Regional Plan of New York and Its Environs, 1931.

Adwers, Robert E. *Rudder, Stick, and Throttle: Research and Reminiscences on Flying in Nebraska*. Omaha, Nebr.: Making History, Inc., 1994.

Allen, R. E. "The Municipal Airport Problem from the Viewpoint of the Smaller Cities," in *Federal-City Relations in the 1930s*. New York: Arno Press, 1978.

"Airport Construction Under the CWA Program." *American City* 49 (August, 1934).

"Airport Planning for the Future." *Western Flying* 23 (May, 1943).

"Airports for the West, Part 6: Airparks." *Western Flying* 25 (February, 1945).

American Society of Planning Officials and the American Municipal Association. *The Airport Dilemma: A Review of Local and National Factors in Airport Planning and Financing*. Chicago: Public Administration Service, 1938.

Baker, George F. "Dayton Improves Its Municipal Airport." *Aero Digest* 29 (December, 1936).

Baldwin, J. Kirk. "Analysis of Rules for Federal Airport Aid." *Airports* 11 (February, 1947).

Barrett, Paul. "Cities and Their Airports: Policy Formation, 1926–1952." *Journal of Urban History* 14 (November, 1987).

Barrett, Paul, and Mark H. Rose. "Street Smarts: The Politics of Transportation Statistics in the American City, 1900–1990." *Journal of Urban History* 25 (March, 1999).

Bassett, Edward M. "Zoning Roundtable." *City Planning* 5 (July, 1929).

Bednarek, Janet R. Daly. "False Beacon: Regional Planning and the Location of Dayton's Municipal Airport." *Ohio History* 106 (summer-autumn, 1997).

Bernard, Richard M., and Bradley Robert Rice, eds. *Sunbelt Cities: Politics and Growth Since World War II*. Austin: University of Texas Press, 1983.

Bernsen, Frank E. "Tulsa's Airport Is Tops." *Southern Flight* 13 (May, 1940).

Bilstein, Roger. "Aviation and the Changing West." *Journal of the West* 30 (January, 1991).

Bilstein, Roger E. *Flight in America: From the Wrights to the Astronauts*, rev. ed. Baltimore and London: Johns Hopkins University Press, 1994.

Bingham, Hiram. "The Most Precious Thing in the World." *U.S. Air Services* 10 (August, 1925).

Binney, Marcus. *Airport Builders*. London and New York: John Wiley and Sons Ltd., Academy Editions, 1999.

Black, Archibald. "Air Terminal Engineering." *Landscape Architecture* 13 (July, 1923).

———. *Civil Airports and Airways*. New York: Simmons-Boardman Publishing Company, 1929.

———. "Have You a Landing Field in Your Town?" *Aero Digest* 6 (April, 1925).

Boyer, M. Christine. *Dreaming the Rational City: The Myth of American City Planning*. Cambridge, Mass., and London: MIT Press, 1983.

Braden, Betsy, and Paul Hagan. *A Dream Takes Flight: Hartsfield Atlanta International Airport and Aviation in Atlanta*. Atlanta: Atlanta Historical Society; Athens and London: University of Georgia Press, 1989.

Branch, Harllee. "Airmail Service and Municipal Airports," in *Federal-City Relations in the 1930s*. New York: Arno Press, 1978.

Braun, Hans-Joachim. "The Airport as Symbol: Air Transport and Politics at Berlin-Templehof, 1923–1948," in *From Airships to Airbus: The History of Civil and Commercial Aviation, Volume 1: Infrastructure and Environment*, ed. William M. Leary. Washington, D.C.: Smithsonian Institution Press, 1995.

Brennan, J. W. "Lindbergh Field." *Aero Digest* 21 (September, 1932).

Bridges, Amy. *Morning Glories: Municipal Reform in the Southwest*. Princeton, N.J.: Princeton University Press, 1997.

Brodherson, David, "'An Airport in Every City': The History of American Airport Design," in *Building for Air Travel: Architecture and Design for Commercial Aviation*, ed. John Zukowsky. Munich and New York: Art Institute of Chicago and Prestel-Verlag, 1996.

Brown, Jerold E. *Where Eagles Land: Planning and Development of U.S. Army Airfields, 1910–1941*. New York: Greenwood Press, 1990.

Brummitt, Wyatt. "The Airport Snaps Out of It." *Aero Digest* 17 (December, 1930).

Bullard, J. E. "Financing the Airport Site." *Airports* 3 (November, 1929).

Bullard, J. E., and Avery E. Lord. "Making the Airport Pay for Itself." *Aviation* 27 (November 9, 1929).

Burden, William A. "Air Traffic and Airports in Relation to Urban Planning." *American City* 58 (November, 1943).

———. "The Civil Aeronautics Administration: What It Is and What It Does." *U.S. Air Services* 31 (May, 1946).

"CAA Forging Ahead on Airport Program." *Aero Digest* 37 (December, 1940).

Caldwell, Cy. "Putting Our Airports on Relief." *Aero Digest* 35 (April, 1939).

"Chamber of Commerce Finds Deep Interest in Aeronautics." *U.S. Air Services* 12 (June, 1927).

"Choose Your Coast and Air-Rail to It." *U.S. Air Services* 13 (June, 1928).

"Cities Seek National Airport Program." *American City* 52 (August, 1937).

"City and Federal Government Cooperate in Creating Extensive Airport." *American City* 38 (February, 1928).

Clarke, Gilmore D. "The Airport Is Specialized Commercial Space." *City Planning* 6 (April, 1930).

"Commercial Airports New the Capital." *U.S. Air Services* 14 (May, 1929).

Committee on the Regional Plan of New York and Its Environs. *The Graphical Plan: Atlas and Description, Regional Plan, Volume 1.* New York: Regional Plan of New York and Its Environs, 1929.

"Connecticut's New Laws of the Air." *U.S. Air Service* 5 (June, 1921).

Connolly, Brigadier General Donal H. "The Airport Program Takes Shape." *Aero Digest* 39 (August, 1941).

"Cooperative Committee on Airport Zoning Organized." *American City* 42 (April, 1930).

Corn, Joseph. *The Winged Gospel: America's Romance with Aviation, 1900–1950.* New York: Oxford University Press, 1983.

Couzens, Frank. "The Municipal Airport Problem from the Viewpoint of the Larger Cities," in *Federal-City Relations in the 1930s.* New York: Arno Press, 1978.

Coyner, Stratton. "The Job of the Airport Manager." *American City* 42 (March, 1930).

Curley, James M. "Boston: The Northeastern Airport." *Aero Digest* 2 (April, 1923).

"Developing the Buffalo Municipal Airport." *Airway Age* 12 (October, 1931).

Dierikx, Marc, and Bram Bouwens. *Building Castles of the Air: Schiphol Amsterdam and the Development of Airport Infrastructure in Europe, 1916–1996.* The Hague: Sdu Publishers, 1997.

Douglas, Deborah G. "Airports as Systems and Systems of Airports: Airports and Urban Development in America before World War II," in *From Airships to Airbus: The History of Civil and Commercial Aviation, Volume 1: Infrastructure and Environment,* ed. William M. Leary. Washington, D.C.: Smithsonian Institution Press, 1995.

Duke, Donald. *Airports and Airways: Cost, Operation, and Maintenance.* New York: Ronald Press, 1927.

Eckert, S. B. "Philadelphia as a Great Airport." *Aeronautical Digest* 2 (April, 1923).

"Editorial: Airports." *City Planning* 6 (January, 1930).

"Expansion and Improvements to Military and Commercial Airports." *Aero Digest* 37 (October, 1940).

Fairbanks, Robert B. "A Clash of Priorities: The Federal Government and Dallas Airport Development, 1917–1964," in *American Cities and Towns: Historical Perspectives,* ed. Joseph F. Rishel. Pittsburgh, Pa.: Duquesne University Press, 1992.

———. *For the City as a Whole: Planning, Politics, and the Public Interest in Dallas, Texas, 1900–1965.* Columbus: Ohio State University Press, Urban Life and Landscape Series, 1998.

Fairbanks, Robert B., and Kathleen Underwood, eds. *Essays on Sunbelt Cities and Recent Urban History.* College Station: Texas A&M University Press, 1990.

"Federal Aid for Airports." *American City* 53 (January, 1938).

"First Air Port in World Established in Atlantic City." *Aerial Age Weekly* 9 (April 14, 1919).

Fleischman, John. "High Society." *Air & Space* 13 (February/March, 1999).

Forbes, Don. "Airparks for Tomorrow." *Western Flying* 24 (February, 1944).

Ford, George B. "Location, Size, and Layout of Airports." *American City* 37 (September, 1927).

"$45,000,000 Airport Program Launched." *National Aeronautics Association Magazine* 14 (July, 1936).

"4000 Airports for U.S. Visioned Under New Plan." *Aero Digest* 37 (October, 1940).

Frank, Carrolyle M. "Who Governed Middletown? Community Power in Muncie, Indiana, in the 1930s." *Indiana Magazine of History* 75 (December, 1979).

Freeman, Harry J. "Establishment of Municipal Airports as 'Public Purpose.'" *National Municipal Review* 18 (April, 1929).

Friedman, Paul D. "Birth of An Airport: From Mines Field to Los Angeles International, L. A. Celebrates the 50th Anniversary of Its Airport." *Journal of the American Aviation Historical Society* 23 (winter, 1978).

Gale, Charles H. "America's Airport Problem to Date." *Aviation* 29 (December, 1930).

———. "The First National Airport Conference." *Aviation* 26 (June 1, 1929).

———. "The Second National Airport Conference." *Aviation* 28 (May 24, 1930).

Gelfand, Mark I. *A Nation of Cities: The Federal Government and Urban America, 1933–1965.* New York: Oxford University Press, 1975.

Goc, Michael. *Forward in Flight: The History of Aviation in Wisconsin.* Friendship, Wis.: Wisconsin Aviation Hall of Fame and New Past Press, Inc., 1998.

Goldberg, Alfred. "Expansion of Aircraft Production," in *The Army Air Forces in World War II, Volume 6: Men and Planes,* ed. Wesley Frank Craven and James Lea Cate. Washington, D.C.: Office of Air Force History, New Imprint, 1983.

Goodrich, E. P. "Airports as a Factor in City Planning." Supplement to *National Municipal Review* 17 (April, 1928).

Grant, Lieutenant Colonel U.S., III. "Airports and Public Parks." *City Planning* 6 (January, 1930).

Hallion, Richard P. *Legacy of Flight: The Guggenheim Contribution to American Aviation.* Seattle and London: University of Washington Press, 1977.

Hancock, John. "The New Deal and American Planning: The 1930s," in *Two Centuries of American Planning,* ed. Daniel Schaffer. Baltimore: Johns Hopkins University Press, 1988.

———. "'Smokestacks and Geraniums': Planning and Politics in San Diego," in *Planning the Twentieth Century American City,* ed. Mary Corbin Sies and Christopher Silver. Baltimore and London: Johns Hopkins University Press, 1996.

Hanks, Donoh W., Jr. "Neglected Cities Turn to U.S." *National Municipal Review* 35 (April, 1946).

Hardie, George A. *Milwaukee County's General Mitchell International Airport.* Milwaukee, Wis.: Friends of the Mitchell Gallery of Flight, Inc., 1996.

Hawley, Ellis W. *The New Deal and the Problem of Monopoly: A Study in Economic Ambivalence.* Princeton, N.J.: Princeton University Press, 1966, 1969.

Heermance, A. H. "Miami Has an Organized System of Airports." *American City* 48 (January, 1933).

Hegardt, G. B. "Development and Management of Oakland Municipal Port." *Airports* 3 (July, 1929).

"Henry Ford's Concrete Airport Runway Dedicated." *U.S. Air Services* 14 (April, 1929).

Heppenheimer, T. A. *Turbulent Skies: A History of Commercial Aviation.* New York: John Wiley and Sons, Inc., 1998.

Hester, Clinton M. "The Civil Aeronautics Act of 1938." *Journal of Air Law* 9 (July, 1938).

Holme, John C., Jr. "Surveying the Airport Problem in New York City, Part 1." *Aviation* 28 (January 11, 1930).

———. "Surveying the Airport Problem in New York City, Part 2." *Aviation* 28 (January 25, 1930).

Hood, Clifton. *722 Miles: The Building of the Subways and How They Transformed New York.* Baltimore and London: Johns Hopkins University Press, 1993.

Horgan, James J. *City of Flight: The History of Aviation in St. Louis.* Gerald, Mo.: Patrice Press, 1984.

Hoyt, Kendall K. "The Airport Program Makes a Start." *National Aeronautics* 18 (November, 1940).

Hubbard, Henry V., et al. *Airports: Their Location, Administration, and Legal Basis.* Cambridge, Mass.: Harvard University Press, 1930.

Johnson, David A. *Planning the Great Metropolis: The 1929 Regional Plan of New York and Its Environs.* London: E&FN Spon, 1996.

———. "Regional Planning for the Great American Metropolis: New York Between the World Wars," in *Two Centuries of American Planning*, ed. Daniel Schaffer. Baltimore: Johns Hopkins University Press, 1988.

Johnson, Colonel J. Monroe. "Airports and the Bureau of Air Commerce." *Federal-City Relations in the 1930s.* New York: Arno Press, 1978.

Kantor, Harvey A. "Charles Dyer Norton and the Origins of the Regional Plan of New York," in *The American Planner: Biographies and Recollections*, 2nd ed., ed. Donald A. Krueckeberg. New Brunswick, N.J.: Center for Urban Policy Research, 1994.

Karsner, Douglas. "Aviation and Airports: The Impact on the Economic and Geographic Structure of American Cities, 1940s–1980s." *Journal of Urban History* 23 (May, 1997).

Kingerly, Robert. "Zoning for Airports." *Airport Construction and Management* 2 (July, 1930).

Knauth, Arnold, et al., eds. *1928 U.S. Aviation Reports.* Baltimore: United States Aviation Reports, Inc., 1928.

———. *1929 U.S. Aviation Reports.* Baltimore: United States Aviation Reports, Inc., 1929.

———. *1930 U.S. Aviation Reports.* Baltimore: United States Aviation Reports, Inc., 1930.

———. *1931 U.S. Aviation Reports.* Baltimore: United States Aviation Reports, Inc., 1931.

———. *1932 U.S. Aviation Reports.* Baltimore: United States Aviation Reports, Inc., 1932.

———. *1933 U.S. Aviation Reports.* Baltimore: United States Aviation Reports, Inc., 1933.

———. *1934 U.S. Aviation Reports.* Baltimore: United States Aviation Reports, Inc., 1934.

———. *1935 U.S. Aviation Reports.* Baltimore: United States Aviation Reports, Inc., 1935.

———. *1936 U.S. Aviation Reports.* Baltimore: United States Aviation Reports, Inc., 1936.

———. *1937 U.S. Aviation Reports.* Baltimore: United States Aviation Reports, Inc., 1937.

———. *1938 U.S. Aviation Reports.* Baltimore: United States Aviation Reports, Inc., 1938.

———. *1939 United States Aviation Reports, with English and Canadian Statutes and Decisions.* Baltimore: United States Aviation Reports, Inc., 1939.

———. *1941 United States Aviation Reports, with English and Canadian Statutes and Decisions.* Baltimore: United States Aviation Reports, Inc., 1941.

———. *1945 United States Aviation Reports, with English and Canadian Statutes and Decisions.* Baltimore: United States Aviation Reports, Inc., 1945.

———. *1946 United States Aviation Reports, with English and Canadian Statutes and Decisions.* Baltimore: United States Aviation Reports, Inc., 1946.

Kneer, Hugh J. "Airports Must Improve Service." *U.S. Air Services* 13 (October, 1928).

Komons, Nick A. *Bonfires to Beacons: Federal Civil Aviation Policy Under the Air Commerce Act, 1926–1938.* Washington, D.C.: Smithsonian Institution Press, 1989.

Kramer, George N. "From Beans to Planes in One Year: The Story of Metropolitan Airport, Lost Angeles, One of the Busiest Western Air Terminals." *Airway Age* 11 (April, 1930).

Kuster, W. Gordon. "The Civic Organization's Part in Local Airport Programs." *Aero Digest* 15 (November, 1929).

Lambert, Major Albert Bond. "St. Louis Has an Aeronautical History." *U.S. Air Service* 8 (September, 1923).

Lane, D. R. "A New Air Harbor in Central Ohio." *Airports* 3 (August, 1929).

"Large-Scale Improvement Program Modernizes Strategic Airports." *Aero Digest* 39 (September, 1941).

Launius, Roger D. "A New Way of War: The Development of Military Aviation in the American West, 1908–1945." *American Aviation Historical Society Journal* 41 (fall, 1996).

Leary, William M. *Aerial Pioneers: The U.S. Air Mail Service, 1918–1927.* Washington, D.C.: Smithsonian Institution Press, 1985.

Lehigh Portland Cement Company. *American Airport Designs.* New York: Published for the Lehigh Portland Cement Company, Allentown, Pa. by Taylor, Rogers, and Bliss, 1930. Rpt., New York: American Institute of Architects Press, 1990.

Lenton, R. E. "Airways and Airports for the Philadelphia Region." *Airports* 4 (June, 1930).

Long, William P. "The Development of the Boston Airport." *American City* 48 (April, 1933).

Lotchin, Roger. *Fortress California, 1910–1961: From Warfare to Welfare.* New York: Oxford University Press, 1992.

MacDonald, Austin F. "Airport Problems of American Cities." *Annals of American Society of Political and Social Sciences* 151 (September, 1930).

Mayer, Major Albert. "Will Cities Come of Air Age?" (Part 1). *American City* 59 (August, 1944).

McMullen, A. B. "Airports: Development and Problems." *Journal of Air Law* 9 (October, 1938).

Miller, Jeff. *Stapleton International Airport: The First Fifty Years.* Boulder, Colo.: Pruett Publishing Company, 1983.

Monkkonen, Eric H. *America Becomes Urban: The Development of U.S. Cities and Towns, 1780–1980.* Berkeley and Los Angeles: University of California Press, 1988.

Moseley, Major C. C. "Hitch Your Airport to the Stars." *Aviation* 34 (November, 1935).

Mueller, Robert. *Air Force Bases, Volume 1: Active Air Force Bases Within the United States of America on 17 September 1982.* Washington, D.C.: Office of Air Force History, 1989.

Muhlenberg, Major H. C. K. "Seattle's Fine Flying Field at Sand Point." *U.S. Air Services* 9 (February, 1924).

"Municipal Airport at New York." *Airway Age* 12 (June, 1931).

"Municipal Airports and Federal Responsibility." *American City* 52 (March, 1937).

"Municipal Airports — Liability for Negligence in Operation." *National Municipal Review* 21 (May, 1932).

"Municipal Landing Fields for Air Service." *American City* 21 (July, 1919).

"Municipal Progress Since 1909." *American City* 58 (January, 1943).

Nash, Gerald D. *The American West in the Twentieth Century: A Short History of an Urban Oasis.* Englewood Cliffs, N.J.: Prentice-Hall, 1973.

———. *The American West Transformed: The Impact of the Second World War.* Bloomington: Indiana University Press, 1985.

"Nation's Capital Working for Ideal Airport." *U.S. Air Services* 12 (January, 1927).

"New Airport at National Capital." *Airway Age* 11 (August, 1930).

"New Jersey Governor Opposes Leasing Park Lands for Airport." *American City* 40 (February, 1929).

"New Landing Field at Pittsburgh." *U.S. Air Services* 10 (May, 1925).

"New York Dedicates Its Airport." *Aviation* 30 (June, 1931).

Nolen, John. "Civic Planning for Airports and Airways." *S.A.E. Journal* 22 (April, 1928).

———. "Under What Jurisdiction Should Public Airports Be Placed?" *City Planning* 6 (April, 1930).

O'Brien, Robert L. "State Control of Airports: How Massachusetts Does It." *Airports* 4 (January, 1930).

Olislagers, Robert P. *Fields of Flying: An Illustrated History of Airports in the Southwest.* Encinitas, Calif.: Heritage Media Corp., 1996.

Osborne, Richard E. *World War II Sites in the United States: A Tour Guide and Directory.* Indianapolis, Ind.: Riebel-Roque Publishing, 1996.

Perry, David C., and Alfred J. Watkins, eds. *The Rise of Sunbelt Cities.* Beverly Hills, Calif.: Sage, 1977.

Pisano, Dominick A. *To Fill the Sky with Pilots: The Civilian Pilot Training Program, 1939–1946.* Urbana and Chicago: University of Illinois Press, 1993.

Pond, Oscar L. *A Treatise on the Law of Public Utilities including Motor Vehicle Transportation, Airports, and Radio Service,* vol. 1, 4th ed., rev. and enlarged. Indianapolis, Ind.: Bobbs-Merrill, 1932.

Powell, Garland W. "The Maryland State Aviation Commission." *U.S. Air Service* 5 (April, 1921).

Pritchard, Robert J. "The Civil Aeronautics Act." *Western Flying* 18 (July, 1938).

"The Problem of the Airport." *National Aeronautics* 17 (July, 1939).

Pryor, Edwin W. "Wichita's Municipal Airport." *Aero Digest* 18 (April, 1931).

Public Works Association. *History of Public Works in the United States, 1776–1976.* Chicago: American Public Works Association.

"PWA to Finance 2,000 New Aircraft Landing Fields Throughout the United States." *American City* 49 (January, 1934).

"Quarterly Review of Decisions: Aeronautics." *Air Law Review* 10 (July, 1939).

Randolph, Jennings. "Congress and the Challenge of Aviation." *Aero Digest* 48 (January, 1945).

"Recent Improvements in Airports Vital to Defense." *Aero Digest* 39 (December, 1941).

Regional Planning Federation of the Philadelphia Tri-State District. *The Regional Plan of the Philadelphia Tri-State District.* Philadelphia: Press of William F. Fell Co., 1932.

Rhyne, Charles S. *Airports and the Courts.* Washington, D.C.: National Institute of Municipal Law Officers, 1944.

———. *The Civil Aeronautics Act Annotated.* Washington, D.C.: National Law Book Company, 1939.

Rieman, Charles. "Chicago: The Nation's Airport." *U.S. Air Service* 8 (February, 1923).

Rohlfing, Charles C. *National Regulation of Aeronautics.* Philadelphia: University of Pennsylvania Press, 1931.

Rothfield, Solomon. "The Law May Get You. . . ." *Aviation* 39 (June, 1940).

———. "To Sue or Not to Sue." *Aviation* 39 (November, 1940).

Rowe, Frank Joseph, and Craig Miner. *Borne on the South Wind: A Century of Kansas Aviation.* Wichita, Kans.: Wichita Eagle and Beacon Publishing Company, 1994.

Sale, Kirkpatrick. *Power Shift: The Rise of the Southern Rim and Its Challenge to the Eastern Establishment.* New York: Random House, 1975.

Schlang, David. "Notes, Aeronautics: Airport-Operation as a Nuisance-Injunctions." *Air Law Review* 4 (January, 1933).

Schmidt, Robert W. "Preventing Ghost Towns of the Air." *Western Flying* 26 (January, 1946).

Scott, Mel. *American City Planning Since 1890.* Berkeley and Los Angeles: University of California Press, 1969.

Shaw, B. Russell. "What Is an Airport?" *Airports* 1 (December, 1928).

Smith, Frank Kingston, and James P. Harrington. *Aviation and Pennsylvania.* Philadelphia: Franklin Institute Press, 1981.

Smith, Henry Ladd. *Airways: The History of Commercial Aviation in the United States.* Washington, D.C.: Smithsonian Institution Press, 1991.

Smith, W. Sumpter. "The WPA Airport Program." *Journal of Air Law* 7 (October, 1936).

Smythe, Allen M. "A Municipal Airport for Washington." *Aeronautic Review* 7 (January, 1929).

Sneed, Preston. "The Problem of Revenues at a Municipal Airport." *Southern Aviation* 2 (July, 1931).

Somervell, Brehon B. "New York Municipal Airport." *Civil Engineering* 10 (April, 1940).

————. "Servicing a Modern Airport." *Civil Engineering* 10 (May, 1940).

"The Springfield Airport Authority." *American City* 62 (February, 1947).

"States Would Control Federal Airport Grants," *National Municipal Review* 36 (January, 1947).

Stewart, A. T. "Regional Aviation Conferences." *Journal of Air Law* 2 (January, 1931).

Strohmeier, William D. "More Fun at the Airport." *Aviation* 39 (November, 1940).

Stromme, George. "$200,000 Airpark." *Western Flying* 26 (January, 1946).

Swander, O. J. "Exceptional Site, Landscaping, Lighting, and Buildings Characterize Wichita Airport." *American City* 44 (April, 1931).

Toll, Seymour. *Zoned American.* New York: Grossman Publishers, 1969.

"T. P. Wright Announces 1947 Airport Allotments." *Airports* 11 (February, 1947).

"Transcontinental Air-Rail Service Becomes a Fact." *U.S. Air Services* 14 (July, 1929).

Trimble, William F. *High Frontier: A History of Aeronautics in Pennsylvania.* Pittsburgh: University of Pittsburgh Press, 1982.

"Tulsa's Air Terminal." *Airports* 1 (November, 1928).

"200 Airports in New CAA Program." *Aero Digest* 38 (January, 1941).

"278 Defense Airports Under Construction." *Aero Digest* 39 (October, 1941).

"200,000,000 Worth of Airports." *Western Flying* 20 (September, 1940).

Valentine, Leslie. "The Development of the Omaha Municipal Airfield, 1924–1930." *Nebraska History* 62 (winter, 1981).

Van der Linden, F. Robert, "Progressives and the Post Office: Walter Folger Brown and the Creation of United States Transportation," in *From Airships to Airbus: The History of Civil and Commercial Aviation, Volume 2: Pioneers and Operations,* ed. William F. Trimble. Washington, D.C.: Smithsonian Institution Press, 1995.

Vietor, Richard H. K. *Contrived Competition: Regulation and Deregulation in America.* Cambridge and London: Belknap Press of Harvard University Press, 1994.

"Virginia Realizing Plan for System of Airports." *American City* 41 (July, 1929).

Voigt, Wolfgang. "From the Hippodrome to the Aerodrome, from the Air Station to the Terminal: European Airports, 1909–1945," in *Building for Air Travel: Architecture and Design for Commercial Aviation*, ed. John Zukowsky. Munich and New York: Art Institute of Chicago and Prestel-Verlag, 1996.

Walker, Lois E., and Shelby E. Wickam. *From Huffman Prairie to the Moon: The History of Wright Patterson AFB*. Washington, D.C.: Government Printing Office, 1986.

"Washington National Airport." *Aero Digest* 38 (June, 1941).

Weir, L. H. "The Airport as Transportation Terminal." *City Planning* 6 (April, 1930).

Wenneman, Joseph H. *Municipal Airports*. Cleveland, Ohio: Flying Review Publishing Company, 1931.

Wentworth, R. Preston. "Have You a Little Landing Field in Your Community?" *U.S. Air Service* 4 (August, 1920).

West, Richard Lincoln. "Making an Airport Pay." *Airway Age* 11 (September, 1930).

"What About the Los Angeles Airport?" *Western Flying* 18 (November, 1938).

"What Will Your Town Do?" *U.S. Air Service* 4 (November, 1920).

Wheat, George Seay, ed. *Municipal Landing Fields and Air Ports*. New York and London: G. P. Putnam's Sons, Knickerbocker Press, 1920.

"Where Plane and Train Meet." *U.S. Air Services* 14 (July, 1929).

Whitnall, Charles. "Municipal Airports." *National Municipal Review* 15 (February, 1926).

"Why Not Compulsory Ratings for Airports?" *U.S. Air Services* 17 (December, 1932).

Wilson, John R. M. *Turbulence Aloft: The Civil Aeronautics Administration Amid Wars and Rumors of War, 1938–1953*. Washington, D.C.: United States Department of Transportation, Federal Aviation Administration, 1979.

Wines, James P. "The Airport on a Paying Basis." *Aviation* 28 (June 21, 1930).

Wood, John Walter. *Airports: Some Design Elements and Future Developments*. New York: Coward-McCann, 1940.

Woodhouse, Henry, ed. *Textbook of Aerial Laws and Regulations for Aerial Navigation, International, National and Municipal, Civil and Military*. New York: Frederick A. Stokes Company, 1920.

"A Year-End Message from the American Municipal Association." *American City* 53 (January, 1938).

Young, David, and Neal Callahan. *Fill the Heavens with Commerce: Chicago Aviation, 1855–1926*. Chicago: Chicago Review Press, 1981.

"Your New Airport—Why, Where, and How." *American City* 60 (June, 1945).

"Zoning Laws to Regulate Buildings Near Airports." *American City* 55 (May, 1940).

Zukowsky, John, ed. *Building for Air Travel: Architecture and Design for Commercial Aviation*. Munich and New York: Art Institute of Chicago and Prestel-Verlag, 1996.

Documents and Archival Sources

Airways Section, Training and War Plans Division, Office of the Chief of Air Service. "Airways and Landing Facilities." *Air Information Circular* 5, no. 404 (March 1, 1923).

Annual Report of the Postmaster General for the Fiscal Year Ended June 30, 1920. Washington, D.C.: Government Printing Office, 1920.

Blakemore, Porter R., and Dana C. Linck. *Historic Structures Report, Historical Data Section, Archeological Data Section, Floyd Bennett Field, Gateway National Recreation Area,*

Volume 1. Denver, Colo.: U.S. Department of the Interior, National Park Service, Denver Service Center, Mid-Atlantic/North Atlantic Team, Branch of Historic Preservation, n.d.

Bonwell, Charles Clifton. "Technology and the Terminal: St. Louis's Lambert Field, 1925–1974." Ph.D. diss., Kansas State University, 1975.

"Brief History of Billy Mitchell Field, Milwaukee, Wisconsin." Compiled by Historical Officer, CWO Roland W. Beck-W-2111052, Billy Mitchell Field, Milwaukee, Wis., to 31 August 1944. (Microfilm copy available at United States Air Force, History Support Office, Bolling AFB, Washington, D.C.)

"Brief Prepared by Meyer C. Ellenstein of Newark, N.J., in support of the retention of the Newark Metropolitan Airport as the Eastern Airmail Terminal." Printed and distributed by Fidelity Union Trust Company, June 20, 1935.

Brodherson, David Phillip. "What Can't Go Up Can't Come Down: The History of American Airport Policy, Planning, and Design." Ph.D. diss., Cornell University, 1993.

Champie, Ellmore A. *The Federal Turnaround on Aid to Airports, 1926–1938.* Washington, D.C.: Department of Transportation, Federal Aviation Administration, Office of Management Systems, Agency Historical Staff, 1973.

Chief of Air Corps. *Annual Report of the Chief of the Air Corps for the Fiscal Year Ending June 30, 1927.* Washington, D.C.: Office of the Chief of Air Corps, 1927.

Chief of Air Service. *Annual Report of the Chief of the Air Service for the Fiscal Year Ending June 30, 1921.* Washington, D.C.: Office of the Chief of Air Service, 1921.

———. *Annual Report of the Chief of Air Service for the Fiscal Year Ending June 30, 1922.* Washington, D.C.: Office of the Chief of Air Service, 1922.

———. *Report of the Chief of Air Service for the Fiscal Year July 1, 1922, to June 30, 1923.* Washington, D.C.: Office of the Chief of Air Service, 1923.

City of Omaha. "Ordinance No. 11170." October 11, 1921. (Copy in City of Omaha Recorder's Office, City-County Building, Omaha, Nebr.)

———. "Ordinance No. 13508." June 19, 1928. (Copy in City of Omaha Recorder's Office, City-County Building, Omaha, Nebr.)

———. "Ordinance No. 13581." December 26, 1928. (Copy in City of Omaha Recorder's Office, City-County Building, Omaha, Nebr.)

Civil Aeronautics Authority. "Airport Survey: Letter from the Civil Aeronautics Authority Transmitting Recommendations as to the Desirability of Federal Participation in the Construction, Improvement, Development, Operation, and Maintenance of a National System of Airports." Washington, D.C.: Government Printing Office, 1939.

Committee on Interstate and Foreign Commerce. *Hearings Before the Committee on Interstate and Foreign Commerce, House of Representatives, Seventy-Ninth Congress, First Session on H.R. 3170: A Bill to Provide Aid for the Development of Public Airports and to Amend Existing Laws Relating to Air Navigation Facilities, May 15, 16, 22, 23, 24, 25, 29, 30, 31 and June 1 and 5, 1945.* Washington, D.C.: Government Printing Office, 1945.

Committee on the Post Office and Post Roads. *Hearings Before a Subcommittee of the Committee on the Post Office and Post Roads, House of Representatives, Sixty-Ninth Congress, First Session, on H.R. 4326 and H.R. 4642.* Washington, D.C.: Government Printing Office, 1926.

Director of Air Service. *Report of the Director of Air Service to the Secretary of War, 1920.* Washington, D.C.: Government Printing Office, 1920.

Doherty, Richard Paul, "The Origin and Development of Chicago-O'Hare International Airport." Ph.D. diss., Kansas State University, 1975.

Douglas, Deborah Gwen. "The Invention of Airports: A Political, Economic, and Technical History of Airports in the United States, 1919–1939." Ph.D. diss., University of Pennsylvania, 1996.

Futrell, Frank. "Development of AAF Base Facilities in the United States, 1939–1945." U.S. Air Force Historical Study No. 69, USAF Historical Division, Air University, 1951.

Harry F. Guggenheim Papers, Library of Congress.

"History of the Atlanta Army Air Base Army Airport, Atlanta, Georgia, Part 1 (Covering the Period 1939 to 7 December 1941)." 13 July 1942. (Microfilm copy available at United States Air Force, History Support Office, Bolling AFB, Washington, D.C.)

"History of the Atlanta Army Air Base Army Airport, Atlanta, Georgia, 1930 to December 7, 1941." Compiled in 1994. (Microfilm copy available at United States Air Force, History Support Office, Bolling AFB, Washington, D.C.)

"History of Billy Mitchell Field, Milwaukee, Wisconsin, 1 January 1945 to 16 January 1945. Compiled by Harold Moffett, 1st Lieutenant, Air Corps, Adjutant. Microfilm copy available at United States Air Force, History Support Office, Bolling AFB, Washington, D.C.

"A History of the Dayton Army Air Field, Vandalia, Ohio, for the Year 1944." Headquarters, Dayton Army Air Field, Vandalia, Ohio, 1 July 1945. (Microfilm copy available at United States Air Force, History Support Office, Bolling AFB, Washington, D.C.)

"A History of the Dayton Army Air Field, Vandalia, Ohio, for the Year 1944, dated 1 July 1945." Appendix. Headquarters, Dayton Army Air Field, Vandalia, Ohio, 28 January 1946. (Microfilm copy available at United States Air Force, History Support Office, Bolling AFB, Washington, D.C.)

Karsner, Douglas George. "'Leaving on a Jet Plane': Commercial Aviation, Airports, and Postindustrial American Society, 1933–1970." Ph.D. diss., Temple University, 1993.

National Advisory Committee for Aeronautics. *Sixth Annual Report of the National Advisory Committee for Aeronautics, 1920.* Washington, D.C.: Government Printing Office, 1921.

National Aeronautics Association Archives, National Air and Space Museum.

National Air and Space Museum Technical Files, Air Transport Series, Airports, U.S.

Records of the Work Projects Administration, Record Group 69; National Archives, Washington, D.C.

Standard Oil Company. *Community Airports and Air Parks.* Aviation Division, Esso Aviation Products, 1945.

"The Story of the Tucson Airport Authority, 1948–1966, Tucson, Arizona." Prepared under the direction of Charles H. Broman, A.A.E., General Manager T.A.A., December 31, 1966.

U.S. Department of Commerce. *Air Commerce Bulletin* 1, no. 16 (February 15, 1930).

U.S. Department of Commerce, Aeronautics Branch. "Airports: Types of Management, Rentals, Concessions, Field Rules." Information Bulletin No. 21 (2nd ed.), Washington, D.C., March 31, 1928.

———. *Construction of Airports.* Washington, D.C.: Government Printing Office, 1928.

———. "Report of Committee on Airport Zoning and Eminent Domain." Washington, D.C.: Government Printing Office, December 18, 1930.

———. "Suggested City or County Aeronautics Ordinances and Uniform Rules for Airports." *Aeronautics Bulletin,* no. 20 (October 1, 1929).

Valentine, Leslie. "The Development of the Omaha Municipal Airfield, 1924–1930." M.A. thesis, University of Nebraska at Omaha, May, 1980.

Van der Linden, Frank Robert. "Progressives and the Post Office: Air Mail and the Creation of U.S. Air Transportation, 1926–1934." Ph.D. diss., George Washington University, 1997.

War Department, Air Service, Division of Military Aeronautics. "Weekly News Letter." [Bound copies of the "Weekly News Letter" are available in the Air Force Command History Office Library, Bolling AFB, Washington, D.C.]

Works Projects Administration. *America Spreads Her Wings.* Washington, D.C.: Government Printing Office, 1937.

Index

Adams, Thomas, 138
Aeronautical Chamber of Commerce of America, 48–49
Aeronautics Branch. *See* Department of Commerce
Air Commerce Act of 1926, 5, 6, 11, 21, 30, 38, 40, 41, 42, 44–45, 47–48, 51, 57, 62, 72, 116, 120; dock concept, 5, 6, 30, 42, 44
Air Corps (Army Air Corps). *See* military
Air Corps Act of 1926, 21
Air Mail Act. *See* Kelly Act
airparks, 168–69
airport administration, 58–61, 180
Airport and Airway Development Act, 180–81
Airport and Airway Revenue Act, 180
airport conferences, 48–50, 84
airport enabling acts and regulations (state), 15, 17, 27–29, 38–39, 43–44; California, 57; Connecticut, 39; Indiana, 28; Kansas, 28, 38–39, 50–51; Kentucky, 28–29, 38, 43; Maryland, 38–39; Massachusetts, 29; Michigan, 43; Minnesota, 28–29; Nebraska, 28; New York, 38–39; Ohio, 28, 38; Pennsylvania, 28; Virginia, 43–44; Washington, 28; Wisconsin, 28
airport management, 12, 48–50, 84
airport rating system, 45–47, 76, 103
Airport Trust Fund, 180–81
airport zoning, 10, 122, 125, 144–50
Air Service (Army Air Service). *See* military
Air Service Reserve Flying Field Program, 18, 22–24, 26, 29

Airway bulletins, 23. *See also* information circulars
Akron, Ohio, 58
Albany, N.Y., 58
All American Airlines, 165
Allegheny County. *See* Pittsburgh, Pa.
Allegheny County Airport. *See* Pittsburgh, Pa.
Allen, R. E., 120
American Airlines, 112–13, 161
American Municipal Association, 118–19, 140–43, 173, 175
American Society of Planning Officials, 140–43
Army. *See* military
Army Air Forces Technical Base. *See* Dayton, Ohio
Army Corps of Engineers. *See* military
Arnold, General Henry H. "Hap," 154
Ashburn Field. *See* Chicago, Ill.
Atlanta, Ga., 5, 12, 25–27, 31, 56, 87–88, 159–60, 180; Atlanta Army Air Base, 160; Hartsfield Atlanta International Airport, 5
Atlantic City, N.J., 16, 58, 158; Atlantic City Air Port, 16–17
Augusta, Ga., 120
aviation enthusiasm. *See* winged gospel

Baltimore, Md., 116, 134
Bangor, Maine, 158–59
Barren Island. *See* New York City
Barrett, Paul, 149
Bassett, Edward M., 144–45

JANET R. DALY BEDNAREK is an associate professor of history at the University of Dayton. She is author of the book *The Changing Image of the City: Planning for Downtown Omaha, 1945–1973* and numerous articles and other contributions on aviation and urban history.

ISBN 1-58544-130-9

90000

9 781585 441303